a Catholic Gardener's *Spiritual* Almanac

"Margaret Rose Realy leads the reader by the hand through God's creation in the garden and shows us how to be open to the presence of the Creator. With saints' stories, symbols, biblical reflections, tender anecdotes, and more, this one-of-a-kind book is sure to inspire the gardener in everyone!"

Donna-Marie Cooper O'Boyle
EWTN host and author of *Rooted in Love*

"*A Catholic Gardener's Spiritual Almanac* is precisely what it purports to be: a unique offering that brings together saintly hagiography, serious tips for gardening and outdoor projects, explorations in symbolic meaning, and prompts to contemplation and prayer that are disguised amid talk of planting, pruning, watering, harvesting, and saints."

Elizabeth Scalia
Catholic blogger and author of *Strange Gods*

"You'll grow closer to God as you journey with Margaret Realy in this treasury of faith and gardening. Your year will be rich with faith and will bloom beautifully with this companion by your side."

Sarah Reinhard
Author of *A Catholic Mother's Companion to Pregnancy*

"Margaret Realy nurtures our yearning to be closer to God and his creation, encouraging prayerful presence in both the natural and liturgical seasons as we garden. Her book is a delightful way to garden meaningfully . . . praying as we work. *Ora et labora!*"

Maria Morera Johnson
Cohost of *Catholic Weekend*

a Catholic Gardener's *Spiritual* Almanac

Cultivating Your *Faith* throughout the Year

Margaret Rose Realy, Obl. O.S.B.

AVE MARIA PRESS AVE Notre Dame, Indiana

Founded in 1865, Ave Maria Press is a ministry of the United States Province of Holy Cross.

www.avemariapress.com

Paperback: ISBN-13 978-1-59471-484-9

E-book: ISBN-13 978-1-59471-485-6

Cover images © iStock.

Cover and text design by David Scholtes.

Printed and bound in the United States of America.

Library of Congress Cataloging-in-Publication Data

Realy, Margaret Rose.

  Catholic gardener's spiritual almanac : cultivating your faith throughout the year / Margaret Rose Realy, Obl. O.S.B.

    pages cm

  Includes bibliographical references and index.

  ISBN 978-1-59471-484-9 (alk. paper) -- ISBN 1-59471-484-3 (alk. paper)

  1. Catholic Church--Prayers and devotions. 2. Gardening--Religious aspects. 3. Nature--Religious aspects--Catholic Church. I. Title.

  BX2149.2.R43 2015

  242'.68--dc23

                    2014040091

To David R. Krajewski

Contents

Introduction

> May my teaching drop as the rain, my speech distil as the dew, as the gentle rain upon the tender grass, and as the showers upon the herb.
>
> –Deuteronomy 32:2

When I seek peace or solace in my life I am drawn to a garden. The working in soil and among plants drains pent-up energy. I feel physical release and rejuvenated spiritually as I labor and pray. Walking through a landscape helps slow down and order my thoughts, making room for the Holy Spirit to enter. Whether I am working or walking, I open myself to the presence of God in nature.

It is this opening oneself to the presence of the Creator through creation that I will share with you. People have asked me how I create spiritual gardens that reveal the holy and then asked how they can do the same for themselves. In this book I will guide you to develop this spiritual sense through the seasons of nature and the seasons of our Church.

This book is designed to take your desire to be near God and find a way to make him more apparent through your gardens. We can bring elements of our faith into outdoor spaces to help us focus on prayer, see more clearly relevant Bible passages about nature, and appreciate our Catholic heritage on a deeper level.

Our heritage is rich with stories, tales, and legends of unverifiable historical events. Before monasteries began developing books, our salvation history was passed down by word of mouth, much as we do today in our own families, as we talk and share stories. As Catholics, we too share many stories. We tell stories about our saints, about the symbolism of the Christmas Star or the legend of the cross in the blossom of a dogwood. There are a lot of stories about nature and religion, as varied as the countries and cultures that gave rise to them.

Many of the analogies we use come from nature. Jesus too followed this narrative style as he spoke in parables to express in more concrete ways how a hidden God works visibly in our lives. The words of our faith, written or spoken, are as alive as nature.

The stories we share often contain symbols or associations to a doctrine of our Church. St. Patrick, for example, used the three-leaf clover to teach about the Holy Trinity. We've learned many stories over our lifetimes. There are wondrous Bible stories from the Old Testament of adventure and adversity. We also have the legends of saints, some of whom often stumbled in their humanity, who left us great tales of living a faith-filled life. And then there are the things of nature with stories that lead us to another way of seeing. It is in this sharing that our faith is nurtured.

The richness of the mystery of our faith can, through misinterpretation, slide right into the shadows of the magical. Things such as burying a St. Joseph statue upside down in the yard of a desired house or the bubble effect of a Virgin Mary on the car dashboard both began with devout prayers for guidance and protection and wound up in the alley of superstitions.

We want our homes and gardens to reflect the substance of our Catholic faith, to have our customs rooted in Church teachings. To evaluate a custom, Meredith Gould, in her book *The Catholic Home*, offered three key questions. To those, I will add one of my own:

- Does this custom bring me into a deeper personal relationship with God the Creator, Christ the Redeemer, and Holy Spirit, the Divine Counselor?
- Does this observance reflect, strengthen, and sustain my Christian values and beliefs?
- Does this practice help me express my Christian faith and enhance my participation in the Body of Christ?[1]
- Will it enhance the faith of my family, friends, or community?

In asking these questions we can keep the substance of our beliefs firm, discern what customs best reinforce our faith, and begin to see more clearly, as Pope Benedict XVI said, the living Word of God in creation.

The format of this book is laid out as a monthly guide. I will start with January, in the middle of winter. Following the progression of the natural seasons and of the Church's liturgical year I will take what is familiar to our faith, show how to translate many of these teachings into a garden setting, and tie it together within the cycles of nature and our gardens. The format of the book for each month is as follows:

- a garden theme focused on the Church's monthly dedication;
- liturgical events or topics occurring during the month;
- Bible stories or verses related to the theme;
- stories of saints whose feast days or memorials are within that month, including gardening-related saints;
- practical gardening tips or techniques related to the gardening season;
- faith-filled gardening activities or guides for specific liturgical gardens;

- relevant Bible passages; and
- monthly prayer focus.

The purpose of this book is not to teach gardening techniques. That is a broad subject and covered in many other books and online. If you are a new gardener, look for month-by-month gardening books for your region; Cool Spring Press or Lone Pine Publishing provide basic information with excellent pictures. If you want to create a prayer garden, my first book, *A Garden of Visible Prayer*, will guide you step-by-step.

Honoring the life of Jesus and his Blessed Mother through prayer and meditation over the course of the year is something Christians have done for centuries. There are many saints memorialized throughout our Church year. I like to think of them as those individuals who were brave enough to keep on trying. They are my brothers and sisters. They are real. Some lived simple lives of grace; others were martyred in terrible ways. They all left behind some kernel of knowledge for those of us to come.

There are stories about the lives of saints that tell us of wonders and miracles taking place through nature.[2] Delving into the abundant literature, I found it challenging to cull the list to include only those saints who were gardeners, were farmers, or had miracles associated with plants. As I researched the lives of many saints, it appeared that God's hand seemed to delight most in turning a leaf instead of felling an army.

With this book as a guide, we can expand our prayer lives to include time in a garden. Countless monks and nuns over the span of Christianity have come to know what the Irish refer to as "that thin place" called a garden, where the membrane between God and us is slight. We can too! We are not the first to desire such a union, as this hymn from the 1700s attests:

A lesson in each flower,
A story in each tree and bower,
In every herb on which we tread
Are written words, which, rightly read,
Will lead us from earth's fragrant sod
To hope, and holiness to God.[3]

January: **Seeding**

For there shall be a sowing of peace . . . and the heavens shall give their dew.

−Zechariah 8:12

A seed contains within itself all that is necessary for its future. Its entire code, the DNA for what it will become, is present. A fertile seed, defined as an embryo for plants or animals, will, if properly cared for, grow to completeness.

We can think of January as a time to consider what it is to be seeded. God has brought us forth from our mothers' wombs and planted in our souls the seeds of faith, hope, and love. From our infancy we were nurtured and with the right environment grew in grace. We were taught simple lessons such as the Golden Rule; God's seed of love was planted in our souls.

> The garden−plants, butterflies, toads and snakes−is the ground of humility; it is not dependent upon me for its value in the design of creation.

Traditions and Feasts of January

Our Catholic Church has many traditions to help guide us in our faith. A portion of those traditions is through monthly, weekly, and daily dedications. The month of January is traditionally dedicated to the Holy Name and Infancy of Jesus. Jesus, the seed of the new covenant, the seed of God planted in the Blessed Virgin Mary, was also an infant who had to be nurtured into adulthood. We begin the calendar year by honoring that childhood.

January 1 is layered with meaning. It is the Solemnity of Mary and commemorates the divine motherhood of the Blessed Virgin Mary as the God-bearer, the Holy Mother of God. It is also the Octave Day of the Nativity of the Lord.

Prior to Vatican Council II, January 1 was the Feast of the Circumcision of Christ. Luke's gospel (2:21) records that on this date Mary and Joseph, acting in obedience to the Mosaic Law found in Genesis 17:10–12, brought Jesus to be circumcised on the eighth day of his life. There is a deeper meaning in this action in that it symbolizes and foreshadows the blood Jesus will shed for us on the Cross.

On January 3 we honor the name that Mary and Joseph gave their infant boy at his circumcision, the Feast of the Holy Name of Jesus. From Luke 2:21, "And at the end of eight days, when he was circumcised, he was called Jesus, the name given by the angel before he was conceived in the womb." It is in this naming that we hear for the first time that God is among us. In a few weeks, on the Feast of the Presentation of the Lord, this name will reveal the promised joys and inevitable sorrows associated with it.

For now, we look toward the Nativity Star and the Epiphany of the Lord. Traditionally celebrated on January 6, the Twelfth Day of Christmas, the Feast of the Epiphany is now celebrated on the first Sunday after January 1. On this day we remember when the Magi, having traveled "from afar," finally met the newborn King. I remember as a child this day being called "Little Christmas."

My maternal grandmother was Italian, and in that culture many families celebrated gift giving to children on Epiphany, when gifts are given in a way that relates to the gifts from the Magi. The more popular Christmas celebration in December was honored in our family, but I remember other children receiving three small gifts on this day.

It was also on the evening of Epiphany that the Christmas tree, originally known as the paradise tree, was taken down. The "gifts" we received on that night were the treats that had hung on the tree's boughs. The still safely edible decorations were distributed among the children—I think more to keep us out of the way of the adults who were trying to wrap up the holiday season that, since the onset of Advent, had been in full swing for nearly six weeks!

On the Monday after Epiphany a traditional celebration by peasants in England used to take place. It was called Plow Monday, and here the plowing practices intersect the cycles of seasonal practices and Christian observances. This holiday concluded the twelve-day celebration of Christmas. "Plow Monday signaled a return to work: women resumed their hearth-side spinning, and men anticipated a return to the fields for the year's first plowing, which occurred between Plow Monday (about January 7) and Candlemas (February 2) to allow time for the manure and stubble to decompose before planting began."[1]

Following Epiphany is the Feast of the Baptism of the Lord. Many of us were baptized in our infancy usually within a few days or at the most a couple weeks of our birth. It is a day of celebration for families when our souls are released from the original sin of Adam and Eve and we become daughters and sons of God, members of his Body, the Church. Parents promise to raise their children in the faith and appoint godparents to carry out this promise should they become unable to perform their duty.

Consider adding a holy water font at the entrance to your prayer garden as a reminder of your own baptism and then enter your space having "blessed" yourself with the assurance of your continued growth toward God.

For Jesus, his baptism by John in the Jordan River took place as an adult and signaled the beginning of his ministry. Jesus shows us how to be born from above. The seed of God that was always present in Jesus now germinated. Jesus began his ministry as the Christ, the Son of God. This title is both inspiring to us as his followers and frightening. It is frightening in that his followers realized he was more than a prophet and miracle worker. He *is* the Son of God, able to manipulate the things of the earth and the Evil One. No one had ever been born who could do such things.

January Saints for the Gardener

> If you can look into the seeds of time
> And say which grain will grow and which will not
> Speak then unto me.
>
> —William Shakespeare, *Macbeth*

January 13: St. Mungo (St. Kentigern), ca. 518–603

Patron against Bullies

St. Mungo, also known as St. Kentigern, is not well known, at least in the United States. Born in Scotland, he was an illegitimate child and given the endearing name Mungo (meaning "dear one") by his tutor, St. Serf.

Mungo was a gifted boy and held a special place in the hearts of his teachers. For this, he was often the object of bullying by his peers at the monastery. At a very young age he began performing miracles. The most popular is the story of his bringing a red bird, which was a pet owned by St. Serf, back to life after it was accidently killed by the other children.

Another incident during his childhood happened when he was left in charge of the holy fire in the monastery. The young boy arose from sleep and found all the fires in the monastery had gone out through a treacherous act by his peers.

The boy in his frustration left the building and, into the early dawn of a winter's day, went out into the garden to the surrounding witch-hazel hedge. He took a branch from the bush and, turning to God, raised the branch, made the Sign of the Cross on it, and blessed it. As he finished his prayer and his frozen breath surrounded the branch, flames from heaven ignited the witch-hazel as he held it in his hand. And so Mungo entered the monastery with his little burning bush and relit the fires.

When Mungo traveled to Glasgow he drew together several monks in the region, who were living and farming independently, into a single monastery. He assigned each man duties based on their talents to increase agricultural production to feed the poor. This group of monks became the Glasgow Abbey.

For centuries to come, this saint would be honored for his love and dedication to the people of this region. The weeklong Festival of St. Mungo still takes place today in parts of the United Kingdom.

January 17: St. Antony of Egypt, 1195-1231

Extensive Patronage

St. Antony the Great of Egypt is best known as the father of monasticism. He is also one of only two saints who are the patrons of those who attend to graveyards or memorial gardens. This patronage came about because of a close friendship with another man of solitude, St. Paul, the first hermit.

Legend has it that the Holy Spirit moved St. Antony to leave his place of solitude and travel across the desert to the cave of St. Paul. Shortly after arriving, the elderly hermit died. Antony knew he had to bury his beloved friend but had nothing to dig the grave and could not leave the body to go and acquire the tool he needed. As he prayed to God for a solution to his dilemma, two huge lions came running toward him—poor Antony may have thought he was about to join his friend in death. The beasts stopped short beside the corpse and began to dig until a suitable grave was made. The story tells of how these lions then laid at the feet of St. Antony until he blessed them and, once received, ran back into the desert as the body of St. Paul was placed into the earth.

St. Antony supported himself in his latter years with his gardening and by making mats from the nearby supply of papyrus along the Nile.

Before he became a hermit at thirty-four he was a reluctant farmer, a necessity because of the need to care for his younger sister after the death of their parents. His call to follow the words of the gospel "to go and sell all that he had" led him to relinquish all he possessed, including his land—all three hundred fields. Setting aside enough money for his sister, he gave the remaining land to the people of his village and distributed the money among the poor. Having gained his freedom from worldly goods, he set off for the desert.

St. Antony is often depicted with swine in the background and has the additional patronage of hogs. There are many legends for why this patronage developed, and they include him having been a swineherd on the family farm, that the torments of the devil took on the partial form of a pig, and that pigs were a form of income for an order founded in his name. It seems the latter story has some foundation.

The Order of Hospitallers of St. Antony was founded in the 1100s and treated those who suffered from a common and severe vascular condition called *ergotism*. This disease is a direct result of a fungus that develops on rye seed. When consumed by mammals, the alkaloid buildup causes intense burning sensations in the limbs. The Order of Hospitallers became widespread over much of Western Europe, being skilled at treating those with "St. Antony's Fire." To raise alms they would ring bells, and later these bells were hung around the necks of their pigs that were sold as food to support the order and their cause.[2]

January 22: St. Vincent of Saragossa, ca. 304

Patron of Vintners

This saint was a Spanish martyr who is highly venerated for the manner in which he persisted in faith throughout his persecution. Because of his perseverance in his martyrdom he is reverenced in the Anglican, Eastern, and Catholic Churches.

According to legend, after being martyred his body was discarded into a bog. While it lay exposed ravens protected it from being devoured by wild animals and vultures. The enraged persecutors, seeing that the corpse was not being destroyed, retrieved the body, tied it to a millstone, and threw it into the sea. The next morning the body was found on the shore by St. Vincent's followers and taken to what is now known as Cape St. Vincent. It was there that a shrine was erected over his grave, which continues to be guarded by flocks of ravens.

There are several allusions to why St. Vincent is the patron of vine growers, the first being because his name could be interpreted as "the blood of the wine," *vin sang*. Another is that his feast day falls between the vine's dormant state and appearance of new growth, when pruning is to begin. It is believed that he protects the fields against the frost that often occurs on or near his feast day, January 22, in Burgundy, France. An old proverb by an unknown author says that if the sun shines on his feast day then it will continue to shine throughout the month.

> Remember on St. Vincent's Day,
> If that the sun his beams display,
> Be sure to mark the transient beam,
> Which through the casement sheds its gleam,
> For 'tis a token bright and clear
> Of prosperous weather all the year.[3]

And another proverb says,
> Upon St. Vincent's Day
> Winter begins anew or goes away.[4]

There is also a legend that tells about his donkey. During his travels throughout Spain, Vincent stopped by the edge of a vineyard to talk with the men working there. While he and the vine growers chatted, his donkey nibbled at the young vine shoots. Come the next harvest, it was discovered that the vine stock that had been browsed had produced more fruit than all the others. St. Vincent's donkey had invented the art of vine pruning.[5]

January 25: The Conversion of St. Paul

We know from the Bible that not all who knew of Jesus followed him or believed in his teachings. He was countercultural, a threat to all that had been held holy and sacred, and a threat to the way the People of God had lived for centuries. One man trying to protect his society from *that Jesus* was Saul who became the apostle Paul. We've all fought against change and know how hard it can be to let go of what is familiar. St. Paul took it to the extreme.

When I read about or hear at Mass about the conversion of St. Paul, I think about the canna seed. The canna seed has a very hard outer coat that must be nicked, known as scarification, in order to germinate. Scarification is the process of breaking down this protective seed coat either by natural means such as freezing and thawing or by purposefully scratching or nicking the seed. Once the hardened coat has a crack, it can break open and begin new life. For me the story of Saul's conversion in Acts 22:3–16 is God's scarifying a hardened heart.

January in the Garden

> Let us praise God, who plants the seeds and reaps the harvest. Blessed be God forever.
>
> *—A Book of Blessings*

Practical Gardening: Seeds

The word *seed* is both a noun and a verb. Technically, as a horticultural noun, it is a small, hard fruit or a mature fertilized plant ovule consisting of an embryo and its food source and having a protective coat.

If you are like me, you love seed catalogs; they evoke such hope! I peek at them quickly as they come into the house and then set them in a basket next to my reading table. When I have a block of time, which is easier to find in the winter, I pick up the stack, peruse their colorful pages, and dream.

And that is when I, and most of my gardening friends, get into a world of trouble. I have learned over the years that it is easier to abstain than to moderate. Here, I am going to try to help you moderate the length of your purchase order form.

It's true that it's less costly to grow plants from seeds than to buy them in flats. But most of us don't have grow-tables in our homes and instead use tables next to windows with southern exposure. So consider the available space in your home for trays of seedlings—and don't forget about pets or kids assaulting your growing efforts.

Besides the space in your home, consider the space in your garden. Can you really plant three kinds of cucumbers, four different heirloom tomatoes, and a dozen herbs? Is there enough space for five kinds of blue flowers, and are they honestly going to be as blue as the catalog pictures? You know darn well that if all the seeds germinate you're going to have a hard time tossing the extras into the compost pile.

With so many options, consider purchasing only new varieties or old favorites. I love cucumbers and can buy one or two plants at local greenhouses. But what I can't buy locally are the lovely round lemon cucumbers, so I'll order the seeds. Also, think about growing a new plant that was just introduced into the market and offers a twist.

Another thing to consider is the level of difficulty in germinating seeds. I have the darnedest time holding onto seeds to scarify them with sandpaper or (yikes!) a knife. And using a heating pad under a flat of Bells of Ireland to keep them warm is not the most brilliant of ideas no matter how many layers of protective plastic is used. Check instructions for propagation method. If it's only one sentence long and contains the words "easily germinated," go for it.

And speaking of instructions, double-check references for growing conditions; many catalog suppliers really stretch the truth not only about what USDA hardiness zone a plant will grow in but also about the size of the flower or its invasive tendencies. Get suspicious when plants have extremely close-up pictures of flowers, have descriptive words such as vigorous grower or naturalizing, or suggest they grow well in a protected site.

This lovely blessing for the planting of seeds comes from the *Book of Blessings*:

> Let us praise God, who plants the seeds and reaps the harvest. Blessed be God forever.
>
> Today we seek God's blessing on these seeds and the crops they will produce. Christ reminds us that, unless the seed is planted in the earth and dies, it will not yield fruit. As these seeds grow and are cared for, may they be signs of the new life that comes from God. Amen.[6]

Faith-Filled Gardening: Creating a Bible Garden

The other way we often use the word *seed* is to indicate the source or a beginning of something. At the very beginning of our lives our souls are seeded with that essence that is God. Over time, faith germinates and we bear fruit.

The Bible is the Word of God, his spoken and written seeds of our faith. The Bible, from Genesis to Revelation, is a book of gardens, lived in and taught through. We experience the invisible God while in relation to his created world. However, for most parts of the world, the culture is no longer agrarian. Over time we have lost the sense of biblical passages that were so readily understood by those who worked and cultivated the land.

Biblical analogies using plants and nature give us a richer understanding of God's working in the everyday events of our lives. There are many books written on the where, when, and why of the plants mentioned in the Bible. Here I will be talking about how a Bible garden is different from other gardens. By its very definition, scriptural analogies will be brought to new life as you grow the referenced plants.

There really are no hard and fast rules when designing a Bible garden. If you live in an area where your weather is similar to the Mediterranean region, you have the advantage of growing Bible plants that are truer to their native species. However, if you live in a region that is not, modern cultivars of the same species or plants with similar form and texture can be grown instead.

Having a larger space for a Bible garden allows you to have more variety. For those with small prayer spaces, try adding a few Bible plants into the existing landscape that will add interest to the landscape and also hold personal meaning for you. There are several references on plants of the Bible available on the market. Check your public library or the Internet for additional resources.

Another way to bring Mediterranean plants into a colder hardiness zone is to bring species grown in a hothouse outdoors during the summer months. Container gardens are very popular, and if you have a patio or small deck, they give an added element of visual interest coupled with religious significance.

Besides containers, there are other ways to incorporate Bible plants into your landscape. One is with a full, visually pleasing landscape design where most of the plants are somehow related to scripture passages. Creating a landscape that fully reflects these plants could be organized in groups, such as flowers, grains, vegetables and fruit, spices and herbs, water plants, and trees and shrubs.

To enhance the prayerful nature of your garden, include an arbor for grapevines and a bench to sit on while you read the Bible. Add a table for writing in a prayer journal.

Another way to design with plants in a Bible garden is to interplant them among the flowers and foliage of your existing garden. For the home garden, this is the easiest and most common method. Position individual plants in a small group in your garden and label each with its name and biblical reference. With other plants, such as grains or poppies, create a small patch or minifield by mixing different species together. This will work as long as the plants have the same needs for water, sunlight, shade, and drainage. A single-specimen tree for shade is also a nice touch.

My personal favorite for a small Bible garden was a narrow strip between a fence and walkway that included a full season of plants referencing the Bible. At one end of the garden were a few wrought-iron angels hanging on the fence and gazing balls in various sizes arranged on the ground, suggesting the planets and the beginning of creation. At the other end of the walkway were a cross and a large boulder.

The garden included a curly willow behind the boulder and dwarf pines planted where space permitted. During Christmas a moderately sized Nativity scene was erected in the garden where it could be seen from the kitchen window and guests could see it when they came to the door.

This small Bible garden came to life in early spring with Star-of-Bethlehem, crocus, spring-blooming anemone, and daffodils. These were followed shortly after by tulips and then field poppies. The clumps of barley and wheat were poking through the soil as the thistles and salvia began to flower along with the daisies and lilies. Hollyhocks growing closest to the fence in late summer created a lovely backdrop for the grains. And the silvery blue rosemary bush, present at both our Lord's birth and his death, lined the walkway for the entire route.

Select plants mentioned in a meaningful verse of scripture to personalize your space. You can label plants from the Bible with handwritten tags. But why not go one better and use a lettering kit and make stepping-stones or bricks. Using a long narrow form to hold the cement and create a rectangular brick, letter out the location of the verse for a particular plant in the cement. When it is dry, place it beside the plant. These bricks look very charming when they are set along the edges of a garden path. One tends to stop and take more notice of the flower, and maybe it will make you or a visitor remember the verse or want to look it up later.

A frequently mentioned plant in the Bible that demonstrates the connection between God and his children is the vine *vitis*, better known as the grape. Because of its many allusions to understanding our relationship with God, this vine should be included in a Bible garden if your space allows.

Plant a grapevine so it will climb on a garden arbor or pergola at the entrance to your garden. I have found that the care and pruning of these vines have helped bring to life God's ways in the care and development of my own faith.

The following is a compiled list of biblical plants. Some are found in the Holy Land now and during Jesus' time. Others are mentioned in the Bible, and some are associated with an event or a similar species.[7] This extensive list includes not all plants but rather only those that are more frequently used and fairly well known.

Biblical Plants

Flowers and Grasses

Anemone, lily-of-the-field, *Anemone coronaria*

Bedstraw, *Galium sp.*

Cane, *Arundo donax*

Cattail, *Typha domingensis, T. latifolia*

Cranesbill, Herb Robert, Red Robin, *Geranium robertianum*

Crocus, *Crocus sp.*; saffron comes from *Crocus sativus*

Cyclamen, *Cyclamen indicum*

Dandelion, *Taraxacum officinale* (considered a food source)

Flax, *Linum usitatissimum*

Flower-of-an-hour, trailing hibiscus, *Hibiscus trionum*

Gladiolus (rose of the Plains of Sharon), *Gladiolus italicus* or *G. atroviolaceus*

Hyacinth, *Hyacinthus sp.*

Ice plant, fig marigold, *Mesembryanthemum crystallinum*

Iris, yellow flag, *Iris pseudacorus*

Larkspur, *Delphinium ajacis*

Lily, Turk's Cap lily, *Lilium chalcedonicum*; the Madonna lily, *L. candidum. Lilium sp.* is not
    biblical, being introduced in Marian paintings long after Christ's time.

Loosestrife, *Lythrum salicaria*

Love-in-a-mist, *Nigella sativa*, or modern fennel flower, *N. damascene*

Lupine, *Lupinus sp.*

Mallow, *Malva sylvestris*; also refers to the saltbush (saltwort)

Marshmallow, *Althea officinalis*

Meadow saffron, autumn crocus, *Colchicum autumnale*

Myrtle, *Myrtus communis*

Narcissus, *Narcissus tazetta* and others

Nightshade, hoary nightshade, a poisonous weed, *Solanum incanum*, also *S. sodomaeum*

Papyrus, bulrush, *Cyperus papyrus*

Peony, wild peony, *Paeonia officinalis*

Persian buttercup, *Ranunculus asiaticus*

Pheasant's eye, *Adonis sp.*

Pincushion flower, *Scabiosa sp.* (aka *Cephalaria sp.*)

Poppy, *Papaver rhoeas, P. somniferum*

Reed, *Phragmites australis* or possibly *Arundo donax*

Rose of Sharon references the narcissus, tulip, gladiola, and oleander. Rose was a generic
    term for flowering plants with bulblike structures. There are several species of *Rosa*
    (roses) that grow in the Holy Land and are not mentioned in scripture but may be
    included as "flowers of the field."

Rushes, sedges, *Scirpus sp., Juncus sp.*

Star-of-Bethlehem, *Ornithogalum umbellatum*

Sternbergia, autumn daffodil, *Sternbergia lutea*

Sweet flag, *Acorus calamus*

Tares, darnel, poisonous weed resembling wheat, *Lolium temulentum*

Thistle, a lot of various cultivated and native species that are prickly

Thorn, various plants: *Sarcopoterium spinosum, Zizyphus spina-christi, Paliurus spina-christi*, though not of the Holy Land, *Euphorbia milii* is called crown of thorns.

Tulip, *Tulipa sp.*

Tumbleweed, *Gundelia tournefortii*

Violet, *Viola odorata*

Water lily, *Nymphaea alba, N. caerulea, N. lotus*

Wild gourd, bitter apple (poisonous), *Citrullus colocynthis*

Willow herb, *Epilobium hirsutum*

Trees and Shrubs

Acacia, setim wood, shittah tree, *Acacia seyal* or *A. tortilis*

Acanthus, *Acanthus spinosus*

Almond, *Prunus communis* or *Amygdalus communis*

Bay laurel, *Laurus nobilis*

Bramble, *Rubus sanctus, R. ulmifolius*

Buckthorn, *Rhamnus palaestina*

Carob, *Ceratonia silique*

Cedar, *Cedrus libani*

Cotton, *Gossypium sp.*

Cypress, *Cupressus sempervirens*; also thyine wood, *Tetraclinis articulata*

Eaglewood, aloeswood tree, *Aquilaria agallocha*

Ebony or persimmon, *Diospyros sp.*

Frankincense, *Boswellia thurifera*

Henna, *Lawsonia inermis*

Juniper, algum/almug, heath, cedarwood; *Juniperus sp.*

Myrrh is a resin that comes from *Commiphora* or *Cistus* plants

Oak, *Quercus sp.*

Oleander, *Nerium oleander*

Pine, *Pinus sp.*

Pistachio, *Pistacia vera*

Plane tree, ash, *Platanus orientalis*

Poplar, *Populus sp.*

Saltbush, sea orach, *Atriplex halimus*

Sweet storax, stacte, *Styrax officinalis*

Sycamine, black mulberry, *Morus nigra*

Tamarisk, *Tamaris aphylla*

Terebinth, *Pistacia palaestina* or *P. atlantica*

Walnut, *Juglans regia*

White broom, *Retama raetum*

Willow, *Salix alba*

Fruits and Grains

Apples, *Pyrus malus*

Apricots, *Prunus armeniaca*

Barley, *Hordeum vulgare*

Bramble, *Rubus sanguineus*

Caper, *Capparis spinos*

Date, *Phoenix dactylifera*

Fig, *Ficus carica*

Grape, *Vitis vinifera*

Millet, *Panicum miliaceum*, or possibly *Sorghum vulgare*

Muskmelon, *Cucumis sp.* (bitter apple melon, *Citrullus lanatus*)

Olive, *Olea europaea*

Palm, *Phoenix dactylifera*

Pomegranates, *Punica granatum*

Sorghum, *Holcus sorghum*

Watermelon, *Citrullus vulgaris*

Wheat, *Triticum aestivum*

Vegetables

Broad bean, *Vicia faba*

Chicory, endive, *Cichorium intybus, C. endivia*

Cucumber, *Cucumis sativus*

Garlic, *Allium sativum*

Leek, *Allium porrum*

Lentil, *Lens culinaris, L. esculenta*

Lettuce, a generic term for a number of sweet or bitter leafy greens

Onion, *Allium cepa*

Shallot, *Allium ascalonicum*

Watercress, *Nasturtium officinale*

Herbs

Aloe, *Aloe vera, A. succotrina*

Anise: mistaken translation for dill

Balm-of-Gilead, *Commiphora opobalsamum* or *Cistus sp.*; there are multiple trees listed as used for balm

Black cumin, fennel flower, *Nigella sativa*

Cane, sweet cane, *Saccharum officinarum*

Castor bean, gourd, *Ricinus communis*

Cinnamon, *Cinnamomum sp.*

Coriander, *Coriandrum sativum*

Cumin, *Cuminum cyminum*

Dill, *Anethum graveolens*

Hyssop was often used as a generic name for several plants.

Mandrake, *Mandragora officinarum*

Marjoram, *Origanum aegyptiacum*

Mint, *Mentha longifolia* and other species

Mustard, black mustard, *Brassica nigra*; prickly wild mustard, charlock, *Brassica arvensis* or *Sinapis arvensis*

Nettle, *Urtica sp.*

Parsley, *Petroselinum sp.*

Rue, *Ruta chalepensis*

Saffron, *Crocus sativus*

Sage, *Salvia offisinalis*

Spikenard, *Nardostachys jatamansi*

Wormwood, *Artemisia herba-alba, A. monosperma,* and others

___

When choosing plants for a Bible garden, match them to what holds meaning for you. Maybe it's the symbolism of the plant, its reference in the Bible, or its meaning in the language of flowers.

Biblical Reflections

Yet I planted you a choice vine, wholly of pure seed. How then have you turned degenerate and become a wild vine?

—Jeremiah 2:21

Your Teacher will not hide himself any more, but your eyes shall see your Teacher. And your ears shall hear a word behind you, saying, "This is the way, walk in it," when you turn to the right or when you turn to the left. . . . And he will give rain for the seed with which you sow the ground, and grain, the produce of the ground, which will be rich and plenteous.

—Isaiah 30:20–21, 23

For my thoughts are not your thoughts, neither are your ways my ways, says the Lord. For as the heavens are higher than the earth, so are my ways higher than your ways and my thoughts than your thoughts. For as the rain and the snow come down from heaven, and return not thither but water the earth, making it bring forth and sprout, giving seed to the sower and bread to the eater, so shall my word be that goes forth from my mouth; it shall not return to me empty, but it shall accomplish that which I purpose, and prosper in the thing for which I sent it. For you shall go out in joy, and be led forth in peace."

—Isaiah 55:8–12

Having purified your souls by your obedience to the truth for a sincere love of the brethren, love one another earnestly from the heart. You have been born anew, not of perishable seed but of imperishable, through the living and abiding word of God; for "All flesh is like grass and all its glory like the flower of grass. The grass withers, and the flower falls, but the word of the Lord abides for ever." That word is the good news which was preached to you.

—1 Peter 1:22–25

He who sows sparingly will also reap sparingly, and he who sows bountifully will also reap bountifully. Each one must do as he has made up his mind, not reluctantly or under compulsion, for God loves a cheerful giver. And God is able to provide you with every blessing in abundance, so that you may always have enough of everything and may provide in abundance for every good work. As it is written, "He scatters abroad, he gives to the poor; his righteousness endures for ever." He who supplies seed to the sower and bread for food will supply and multiply your resources and increase the harvest of your righteousness.

—2 Corinthians 9:6–10

What you sow does not come to life unless it dies. And what you sow is not the body which is to be, but a bare kernel, perhaps of wheat or of some other grain. . . . So is it with the resurrection of the dead. What is sown is perishable, what is raised is imperishable. It is sown in dishonor, it is raised in glory. It is sown in weakness, it is raised in power. It is sown a physical body, it is raised a spiritual body. If there is a physical body, there is also a spiritual body.

—1 Corinthians 15:36–37, 42–44

In Mark's gospel, all of chapter 4 speaks of the parable of the seeds, the sower, and those among the weeds.

Prayer Focus for January

> The seed is the Word of God, Jesus is the sower. I am the
> farmer who makes ready the soil of my soul to receive
> the seed.

Think of a seed and all that is contained within its coating; all of
what it will be is there. Now think about how God plants his seeds
in our soul and how we must allow those seeds to germinate and
grow. Consider how you can encourage those seeds to grow. In what
ways can you plant seeds of faith in our world? What about inviting
someone into your Bible garden and sharing with her or him the
stories of the plants you grow there?

February: **Light**

God illuminates the universe with the brilliance of
the sun and illuminates humanity with the splen-
dor of his Word.... It is almost like a double sun.

–St. John Paul II

Simply put, all things would cease if there were no light. It was the
first thing created for our watery planet before land was formed.
God established vegetation on the third day, and on the fourth day
of creation, light was divvied up into stars and moon and sun, and
the seasons were set into motion (Gn 1:1–5, 14–19). The seasons,
which have varying lengths of sunlight, are the necessary cycles
for sprouting, growing, and bearing fruit. For proper development
plants need balanced periods of growth and rest; light and dark are
essential.

We need light to live. The things of the earth need sunlight, and
the things of the spirit need the light of God.

In February the hours of sunlight "grow," increasing incremen-
tally into spring. In the Catholic tradition, this month is dedicated to
the Holy Family and the time in which Jesus, the Light of the World,
grew within his family.

Traditions and Feasts of February

> As a seed, we do not know what will be made of us. We
> need to be willing to wait in an unknown darkness.

The first encounter we have with the Holy Family in our February
liturgies is on February 2, the Presentation of the Lord, also known as
the Feast of the Purification of Mary, and Candlemas. The gospel for
this day tells about Mary and Joseph bringing Jesus to the Temple in
accordance with the Jewish custom and, more likely, from the desire
of their hearts. They came to thank God for his gift of a wondrous
baby boy, the light of their lives.

But one who was clearly illuminated by Mary's baby was the
holy man Simeon. He knew, in a way only Mary knew before him,
that the essence of God was there in his arms. For decades he and the
Chosen People had longed and prayed, yearning for the Emmanuel,
God with us, to come. On that day Simeon held against his chest the
promised gift of God himself, the arrival of the Light into the world,
a gift to rouse a flame in every soul. The power and intensity of the
Holy Child, warm and swaddled against the flesh of his arms, made
Simeon's joy boundless! And the Temple echoed his joy.

Candlemas is the celebration of the coming of the Light into
the world. In Poland, the candles brought from home to be blessed
at church are decorated with symbols and ribbons (comparable to
Hispanic *milagros* crosses). In Poland, the custom is to let a blessed
candle burn all night before an icon of Our Lady who, when the
world still had forests, was relied upon to keep the wolves away
during the cold nights of winter.

Now, our "wolves" tend to be of a different sort. But the pious
burning of a blessed candle, with prayers offered to Our Lady, still
might help keep these wolves at bay.[1]

Light

"Light is the symbol of joy (luminous thoughts give us thrills), of life (light vivifies living creatures), and of happiness (days of light are days of happiness). Jesus is the giver of light; in redemption he brings to the believer truth, blessing, and peace. . . . Christ himself repeatedly announced, 'I am the Light of the world. . . .' The sense is clear. In the divine economy we must believe in Christ to be possessed of the light of life."[2]

Not long after the presentation of Jesus, the Holy Family was enlightened by a dream that their child's life was in danger. February 17 is the traditional date when we commemorate their flight into Egypt.

There are several stories about how the Holy Family was protected as they fled from Herod. One legend is called the grain miracle. The Holy Family was fleeing to Egypt with Herod's soldiers not far behind. The Blessed Mother saw a man in the act of sowing seeds and instructed the farmer that if soldiers came looking for her and her family he should tell them that he saw them pass by while he was sowing. Immediately after Mary left, the freshly sown seeds sprouted and grew tall. When the soldiers arrived and asked the farmer if he had seen a mother and child pass by, he truthfully answered, "Yes, when I first began to sow the seed." The soldiers turned away and went in another direction, assuming the seed had been planted months ago.[3]

Another legend is of the giant juniper tree, *Juniperus thurifera*, a massive native tree in the Holy Land. The story begins with the soldiers pursuing Joseph, Mary, and the baby Jesus. Frightened by Herod's men getting closer, the little donkey that the Holy Family rode turned and at nearly full gallop headed toward the juniper. Immediately the tree miraculously opened up its branches like arms and enfolded them. There in the shadows of the tree they were safely hidden from the pursuing soldiers. In gratitude, Mary gave the tree her blessing, and a custom that still exists today is that juniper boughs are placed in stables and barns on Christmas.

On February 11 we celebrate the memorial of Our Lady of Lourdes. In 1858 the Blessed Mother appeared eighteen times to St. Bernadette Soubirous. It was during these apparitions, when in desperation Bernadette begged for a way to tell others that Mary was visiting her, that Our Lady, looking to the heavens, conferred upon herself this name: "I am the immaculate conception."

After the apparitions ended, Bernadette became part of a nearby religious order, the Sisters of Charity of Nevers. She remained with them until her death at age thirty-five. Though Bernadette was engaged by the Blessed Virgin Mary to bring forth to the world the healing waters at Lourdes, she was never cured by them of her many illnesses and died relatively young. St. Bernadette's body remains incorrupt to this day, enshrined in the St. Gildard Convent's chapel in Nevers.

During February we also celebrate the Feast of the Chair of St. Peter on the twenty-second. This feast day helps us to remember the mission of teacher and pastor conferred by Jesus on Peter and how this mission to light the way for his followers has continued in an unbroken line down to the present pope. We celebrate the unity of the Church, founded upon the Apostle Peter, and renew our assent to the magisterium of the Roman pontiff.

When I read in the Bible about St. Peter I love the transitional meanings of his names. Simon was his name as the master fisherman whom Jesus called. The name Simon in Hebrew means "he who hears." Simon did indeed hear the Word of God spoken through Jesus and heard God's enlightening his soul when he responded to Jesus' question "Who do you say that I am?" by answering, "You are the Christ." It is here that Jesus renames him Kephas (*ke-pha* meaning stone; Mt 16:18, "You are Peter, and on this rock I will build my church"), which in Greek is Petros; in English, Peter.

February Saints for the Gardener

> The people who walked in darkness have seen a great light; those who dwelt in a land of deep darkness, on them has light shined.
>
> —Isaiah 9:2

February 1: St. Brigid, 453–523

Extensive Patronage, Many Related to Farms

The saints shared the light of Christ in their world. One well-known saint is St. Brigid, one of the founders of Christianity in Ireland and the subject of numerous legends. She holds a place of honor among the Irish nearly equal to that of St. Patrick.

St. Brigid was the daughter of Dubtach, a pagan Scottish king, and his slave Brocca. Brocca was sold to an Irish druid landowner while pregnant with Brigid. The association of Brigid and miracles with cows begins at her birth. The story is told that one morning at sunrise while her mother was carrying milk to the druid's house, she went into labor. Brocca's birthing of Brigid was so sudden and fierce that she gave birth to the future saint on the druid's doorstep with one foot outside and one foot inside the threshold.[4] Her birth was considered to be a symbolic first step beyond the order of the druid and into Christianity.

Brigid saw the goodness of God in all creation but delighted most in God's love when she saw cows. In her century, cows were considered a source of sustaining life. As a child she was nourished by an unusually marked all-white cow with red ears. It is this same cow that she is often pictured riding across Ireland as she blesses homes on her feast day.

St. Brigid was well known for her generosity to the poor, much to her pagan father's frustration. She often gave them milk, butter, and bread. The miracle of her generosity is that no matter how little milk came from the cow or how much she gave away, there was always at least as much left for the larder.

One legend tells of a time when Brigid acted in defiance of her father's command and carried her butter and bread to those in need. Spotted by her father's soldiers, she knew that if she were caught with the basket of food she would suffer severe punishment for her disobedience. She fervently prayed as the soldiers yanked off her cloak. Miraculously they found only a basket of roses clasped in the young girl's hands.

Eventually Brigid, who refused to marry, became a nun. Immediately she set about converting her homeland to Christianity. A tactic for the conversion of her countrymen from paganism was in Christianizing their customs and the items they worshipped. Oak trees held specific ritualized meaning in the druid culture. To debunk those magical associations, Brigid built her monastery from this tree and the site was called church of the oaks, Cill Dara, or more commonly, Kildare.

A favorite story about Kildare tells of how St. Brigid acquired the land upon which her abbey was built. The saint had such a reputation for good works that the local chieftain was obligated to fulfill her request for land. Mockingly he told her she could have as much land as her cloak could cover. With a knowing smile, St. Brigid confidently swirled her cloak to the ground, where it began to miraculously increase, much to the chieftain's dismay, and did not stop spreading until it covered the hillside she had prayed to obtain for her abbey.

Imbolc, or St. Brigid's Day, was a Celtic festival marking the beginning of spring. The word is derived from the Old Irish *i mbolg*, "in the belly," referring to the pregnancy of ewes during that time of year. Imbolc is traditionally a time of foretelling the weather. The old tradition of watching to see if badgers or serpents came from their winter dens is perhaps a precursor to our North American Groundhog Day.

A Farmer's Invocation to St. Brigid

Dear Saint Brigid, my hope of spring,
Bless these little fields of mine;
Bless the pastures and the trees;
Bless the butter and the cheese;
Bless the cows with coats of silk;
Bless the brimming pails of milk;
Bless the hedgerows, and I pray;
Bless the seed beneath the clay;
Bless the hay and bless the grass;
Bless the seasons as they pass;
With your blessings, we will prevail,
Dear St. Brigid, Mary of the Gael.[5]

February 23: St. Serenus the Gardener, ca. 307

Patron of Gardeners

February 23 is the memorial of St. Serenus the Gardener, who died in 307. He was Grecian and a caretaker of beautiful gardens. He left behind all that he had including his friends and country to serve God.

To live as a hermit, he bought a garden in Sirmium in Pannonia (modern-day Serbia); he cultivated the garden and lived on the fruits and herbs it produced. The beauty of his garden was well known throughout the region, and many villagers would take delight walking about the grounds of this neighborhood hermit's garden.

For a while he had to abandon his lovely garden and hide from the persecutions taking place during the early 300s. During those years, under the reign of Galerius and Diocletian, Christians were compelled to sacrifice to Roman gods or face imprisonment, torture, and execution. For a short period Constantine, on taking the imperial office in 306, attempted to restore Christians to full legal equality.

When that campaign to eliminate Christians lessened, Serenus returned to his hermitage and immediately began work to restore his overgrown plot to its previous charm.

One day around noon, he found a woman and her daughters walking in the gardens. Because it was during the time of day when Romans were rarely seen out and about, let alone a wife of a Roman gentleman, he suggested they leave and return when it was cooler, and the woman took offense. Her husband, wanting to avenge the insult to his wife, had Serenus arrested. Though he was acquitted, the courts learned that he was a Christian, and because the Emperor Maximian was ruling at that time, Serenus was martyred when he refused to worship pagan gods.

The gardens of the dark ages were utilitarian in their function, and it was unusual for them to be arranged in an aesthetically pleasing manner as Serenus had done. The plants he grew would have included herbs for cooking, for the household, and for medicinal purposes. He was known to use the food from this garden to feed the poor.

St. Valentine, February 14

It is believed that the custom of men and women writing love letters to their valentine started on Valentine's Day in about 1477. This stems from the English, who associated lovers with that day because "every bird chooses him a mate" by that day. Other romance traditions have become attached to this feast, including pinning bay leaves to your pillow on the eve of St. Valentine's Day so that you will see your future mate that night in your dreams.[6]

St. Lucy

Her name means "light." The Feast of St. Lucy is celebrated on December 13 when we are approaching the winter solstice. It is associated in popular tradition with spiritual light. Read more about this saint in the December chapter.

February in the Garden

> Christians . . . who truly know the ancient symbols of the
> Church's doctrine and rites are Christians who are deeply
> rooted in the faith.
>
> –Mike Aquilina

Practical Gardening: Sunlight and Shade

When it comes to gardening we know how important sunlight is. The vibrant colors of full-sun flowering beds are often breathtaking. We can also create lovely gardens that are not in full sun. Plants vary in their needs for light, from dappled shade to woodlands.

For February, let's focus on some of the low-light or shade environments you may have in your garden areas, how to identify the type of shade, and what to consider if your area is dry, moist, or really wet.

Defining a low-light garden usually begins with the quantity and quality of light in the area.

Woodland or Heavy Shade

This is an area where sunlight is blocked or covered by trees or structures all day. This is the most challenging and rewarding of gardens to develop. In late summer I love to sit in a cool shade garden while looking out into an illuminating sunny landscape. The contrast offers many metaphors for prayer.

Light, Dappled, or High Shade

In this environment the sun is filtered through high branches all day. Most of us have this type of shade, especially if we live in a suburban area.

Afternoon Shade

This is an area that has gentle sun in the morning and heavy to light shade all afternoon from structures or trees. This is the easiest light condition in which to develop a shade garden and offers early morning and late-day opportunities to pray while protected from harsh sunlight.

Morning Shade

Here an area has heavy to light shade in the morning from structures or trees and full, hard sun all afternoon. This type of a garden would be considered full sun to minimal shade. Most shade plants will not tolerate this type of an environment; the afternoon sun is too harsh.

Sunny Area

Here there is full sun from dawn to sunset.

The next step to consider in the shade garden is the relative moisture-retaining qualities of the soil.

Dry Shade

These areas exist between buildings that block rainfall, on shaded slopes, or in some heavily wooded areas. Very specific plants are required for dry shade. A small area of dry shade may be improved by creating a raised bed or amending the area to hold more moisture by adding peat or compost. With dedicated effort and watering, you can broaden the type of plant materials that will grow in this location. For larger areas, use the right plant in the right place.

Moist and Well-Drained Shade

This is a more common environment in suburban yards. It is rich in organic matter and has a nice soil composition that holds moisture without becoming heavy. This offers the broadest range of plantings, especially when the shade is not heavy and dense.

Faith-Filled Gardening: Creating Symbolic Elements

I like shade gardens, especially when there is a path meandering through. A lovely touch to a path is making your own stepping-stones. In creating these pavers, why not include simple Christian images or symbols in them that will remind you of the Light of the World?

The meanings, origins, and ancient traditions surrounding Christian symbols date back to early times when most ordinary people were not able to read or write and printing was unknown. As author Mike Aquilina notes in his book *Signs and Mysteries*, "The relationship of the sign to the signified can be complex. It can arise from historical association, social convention, or mere physical resemblance. Sometimes several of these factors enter the equation."[7]

There are symbols, such as a fish, star, or cross, whose images we recognize in line drawings. These definitive symbols translate well into a garden setting. Their representative shapes can be worked with wood, mosaics, stones, or any other kind of weather-resistant materials.

As you read through the description of each symbol, think about which ones have meaning for you and will incorporate well into your yard. In a garden for families with children, use images of animals and nature. You can also make a lovely walkway using stepping-stones where each step represents a different Christian cross. The combinations and ways to display them are limitless.

Images

Butterfly

A symbol of the Resurrection. From a seemingly lifeless cocoon, it is transformed into another phase of life.

Dolphin

Historically, the dolphin was thought to have human qualities. Fishermen saw them as guides, rescuers, and friends. Sometimes they are drawn in pairs representing Christians, or singly representing Christ, much like the line drawing of a fish. The dolphin is often paired with other symbols, especially the anchor.

Dove

Representative of the Holy Spirit and a harbinger of hope. For the faithful, it signified the release of the soul at death. It has also been used to signify peace.

Egg

A symbol of the Resurrection and new life. It also recalls the story of Creation.

Fish

The oldest symbol of Jesus as Eucharist. The first letter of each word from the Greek phrase "Jesus Christ Son of God Savior" spells *fish* (Iehthys).

Lamb

This symbol has many interpretations but is most often associated with the paschal sacrifice, with Jesus as the paschal lamb of God. When he is portrayed holding a cross, people recognize this as his triumph over death. A lamb also reminds Christians that sheep need a shepherd to guide and feed them. Often used on the tombstones of children, it represents innocence.

Peacock

A symbol of immortality because it was believed that its flesh did not decompose. Also associated with the Resurrection of both Christ and Christians because it sheds its old tail feathers each year and grows even more elaborate new ones by Easter. The tail feather pattern is symbolic of the eye of God.

Pelican

It was believed that during times of famine, the pelican wounded itself in its breast to feed its young with its own blood. Thus, it is the symbol of the Redeemer who gave his blood to save us. It also symbolizes atonement.

Rainbow

Represents God's faithfulness to his followers. Because it is composed of seven colors, it also symbolizes the seven sacraments.

Rooster, Cock

Symbolizes watchfulness and vigilance, and hope in the coming of dawn. Two roosters together will fight, and so a rooster also indicates a Christian who is called to fight the good fight for the gift of faith.

Rose

The symbolism changes depending on the type, the number of petals, and the color of this flower. Generally it stands for faith. The Christmas Rose of the Nativity, or Messianic Rose, shown here has a central Epiphany star, five petals for the five wounds, and trefoil calyx tips for the Holy Trinity; often a Latin cross of the crucifixion is drawn on the calyx.

Shell, Scalloped

Symbolizes baptism, and if seen with three droplets it represents the Holy Trinity.

Turtledove

Symbolic of Christian fidelity. These birds are faithful to only one mate for life.

Wheat Sheaves

There are several meanings to wheat: Jesus is the eucharistic bread of life, the miracles of the multiplication of loaves, Jesus' death as seed to germinate new life, and our own death to self.

Symbols

Alpha and Omega

A recognizable symbol by nearly all Christians, alpha as the first and omega as the last letters of the Greek alphabet, representing God as the one who is the first and last.

Anchor

Symbolizing hope and stability, fishers of men, and anchored safely in faith. The shank is representative of the Latin cross. Often seen with other symbols such as the dolphin, fish, and boat.

Chi-Rho (Chi = X, Rho = P), *Labarum*

An old and very recognizable monogram of Christ; the "*X*" and "*P*" are the first Greek letters in the title *Christos*. An interesting historical fact is that this symbol was used to mark text much in the same way we use an asterisk.

IHS

This monogram is the abbreviation for Jesus' name during that era, *IESUS*. When appearing with periods, I.H.S., it is the acronym for the Latin phrase *Iesus Hominum Salvator*, Jesus, Savior of man.

Keys

Symbolize papal authority, the keys to the kingdom of heaven, and the Church's power to bind or loose human error.

Lamp

Symbol of the illumination of God's Word.

Nails

Three nails were used to crucify Jesus. Nails are often incorporated into paintings of the child Jesus.

Quatrefoil

A shape found in nature, especially in flower petals, it was adopted to represent the four evangelists: Matthew, Mark, Luke, and John.

Ship

Symbol of the Church with many meanings, for example, Mary as the Church safely bearing the faithful toward her son, and Noah's ark as a ship's hold of safety while all those outside were destroyed. The interior of a church is called the nave (Latin, *navis,* ship).

Star

Shown here is the Epiphany star, always represented with one of its points at the apex, and is a reminder of the five wounds of Christ. The four-point star, often used in art as the star over the place where the child Jesus was born, is called the Bethlehem or natal star. The eight-pointed star is known as the Star of Redemption, while the six-pointed star, two triangles interlocked, is called the Star of David.

Torch

Symbolizes the light of truth being carried into the world. Also the symbol of the Dominicans, the order of preachers.

Triquetra or Trefoil

A symbol of the Holy Trinity.

Crosses

Baptismal Cross

The number eight represents regeneration or resurrection. Many baptismal fonts are eight sided for this reason. The eight points are made from the Greek cross overlaid with the Greek letter X, which is the first letter in the Greek word for Christ.

Byzantine Cross

Used in Eastern Orthodox Churches, the smaller crossbar at the top is for the inscription INRI, and the lowest crossbar is for Jesus' feet.

Celtic Cross, Cross of Iona

There are many tales, so typical of the Celts, associated with the design of this cross. The basic symbolisms present here are a Latin cross (tall) or Greek cross (short) with a circle for eternity forming four chambers representing the evangelists.

Evangelists' Cross

A Latin cross set on top of the four Gospel books, or steps, of the evangelists.

Graded Cross

A Latin cross set on top of the three theological steps of virtue: faith, hope, and charity.

Greek Cross

The original cross symbol, with arms of equal length, was easily disguised by Christians during eras of persecution.

Jerusalem Cross or Crusaders' Cross

Constructed of five Greek crosses signifying the five wounds. Can also stand for the four evangelists with Christ at the center. When seen with Greek initials instead of four smaller crosses, it is called the Conqueror's Cross.

Latin Cross, *Crux immissa*

The most commonly used cross, it came into use in the second or third century. It is in the shape of the crucifixion cross upon which Jesus was nailed.

Maltese Cross

The eight outer points represent the Beatitudes. It is the symbol of the Christian warriors, Knights of Malta or Knights Hospitaller.

Papal Cross

The crossbars represent the pope's role as the bishop of Rome, patriarch of the West, and the successor of St. Peter. This particular cross configuration is also a reminder to its viewers of the three crosses erected on Calvary.

Patriarch's Cross, Lorraine Cross, Caravaca Cross, and Other Names

Used by Roman Catholic archbishops. Positioning of the second crossbar connotes different representations, and as a result, this cross has various names.

Slavonic Cross

Used in Russian Orthodox Churches. The smaller crossbar at the top is where the inscription INRI would have been nailed up, and the lowest crossbar at an angle suggests the way Jesus' intense suffering dislodged the woodworking. The angled footrest has other meanings as well: the fate of sinners, the good and bad thieves on either side of Christ, and the cross on which St. Andrew was crucified.

St. Andrew's Cross, Swiss Cross, *Crux decussata*

St. Andrew was crucified on a cross of this construction. This cross looks like the Roman numeral ten, so it has the name of *decussis*, which is the word for the number ten.

St. Brigid's Cross

An easy handmade cross created by St. Brigid from Ireland.

Tau or Thau Cross, *Crux commissa,* Franciscan Cross

Named after the Greek letter it resembles. The word *commissa* means joined or attached. Sometimes called the Old Testament cross.

Creating Stepping-Stones

To make your own stepping-stones using these symbols, begin by gathering the items you want to embed into your stepping-stone. Shells, glass cabochons, stained-glass pieces or broken pottery for mosaics, small rocks, metal objects, and so on; the list is endless. The objects need to be weatherproof and sturdy enough so that they will not break when someone steps on them.

You can purchase garden stone kits that include forms or lettering sets.[8] To make your stones, find a place where you can work with little damage if you spill or soil something. If the outdoor workspace cannot be hosed off and you do not want cement stains to remain, be sure to cover the work surface with newspapers or a plastic tablecloth.

An inexpensive way is to create a form using a ten- or twelve-inch pizza box with duct tape wrapped around the perimeter of the box for added support. You can also make a wood frame, but be sure to line it with plastic along the sides so the cement will not adhere to the wood. A saucer from a large plastic plant container also works well as a starter modeling form, but be sure to line it with plastic or smear it with petroleum jelly so the cement will come out when it is dry. These homemade stepping-stones will look more rustic and naturalistic than ones purchased from hobby and craft shops.

You will need a three-gallon bucket or basin for mixing cement, a hose or bucket of water, waterproof gloves to protect your hands from the acid in the cement, and something to cover your face. Cement is caustic and always sends powder into the air when it is disturbed, so protect your eyes and nose until the cement is well mixed.

As with cooking a recipe in the kitchen, have all your "ingredients" ready before you start mixing, including the forms for the stones, objects for embedding, a trowel or screed for smoothing, and a narrow plastic plant tag or similar object for writing. Adding a piece of wire hardware cloth cut slightly smaller than the size of your stone will help reinforce the cement, though this is rarely necessary.

A ten-pound pail of Quikrete dry cement—either vinyl-reinforced or quick-set mixes—will make about two twelve-by-twelve stones and half of another. For a single twelve-by-twelve stone, scoop just over a third of the powdered cement into your mixing bucket that already contains some water; I start with one cup of water and add a quarter cup more of it at a time as needed. Mix this with your gloved hands until it is about the consistency of dropped cookie dough. If you squeeze a handful of the cement it should hold its form when you open your palm and not squish through your fingers (it's too wet and soupy) or crumble when touched (it's too dry).

Scoop the wet cement from the mixing pail into the mold and press it into place. Smooth the surface and edges. Add the decorative objects, being sure to push them in the cement a good inch in from the edge and deep enough so that the cement will hold them securely. Set the finished stepping-stones in a shaded, dry location to cure for the next one or two days, depending on the thickness of the stones. When they are hardened, release your stones from their molds. If you have used glass or ceramics and you find there is a slight film of cement on them, use a nonmetal scrubber to remove the excess.

Place your stepping-stones in your garden path, at the edge of your flower bed, or at the base of your statue or birdbath. They also make wonderful gifts.

Biblical Reflections

"Let light shine out of darkness," who has shone in our hearts to give the light of the knowledge of the glory of God in the face of Christ. But we have this treasure in earthen vessels, to show that the transcendent power belongs to God and not to us . . . because we look not to the things that are seen but to the things that are unseen.

—2 Corinthians 4:6–7, 18

O dwellers in the dust, awake and sing for joy! For thy dew is a dew of light.

—Isaiah 26:19

I am the LORD, I have called you in righteousness, I have taken you by the hand and kept you; I have given you as a covenant to the people, a light to the nations. . . . And I will lead the blind in a way that they know not, in paths that they have not known I will guide them. I will turn the darkness before them into light, the rough places into level ground. These are the things I will do, and I will not forsake them.

—Isaiah 42:6, 16

And we are writing this that our joy may be complete. This is the message we have heard from him and proclaim to you, that God is light and in him is no darkness at all. If we say we have fellowship with him while we walk in darkness, we lie and do not live according to the truth; but if we walk in the light, as he is in the light, we have fellowship with one another.

—1 John 1:4–7

Then I saw that wisdom excels folly as light excels darkness.

—Ecclesiastes 2:13

Prayer Focus for February

> Let your light so shine before men, that they may see your good works and give glory to your Father who is in heaven.
>
> –Matthew 5:16

We and our physical world would not exist without light; now consider the importance of God's light for our souls. This light is not meant to be kept to ourselves and hidden. In what ways can you illuminate those around you with the light of Christ? Imagine that you had been denied light for a very long time, having lived in shadows. You knew that on a set day you would be liberated. What is the first thing you would want to see? Why? We cannot always be in the intense demanding light of life and like Jesus need a quiet place to go away for a while. How can you create a shady retreat in your own gardens?

March: **Pruning**

I am the true vine, and my Father is the vinedresser. Every branch of mine that bears no fruit, he takes away, and every branch that does bear fruit he prunes, that it may bear more fruit.

–John 15:1–2

Pruning strengthens and enhances a plant in a balanced pattern of growth, beauty, and function. Any vintner, orchardist, or laborer in the field knows the importance of proper pruning for fruitfulness.

The month of March is dedicated to St. Joseph the foster father of Jesus, also known as St. Joseph the Worker. He was one of many holy men who labored for God, and to labor is to undertake something of difficulty. Joseph diligently worked to support and protect his family and to properly rear a Jewish boy to manhood.

Our society at times seems to discourage the importance of marriage and fatherhood. St. Joseph is a beautiful model of a faithful and obedient father dedicated to what was best for his family. He set aside all thoughts of self and willingly shouldered his responsibilities.

Children are somewhat like young saplings or vines that need to be directionally pruned to prevent them from shooting off in wild and unproductive directions. And I'm sure Joseph had his hands full with a perfectly healthy little boy. We know that Jesus was human in every way, and I don't doubt that as with any little boy he was neither perfectly angelic nor fully attentive for more than seven minutes. Joseph, with Mary, would have had to keep their little boy growing properly in their faith. No matter how miraculously Jesus had been conceived, he was still a little boy full of energy, curiosity, and impulses.

Traditions and Feasts of March

> The apple tree spread wide its shade
> To shield the garden from the sun;
> In dappled light the Virgin prayed
> That, cloud or clear, God's will be done.
>
> —Genevieve Glen, O.S.B.

During March, Lent is in progress. It is during this season of Lent that we prune back from our lives that which is not essential. Sometimes it is a challenge to remove from our lives the little things that comfort or delight us.

It is also the time, if you have a home altar, when the nonessential elements are removed until after Easter. I remember a time when clearing my prayer space that I found it hard to remove what was familiar: a white statue of Mary.

The Blessed Mother statue is only twelve inches tall. Finding a place to store it for Lent shouldn't have been that hard. At a Catholic writers conference I'd bought this smaller version of the original from the Asian woman who was the sculptor.

The soft light from the candles in my prayer space enhanced the artist's design. The hands of Mother Mary are against her chest, tipped back in a way that gives the impression of an opening lotus flower. Her head is tilted; her Asian eyes and delicate smile are directed at baby Jesus standing in the blossom of her hands.

Setting the statue on a side table, I changed over the altar. The green linens of Ordinary Time that covered my altar after Christmas are again folded away. The bottles of holy water from Lourdes, Fatima, and my grandmother's cabinet are nestled in a drawer below the altar, along with silk flowers, holy cards, crocheted cross bookmarks, and a small framed picture of Blessed Mother Teresa.

Honoring the traditions of Lent, I've placed deep purple cloths on the altar and over the sacred images on the walls. I hesitated before covering the lithograph of St. Mary Magdalene. This saint has journeyed with me since childhood and we greet each other every morning as I enter the room to pray. I carefully drape a cloth over the print of Divine Mercy and as I do so offer prayers for the precious souls in purgatory. My room feels empty. The absence of others sharing my prayers is pronounced.

Everything is readied except for the twelve-inch Madonna. I hold her tight to my chest as I bend down to look in lower cabinets for storage space. I continue to hold her as I walk from one room to another and then back trying to find a safe place for her to rest. Standing in the prayer room with its purple linens, Mary pressed near my heart, I realized I was tearing up.

A memory had come to the surface of when I was a child. I had a favorite stuffed toy, a sleeping white kitty with an embroidered pink nose and slanted eyes. From bed to sandbox to washer and back to my hands it would travel. A day came when I was to stay with my grandmother, and Kitty was placed in the bottom of a grocery bag, on top of which were my clothes. I wanted to carry Kitty in my arms; I didn't want to let go. As long as I held it—near and tight—I felt safe.

I felt a little silly welling up with tears as I stood there holding the statue. My desiring to hold close a sense of safety was once again evident in the motion of my arms. I didn't want to let go of the Madonna; I didn't want to be without that statue in my sight for the forty days of Lent. I wanted to embrace, as nearly as I could, this side of heaven, the nearness of my Holy Mother.

Letting go, paring down, and pruning back are familiar Lenten themes that often surface at other times of the year and rattle our sense of security. This was certainly true for me in the economic crash that started in 2008. The financial and physical challenges taking place in my life would result in a new writing career. At the time, transformation was hard to endure. As with so many others, I too have learned that the most marvelous transformations at God's hands are taking place in our most desolate of times.

March is also the month when we celebrate the Feast of St. Joseph and the Annunciation. The Solemnity of St. Joseph is on March 19. He was the man set apart by God for a very specific vocation of rearing the Messiah. Whenever God chooses someone to receive a special grace, he provides the person with all that is needed to fulfill the task. For St. Joseph that seemed to be a steady, confident persistence. Throughout the Bible we see in St. Joseph a quiet and willing readiness to do what God had called him to do; he wore not a martyr's crown but the crown of humble perseverance.

The Solemnity of St. Joseph is a widely celebrated feast day for Italians. During the Middle Ages, St. Joseph's intercession saved the Sicilians from a very serious drought. Because of this miracle, the custom developed for all to wear red on his feast day to honor him, in the same way green is worn on St. Patrick's Day, also occurring this month.

On the day of celebration, which usually falls on the weekend closest to March 19, a St. Joseph's table is constructed. The table will have three tiers indicating the Most Holy Trinity, is blessed by a priest, and is laden with food contributed by the community. Different Italian regions celebrate this day in various ways, but all involve special meatless foods: minestrone, pasta with breadcrumbs (symbolizing the sawdust that would have covered St. Joseph's floor), seafood, special desserts, and always, fava beans. Fava beans are considered a special blessing because, during the drought, this bean thrived while other crops failed.

The top tier holds a statue of St. Joseph surrounded by flowers, especially white lilies. The other tiers would include the food, more flowers, candles or figurines, symbolically shaped breads and pastries, twelve fishes symbolizing the apostles, wine symbolizing the miracle at Cana, other edible items that represent hospitality and blessings, and pictures of deceased family members. A basket is set before the St. Joseph table in which the faithful place prayer petitions.

After the meal and with the leftover food secured elsewhere, the St. Joseph table is smashed. Immediately following, three children dressed as the Holy Family will knock on three doors, asking for shelter; this reenactment is called *tupa tupa*, meaning "knock knock." They will be refused at the first two homes and welcomed at the third, in memory of the Holy Family's seeking shelter before Christ was born. The day ends with participants taking home a bag that might be filled with bread, fruit, pastries, cookies, a medal of St. Joseph, a holy card, or a blessed fava bean.[1]

St. Joseph was attentive to the holy words from God that came to him through angels or in dreams. His life was being radically changed, and because God was pruning away Joseph's previous life, Joseph would be strengthened to grow in new ways. Joseph drew strength and courage from his faith during that time of transition. He trusted what was spoken to him and acted upon what he heard, enabling him to care for Mary, who was pregnant with a child he did not father.

The meadow lily, *Lilium candidum*, is strongly associated with St. Joseph. There is a story that, during the birth of Jesus, Joseph's staff burst into lily blooms to prove he was worthy to guard and care for Mary and the infant Jesus. This lily, also called the Madonna lily, is often shown at the annunciation to Mary because it represents purity. Both Joseph and Mary had a purity of heart in following the will of God.

The annunciation to Mary is a solemnity held on March 25. This event, found in Luke 1:26–39 and Matthew 1:18–21, is not only recognized by Roman and Eastern Catholics but also recorded in the Qur'an.

We read in the Bible that the angel Gabriel came to Mary and announced to her what her vocation would be: "You will conceive in your womb and bear a son, and you shall call his name Jesus. . . . The Holy Spirit will come upon you, and the power of the Most High will overshadow you; therefore the child to be born will be called holy, the Son of God" (Lk 1:31, 35). Imagine that for a moment; there you are sitting in your favorite chair, reading the Bible or praying a Rosary, when suddenly a heavenly creature pops in, falling to its knees before you, and says hello. I'm amazed that we weren't told that Mary fainted dead away.

Mary, as did Joseph, received a very clear calling of her vocation ascribed by God. That calling pruned away much of the life she had grown secure with. In the words of Mother Marie des Douleurs, Mary was illumined by the light of certainty because she lived in a state of continual wonder. "It was precisely because she dared to believe [in the all-loving power of God] that she dared to give up everything, or rather that it never occurred to her to let herself be bound by anything."[2]

I wonder how much certainty and confidence we bring when God calls us to do his will and change the plans we had set out for ourselves. For some of us, that redirection to grow in new ways means reassessing what is important in our lives.

Gabriel is the angel of the annunciation. His name means "God is my strength." He was present at the Resurrection; according to traditions in the Greek Orthodox Church, Gabriel appeared to Daniel to tell him of the coming of a Messiah and announced to Zechariah the coming of John the Baptist. This archangel, through God's command, brought mercy, vengeance, death, and revelation. Gabriel is the ruler of the heavenly army of angels and the cherubim. It was Gabriel speaking for God who dictated to Mohammed the Qur'an. In Jewish legend it was Gabriel who dealt death and destruction to Sodom and Gomorrah.

March Saints for the Gardener

> Greatness of soul consists not so much in soaring high and in pressing forward, as in how to adapt and limit oneself.
>
> —Michel Eyquem de Montaigne

March 13: St. Ansovinus of Camerino, d. 840

Patron for the Protection of Crops

Not much is known about the early life of this saint. His story begins after he became a priest and lived as a hermit near Torcello, Italy. The people in the region came to rely on this quiet and unassuming priest for many of their needs. It was not long after he had arrived in the region that miracles began to take place; Ansovinus had been given the gifts of multiplication of food and healing.

St. Ansovinus lived across a river and a bit of distance from the chapel where he would say Mass. Being a poor hermit he did not own a boat, and being a humble man he did not want to ask the neighboring community to come and fetch him from across the water. The story is told that this unassuming priest would offer prayers as he placed his cloak upon the water and then sitting upon it would paddle across the river.

His patronage for the fruitfulness and protection of crops comes from the miracle of his ability to feed the poor from his small plot. It didn't seem to matter how many of the poor came to him or when. He nourished them all with grain and the Word of God, bread that fed both body and soul.

One of his more memorable miracles took place when he had emptied the regional granary at Castel-Raimondo. There were so many people starving during the early Middle Ages in Western Europe that hundreds who had heard of his charity had flocked to him in their need. The beloved St. Ansovinus had already fed thousands who were starving, and still more needed food. As his helpers told him of the emptied hold of grain, I can imagine this dedicated priest kneeling in prayer. I can appreciate the doubt of the workers and their ultimate astonishment when they were told to go back to the granary and found it miraculously filled.

March 17: St. Patrick, ca. 388–463

Extensive Patronage

St. Patrick is a well-known saint, and there are countless books written about him. One of his best-known traits was using the three-leaf clover to teach about the Holy Trinity, pointing to its three leaflets united by a common stalk. Due to his missionary efforts the shamrock became a registered trademark by the government of Ireland.

As a youth Patrick's arrival in Ireland was by force; he was kidnapped by pirates and enslaved there as a shepherd for six years. Before he was kidnapped there are several delightful stories about St. Patrick as a child, foretelling his holiness.

When he was still quite young and tending the sheep of his aunt with his sister, a wolf bounded out of the woods and nabbed one of the lambs. The poor boy was distraught, and when he told his aunt of the incident she scolded him for neglecting his duties. Though stung by her harsh words, he prayed all night to God for the return of his aunt's lost lamb. When he returned to the same pasture the next morning, the thieving wolf ran from the woods and dropped the lamb unharmed at Patrick's feet.

Another story tells of one of his aunt's cows being suddenly possessed by an evil spirit. The cow tore, butted, and charged with her horns, scattering the herd and badly wounding several other cows. The boy Patrick went forward and armed with faith stood before the mad cow, made the Sign of the Cross, and in doing so freed the poor beast of its demon. Patrick then went to the side of each wounded cow and knelt in prayer; blessing them, he restored them all to health. The formerly possessed cow followed him and, when Patrick had finished all of his praying, licked the hands and feet of her deliverer.

St. Vincent of Saragossa

St. Vincent is a patron of vintners, and as we know those who tend to grapevines are well practiced in the purposefulness of pruning. His feast day is January 22; read about him in the January chapter.

Blessing for Fruiting Trees and Vines

Let us pray. We beg You in Your goodness, almighty God, to pour the showers of Your blessing upon these newly budding trees and vines that You have made and that You have been so kind as to nourish with temperate weather and sufficient rain. Bring the fruits of Your earth to full ripeness. Grant, too, that Your people may always give

You thanks for Your gifts, so that You may fill them that are hungry with the fruits of a fertile land and that by sharing the poor and the needy may also praise the glory of Your name, through Christ our Lord. (Then the plants are sprinkled with holy water.)[3]

March in the Garden

Practical Gardening: Pruning

I love to prune. It's like art to me, a hope-filled art. Each cut is intended to produce a directional growth, to form and shape hardwoods for beauty, or to enhance the bearing of fruit.

Sometimes with ornamental trees a whole section of limb that rubs against another needs to be removed, allowing the stronger limb to develop more fully. At other times the interior has become so cluttered with unnecessary branches that they block the light from reaching deep inside. More often if pruning has been done regularly, it is a simple nip here or there to keep things growing as they should.

Spring-flowering shrubs bloom on branches that matured during the previous growing season, also known as year-old wood. By the end of summer, these shrubs have already developed tiny leaf and flower buds that remain dormant over the winter, ready to bloom once spring arrives. If those branches are pruned in the fall, you will eliminate the flowers they'll bear. For this reason, spring-flowering shrubs should always be pruned immediately after flowering. This will give the shrub the entire summer to develop flower buds for next spring.

Some spring-flowering shrubs and vines are as follows: azalea, beauty bush, broom, burning bush, clematis (check cultivar for correct procedure), Daphne, deutzia, dogwood, elder, forsythia, holly, honeysuckle, kerria, lilac, magnolia, mockorange, passion flower, potentilla, flowering quince, rhododendron, spirea, viburnum, weigela, winter jasmine, and wisteria.

Summer-flowering shrubs are slower to leaf out in the spring, being the last in the garden to break dormancy, sometimes not until early summer. If you are a beginner at gardening and think your Rose of Sharon or other summer-blooming shrub is dead, don't dig it up until you've checked for life: scratch a very tiny piece of the bark from a main branch with your fingernail; if you see a hint of green, the plant is alive.

These shrubs flower on growth from the current year, known as new wood, and need to be pruned before new growth begins. Summer-flowering shrubs are pruned in the early spring before the new growth begins.

Summer-flowering shrubs and vines include abelia, American bittersweet, butterfly bush, caryopteris, clethra (summersweet), grapes, hydrangea, potentilla, Rose of Sharon, roses, smokebush, spirea, and trumpet vine, just to name a few.

A lovely story about preservation from pruning is told about the flowering hawthorn of St. Joseph of Arimathea. According to tradition, following the crucifixion of Jesus, St. Joseph of Arimathea, the owner of the tomb in which Jesus Christ's body would lay, was driven from his home and began a journey of conversion. He traveled first to Marseilles and then to Glastonbury in an attempt to bring Christianity to the Britons.

When he and his twelve companions arrived at Wirrial Hill, tired from the journey, he thrust his staff into the hillside as he and his friends lay down to rest. When he awoke, a miracle had taken place: the staff had taken root and begun to grow and flower. This became the site of the Glastonbury Abbey, where the hawthorn blooms every Christmas and spring, almost always near Easter time.

Legend has it that the original hawthorn was cut down by a Puritan soldier in 1653 (who, it is said, surmised it to be an object of superstition—and was blinded when struck in the eye by a splinter). Numerous other versions of the attempted eradication exist.

However, many cuttings were taken from the tree before its destruction. The current hawthorn on the grounds of Glastonbury Abbey is said to be a cutting from the original tree. It was planted in secret after the original was destroyed.[4]

To learn more about pruning techniques, check online or at your library for reference material. Many nurseries have knowledgeable staff members who can also advise you on how to prune a newly purchased plant.

Faith-Filled Gardening: Creating a Lenten Garden

Lent comes providentially to reawaken us, to shake us from our lethargy.

–Pope Francis

Each Church year we remember and celebrate the events that saved us. We make the Word of God, the life of Jesus, the outpouring of the Holy Spirit, and the events of Mary's life present in our everyday lives. They become real! We are enriched by all that is inspired in us through these celebrations.

As Catholics, we begin marking time in the Church year with Advent, then Christmas, and after a brief period of Ordinary Time, we move into Lent. This is followed by all those blessed days of Easter, and then once again it's back to Ordinary Time. Since I live in the northern hemisphere, it seems appropriate to begin our faith-filled gardening with Lent since the liturgy coincides so beautifully with the coming of spring.

Pre-Lent and the Festive Garden

The word *Lent* is derived from Old English *lencten*, which means "lengthen" and refers to the increase of daylight hours. It is a period of transition from late winter to early spring.

Traditionally, the three weeks preceding Lent were a time of carnival-like festivities. It was the time to consume all the foods to be avoided during Lenten fasting, when we wean ourselves away from all that distracts us from our journey with God.

During this carnival period, add additional ornamentation to the garden—a great activity if you have children. Make the garden bright and garish by adding colorful ribbons and handmade ornaments. Think about the excesses in your life and how pretty and possibly useless they might be.

We begin Lent with Ash Wednesday. On Ash Wednesday, after the noon Mass and before 3:00 p.m., silently strip the garden of these accents. You could save some of them for Easter or store them for next year. You can also mark this holy day in the garden by creating your own ashes from some of the smaller decorations you have removed from the carnival-week garden, or from written prayer notes.

The notes can be a collection of prayers containing all the useless things we have accumulated in our hearts that need to be released to make room for God. You can also write prayers of offering. Make a small fire pit of stones in your garden or use a fireproof container or clay chiminea. Prayerfully place your written words inside the container and burn them. Imagine your prayers rising to God in the smoke. Collect these ashes and bury them in the garden, maybe near the foot of your statue of the Virgin Mary.

While you're at it, and if you haven't decided what your personal sacrifice will be for Lent, envision doing deliberate acts of kindness instead of the typical sacrifice of giving up a favorite food or candy.

The elderly, busy single parents, and sick people would sincerely appreciate a little help in their gardens or yard as part of your Lenten practice.

Lenten Garden Elements

Lent is a season of change, a way to atone and become whole, and a time to break out of old patterns in a conscious and creative way. We change the way we see and respond to the world around us.

This transformation can begin with the garden in some very simple ways. Start with a verse or saying displayed where you enter the garden or near the area where you sit. Write the verse on a weatherproof cloth, or stamp a stepping-stone with the words you want to make permanent.

One of my favorite sayings for Lent and, for that matter, all through the year is *vacare Deo*. The literal definition is "to be empty for God." Another way to say it is to be empty of the false self and become available to God to find one's true self. (Hint: This is a good source for the prayer notes you're going to burn.) In the Christian monastic and contemplative tradition, *vacare Deo* is to set aside time from work for meditation and prayer. This dying to self leads us into a Lenten springtime.

During the liturgies of Lent we do not say "alleluia." Alleluia means "Praise the Lord" and is associated with the joy of Easter. We bury this praise deep within our hearts during Lent. Try burying the alleluias in your garden. Take a piece of easily biodegradable paper and write a blessing on it. Mix a packet of seeds with a couple of tablespoons of potting mix and then wrap a small amount of the seed-soil mix in the paper, tying it all together with garden twine. Now bury your alleluia blessings in the garden. You will definitely praise the Lord as your little blessings begin to sprout in spring.

These are also wonderful gift alternatives to the usual Easter baskets filled with candy.

Going through darkness in a tunnel or a long unlit passage is similar to entering into the light of God, and a gate is a passage from one area to another. You can create a shaded tunnel of sorts using a gated arbor or pergola by growing a vine on it; use grapevines for additional symbolism. Do you have a line of trees or evergreens? Create a walkway underneath their boughs by trimming up branches from the lower portion of the trunk. At a retreat center where I volunteer, the evergreens are planted in parallel rows and only the boughs on the inside of the row are trimmed up. It makes an amazing tunnel under the pines and is referred to as the "Cathedral Walk."

Another idea is to place the arbor so it leads to that part of your garden devoted to the Stations of the Cross.

During Lent we are called into deeper prayer, almsgiving, and fasting (PAF) and beyond our usual tithe. To remind us of our call to action, mark a cloth, stepping-stone, or smooth rock with a triangle, symbolizing the Holy Trinity, a heart painted inside to show the love of God, and the three letters of each action, PAF, at each tip of the triangle.

The liturgical color of Lent is purple. Purple ribbons tied in knots on branches or a purple cloth draped across an outdoor table or bench will also enhance your appreciation of the season. And about that table . . . did you include a second chair for Jesus? Drape that chair too and add other personal elements that help you reflect on these forty days.

It is during Lent that we become more acutely aware of the Cross, the strongest of Christian symbols. Make crosses from any number of found objects in a variety of sizes. While doing so, speculate as you make them how, in whatever we do, God can work with us.

Place your crosses, whether handmade or purchased, throughout your garden. As you walk through the garden during Lent you will be reminded of the many ways the Cross influences your life. Plan on "resurrecting" these crosses on Easter Sunday by prayerfully gathering them up and arranging them in a pot. You could also freshen up the crosses and distribute them as Easter garden gifts instead of giving sugared bunnies.

For those who have very small yards, or no yard at all, place a cross made from sticks in a container of sand. During Lent add small stones or twigs and think about the desert experience that Jesus would be facing. As Easter approaches, put some water in the sand and add budding branches or flowers to the container.

Another way to journey through Lent in a very simple way is to gather forty stones or forty sticks and line them along your garden path. Each day as you collect an item and set it in place, ponder what one thing that day you will surrender to God. You could also build a small pile with the sticks to be burned at the end of Lent, at noon on Holy Saturday.

Early Christians observed many more feast and holy days than we do in the twenty-first century. Then and now we eat fish during the Fridays of Lent. In celebration of this practice, place the double-line drawing of a fish, called the *ichthys*, on different materials such as wood, stepping-stones, or tin or plastic discs that can be hung as ornaments from branches in the garden. The ichthys symbol of a fish can be a reflection on that time when Jesus ended his forty days in the desert and called the first disciples to be fishers of men, a meditation on when he fed the five thousand, or a way to stir your thoughts to the time when early Christians who were being martyred used this symbol to distinguish safe places to gather.

As long as you're making simple line drawings, don't forget about drawing a pretzel: "The pretzel is the oldest, traditional, authentically Christian Lenten bread. Some food historians trace its origin back to Roman Christians of the fifth century. Others insist that monks in southern France, or maybe it way northern Italy, cooked up this . . . snack in A.D. 610. The former called them *bracellae*, Latin for 'little arms'; the latter called them *pretiola*, Latin for 'little reward.'. . . . The dough configuration represents arms folded in prayer and the three holes represent the Trinity."[5] So make some pretzel ornaments or trace the pattern into a stepping-stone. You could bake some to share with a friend in the garden as you read Lenten reflections together.

Passion (Palm) Sunday begins this holiest of weeks. To enhance your garden for this day, lay fern fronds or palm branches across your garden path. Think about the crowds who did the same when they welcomed Jesus.

Do you have statuaries, crosses, or icons in your garden? Follow the tradition of the Church, and at the end of Palm Sunday cover these sacramentals with a purple cloth or pillowcase, tying the bottom with a rope. Your garden should appear somber in preparation for the triduum.

Holy Thursday at noon marks the end of Lent, and the triduum leads us into Easter Sunday; this is discussed in the next chapter, April.

Biblical Reflections

I am the true vine, and my Father is the vinedresser. Every branch of mine that bears no fruit, he takes away, and every branch that does bear fruit he prunes, that it may bear more fruit. . . . As the branch cannot bear fruit by itself, unless it abides in the vine, neither can you, unless you abide in me. I am the vine, you are the branches. He who abides in me, and I in him, he it is that bears much fruit, for apart from me you can do nothing. If a man does not abide in me, he is cast forth as a branch and withers; and the branches are gathered, thrown into the fire and burned.

—John 15:1–2, 4–6

Turn again, O God of hosts! Look down from heaven, and see; have regard for this vine, the stock which thy right hand planted. They have burned it with fire, they have cut it down. . . . Restore us, O LORD God of hosts! Let thy face shine, that we may be saved!

—Psalm 80:14–16, 19

Why are you cast down, O my soul, and why are you disquieted within me? Hope in God; for I shall again praise him, my help and my God.

—Psalm 42:11

We are afflicted in every way, but not crushed; perplexed, but not driven to despair; persecuted, but not forsaken; struck down, but not destroyed; always carrying in the body the death of Jesus, so that the life of Jesus may also be manifested in our bodies.

—2 Corinthians 4:8–10

Behold, happy is the man whom God reproves; therefore despise not the chastening of the Almighty. For he wounds, but he binds up; he smites, but his hands heal.

—Job 5:17–18

My son, do not despise the LORD's discipline or be weary of his reproof, for the LORD reproves him whom he loves, as a father the son in whom he delights.

—Proverbs 3:11–12

For the moment all discipline seems painful rather than pleasant; later it yields the peaceful fruit of righteousness to those who have been trained by it.

—Hebrews 12:11

Prayer Focus for March

> For I know the plans I have for you, says the Lord, plans
> for welfare and not for evil, to give you a future and a
> hope.
>
> —Jeremiah 29:11

How often have I doubted the purposefulness of changes in my life
and lost my faith and hope in God's providence? What have my
feelings been when I faced a spiritual crisis? When were the times
of my own resurrections when I thought all was lost? How often
have I failed to see Jesus in the breaking of the bread and accepted
the Eucharist with callousness or indifference? How often have I
not recognized his voice? What does the resurrected Jesus need to
change in my life?

April: **Preparing the Soil**

> What material food produces in our bodily life, Holy Communion wonderfully achieves in our spiritual life. . . . [It] preserves, increases, and renews the life of grace received at Baptism.
>
> *—Catechism of the Catholic Church*

April is known as the Easter month because Easter Sunday often falls within its thirty days. Even if Easter falls in March, the Easter season continues throughout April. It is the time when we are deeply aware of the eucharistic presence and sacrifice of Christ. For this reason, April is the traditional month for devotion to the Eucharist.

We as Catholics are taught the profound nature of the Eucharist as the physical presence of Christ through transubstantiation of the bread and wine. It is awe inspiring when we realize that God chose the things of the earth to express himself to us. From the simplest things of a garden comes the greatest revelation. It is from the grain of wheat and the fruit of the vine that we receive bread and wine.

The *Catechism* reminds us that the mode of Christ's presence under the eucharistic species is unique. It raises the Eucharist above all the sacraments as "the perfection of the spiritual life and the end to which all the sacraments tend." In the most Blessed Sacrament of the Eucharist, "the body and blood, together with the soul and divinity, of our Lord Jesus Christ and, therefore, the whole Christ is truly, really, and substantially contained . . . wholly and entirely present" (CCC, 1374).

The Eucharist is also a call to examine the state of our hearts so that God can nourish our souls—the core of who we are. I see my soul as similar to the earth. It is from this central element that the terrain of my spirit is formed. The soul is the soil in which the seeds of faith are planted, and as all good gardeners know, the condition of soil is critical for proper growth.

All soils nourish some form of life. There are many kinds of soils, and different forms of plant life are specific to the soil's condition; prairie grass will not grow among woodland ferns.

The essence of my spirituality, like the essence of a good garden, depends on a healthy soil, one in which seeds can easily take hold and grow. Fruitfulness depends on soil rich in nutrients, the food of life. For no matter how clear the light or how gentle the rain, without good roots being properly fed, the seeded plant will eventually die.

I have found that there are many types of soil within me. There is the desert sand. When I, like many, wrestle with depression, I often feel that I have entered into a desert wilderness and wander lost on the sands of "What do I do now?" I try to trust God and allow the shifting sands to teach me endurance and a new stability. The desert, though truly inhospitable, nevertheless sustains many organisms specific to that environment, and with God's help, my soul can endure its harsh reality.

As with dense compressed clay, the soil of my soul can be difficult to alter. Even though clay is one of the more mineral-rich soils, the problem lies in freeing up what is useful. When I'm in a bad mood the goodness in me becomes inaccessible. This hardness of heart hinders my receptivity to the Word of God. When seeds specifically suited to clay soils land and germinate, their deep taproot persistently and gently grows into the clay. Eventually the clay is loosened, and the changes allow what is nourishing to be released. God always knows what seeds to send to release what I have bound up.

I have at times felt that a piece of my soul has turned to stone, so hardened from earthly pressures that nothing can penetrate. But rock is purposeful, the stuff of mountains and ocean cliffs. By God's hands the stone can be quarried if you will allow it, repurposed into blocks upon which he will build. It has been written before that amid all the coal, the pressure formed diamonds. The process of breaking down and conversion is as essential to nature as it is to the nature of my soul.

It takes all the soils of my heart's terrain to create a spiritual habitat favorable to receiving the Eucharist and all the varied seeds of grace God offers me. I need to strive in my faith to bring about fruitfulness sweet enough for our Lord, to have a heart composted with the debris of life, the black gold of living on earth.

Traditions and Feasts of April

> Spirituality is a life of grace anchored in the rhythms of the liturgical year's celebrations of the mysteries of Christ ... to which the individual soul is attracted.
>
> —Peter M. J. Stravinskas

Easter is the primary celebration during April. Holy Week begins on Passion (Palm) Sunday. On Holy Thursday the sacred triduum begins with the remembrance of the institution of the Eucharist at the Last Supper. On Good Friday we commemorate the death of Jesus on the Cross. The triduum concludes with the celebration of the Easter Vigil on Holy Saturday night.

Passion (Palm) Sunday

On this day the Church recalls the entrance of the Christ into Jerusalem to accomplish his paschal mystery; a procession into church with palm fronds usually takes place.

We all have memories of picking up palms before we enter the church and, if unconcerned about looking cool, waving them as we sang and processed. What I remember most about Palm Sundays comes from a time when I coordinated the Art and Environment Committee for my home parish.

During the days preceding Holy Week, the packaged palms would arrive and be placed in the priest's cold garage. On Saturday afternoon I would find that someone had courteously brought over the long waxed cardboard boxes and set them in the vestibule to the sacristy. I would push them aside and head upstairs to the massive storage area. Along the east wall under the built-in shelving were the wicker trug baskets that, once filled, would be placed at the entrances to the church.

The afternoon prepping was a solitary effort. I would remove the silk plants and purple cloths of Lent and then change the candle guard of the sanctuary light and altar linens to red. Then I would spread an old white cotton sheet on the floor to keep the palms clean during the next phase: separating the thin sword-like leaves, which are actually the fronds of a palm bud.

After lining up the baskets, I would carry over and set the waxed boxes on the sheet. Then I would release a long, deep sigh before cutting the bands that held the boxes closed. Initially I thought the sigh was because I knew I was about to spend a fair amount of time sitting on the hard floor dividing up fronds. But one cannot sit in the sanctuary only a few yards from the tabernacle and not recognize the presence of Christ. I very soon realized that my sighing was more about the reality of the symbolism of the palms to the ritual to come.

With wire cutters held out at arm's length and my face turned slightly away, I would cut the bands and invariably jump at the loud crack they made being released. It was a chilling reminder of the sound of spikes driven through flesh into the Cross. Lifting the box's lid, I would pick up a bundle of fronds and pull them apart as I reflected on our Lord's journey into Jerusalem.

Jesus knew what was going to happen, and yet he continued toward a certain and terrifying end. Did he dutifully smile from atop his little donkey and wave a greeting to the crowd? Was he somber, looking down and away in prayer to maintain his composure? Did he cry? Tremble? Sitting there in the sanctuary I could only imagine the gamut of emotions that ran through his heart and across his face.

The Easter Triduum

Sometimes called the paschal triduum, these three days bridge the penitential season of Lent and the joyful celebration of the Easter season. Starting with the Mass of the Lord's Supper on the evening of Holy Thursday, it continues through the Good Friday service and concludes on Holy Saturday.

When I was in my thirties, during the first year of my return to the Church, I had decided to embrace the fullness of Holy Thursday and planned to attend all the services. I rose early that morning in eager anticipation of the "holiness" I was sure to receive. I had no idea what I was doing but went off as an adolescent child full of self-assurance. Looking back on that day, I'm confident the Holy Spirit on more than one occasion laughed at my ardent, bumbling love.

I was captivated by all the rituals of the Chrism Mass at the cathedral. The procession of priests was inspiring, the numerous readings, blessings of the oils, and prayers filled me with awe and wonder. I was eager during the long drive home to read the meaning behind all that I had seen; little did I know that it would take a lifetime to grasp.

There were several hours from the time I left the cathedral until the Mass that evening. I had set my heart on maintaining prayer-fulness and offered up all of that day—for what I wasn't sure, but I knew that was what all good Catholics did. After lunch I headed to a small country church where I sat and prayed all the Mysteries of the Rosary. Next stop was a coffeehouse where I sat reading a spiritual book and a bible I'd brought.

The time finally drew near for evening Mass. Arriving at church early, I chose a center-aisle seat near the front. I'm just five feet tall and wanted to see all the service (hoping that the group of widowed women would sit in front of me and not the family with three bas-ketball stars).

After the gospel, the ushers assisted the chosen twelve people in bringing chairs around the altar for the washing of feet. Those selected varied from a young mother with an infant on her lap to a widower in his nineties. The priest stripped to his alb, rolled up his sleeves, and, followed by altar servers, knelt and began the rit-ual. The significance of the priest being a servant to all in his flock touched my heart.

Later, after Communion, a reverent sort of ballet took place. Silently and thoroughly everything was stripped from the sanctuary by the priests, deacons, and altar servers. I did not remember this from my youth and was unsure of what to do next—where was I to focus my prayers? I looked around to other parishioners for a clue, but all were quietly waiting.

Looking back to the altar I saw the ciborium with the Blessed Sacrament. This I knew the significance of and with a sense of eager anticipation followed the procession, with incense encircling our walk, to the place of repose for adoration.

The day had been long, and when the priests came after midnight to return the Blessed Sacrament to the sacristy, I was near tears. Inspiring as it had been, I was exhausted from the full sixteen-hour day. Following others across the dark parking lot, I thought to myself, *I am never going to do that again!* and immediately felt shame for being so selfish toward God. Well, I did do it again but allowed myself travel time between services to go home and rest, a perfect compromise.

On my way to church the next day for Good Friday services, I remembered how as a child, when still attending church with my grandmother, I disliked Good Friday. Slightly before noon she would secure on top of our heads the black lace mantillas, and in silence we would walk the long block from her house to church.

Everything was dark and somber as we entered the nave and walked reverently to the front pews. All of the statues, icons, and even the massive crucifix were veiled in dark red. The gates to the little grottos of vigil candles were closed too. The service was long, and not at all like a Mass, which I often enjoyed, especially after I made my First Holy Communion (and could kneel beside my grandmother at the Communion rail). I didn't like how the church echoed with the loud words of Jesus being tortured. I didn't like having to be still until three o'clock. I didn't like that I had to fast—I was hungry all the time, and for more than just food. Nope, as a kid I didn't like Good Friday one bit!

But I was now an adult returning to a faith that my grandmother had encouraged, and I smiled to myself at the childhood memory as I walked along the parish sidewalk.

I wasn't prepared for the feelings that erupted when I entered the church. My first reaction was *Where is my God?* The corpus had been taken down from the cross, the statues removed, and the icons and paintings were also gone. I felt an overwhelming sense of loss so deep that I began to cry. I immediately tucked myself into a pew and knelt, resting my face in my hands so no one would see my tears. Soon I realized that my weeping was in recognition of the absence of love. The visual assurance of God's love was gone, much like the passing of my grandmother.

In those few moments an adult faith began to form. The seed of faith from my grandmother moved beyond childhood memories and took root in the soil of my heart. The lack of visual elements in the church stimulated a deeper faith, and a new spirituality, all my own, took hold.

Crown Imperial Blossoms

There is a legend about the Garden of Gethsemane and the crown imperial plant, *Fritillaria imperialis*. As Jesus walked into the garden for the last time, all the flowers bowed their heads, except for the flowering crown imperial that held its stiff white blooms high. Our Lord gently placed his hands on the flower and said, "Lily, be not so proud." At that the plant hung its flowering head and blushed with shame. Its tears lingered on its petals. On that day it lost its color of innocence, white, and when you find it growing in its native land, you'll find it is red, although some species are also yellow. If you look inside the drooping flower cups, you can still see the pearl-like tears attached to the top.

April Saints for the Gardener

Even the best of soils must first be plowed and broken before it can become a source of fruitfulness.

April 1: St. Valéry of Leucone, ca. 622

(Variations: Valerian, Gualaric, Wala(e)ric(h)us)

St. Valéry was born to a poor sheep farmer in Auvergne, France. He was a gentle boy who genuinely cared about the well-being of his flock and all the creatures God had made. He developed a deep prayer life while shepherding and, out of a deep desire to grow in spiritual knowledge, memorized the Psalter while doing so.

He eventually chose to be a monk, became a follower of St. Columban of Ireland, and entered the French monastery of Luxeuil.

St. Valéry, as with all the other monks, was assigned a garden at the monastery. His garden flourished so well and produced such a great abundance of food that St. Columban declared it a sign of Valéry's holiness. Valéry also distinguished himself as a horticulturalist. The preservation of his fruit and vegetables against the ravages of diseases and insects that destroyed most other crops was considered miraculous.[1]

St. Valéry was known for his gentleness with animals as well as men. The woodland animals seemed drawn to him and would gather about his cell window, especially birds. When he was about the gardens, the birds would fly and land all over him, eating from his hands and nibbling playfully at his ears.

April 2: St. Urban of Langres, 327–ca. 390

Patron of Vine Growers, Viticulture

There is very little about the early history on St. Urban's life. In 374 he became bishop of Langres, France.

The middle of the fourth century was a time of political upheaval in France, and St. Urban was forced into hiding. During this time he took safe harbor among the family farms of vine growers loyal to the Church. The wine production was very prosperous during the

Roman Empire. As such, there were a number of groves in which the saint could preach and teach while in exile.

While among these growers, he converted several of the workers to Christianity, who then in turn helped him with his ministry to convert others. Due to the vinedressers' help in St. Urban's work and St. Urban's devotion to the consecrated wine turned to the Precious Blood, he developed a deep affection for all the people who made wine, and they loved him in return. Interestingly enough, and not surprisingly, he is also the patron saint of alcoholics.

April 29: St. Catherine of Siena, 1347–1380

Patron against Sickness

It is impossible in a few words to give an adequate portrayal of this saint. At six years old, Catherine had her first vision from heaven, and for the rest of her life she sought how to best please Jesus. Her charity, sufferings, and writings have made her one of the Doctors of the Church. "St. Catherine's spiritual teaching is rooted in her experience of the cell of self-knowledge. She learned there an honest knowledge of God and herself that bore fruit in an acute awareness of the difference between God and the human soul but also of the love that binds on to the other."[2]

Catherine, in her teens and having refused to marry, lived as an anchoress in a solitary life of prayer. During this time Satan assaulted her with intrusive images so vile that at times she felt on the brink of losing her soul. The darkness consumed her for years, and only through fervent prayer was she able to persevere. When at last the horrific imagery ended, she wrote of once again feeling Christ was near—and questioned him about abandoning her! She soon learned that he had been with her, for if he had not been there she would not have found the images so painful and would not have had the strength to overcome them. They had served to purify her heart. Before she was twenty she took her final vows as a Dominican nun.

It wasn't long before Jesus came to her again and asked her to leave the cloister and go into the world to serve, bringing souls to him through her goodness. St. Catherine was filled with dread at the thought of leaving her quiet life and feared she had offended God because he was sending her away from the privacy of prayer and penance. "But His voice sounded in her ears once more, and told her it was not to separate her from Himself that He sent her out, but that she should learn to help others. 'Thou knowest that love giveth two commandments—to love Me, and to love thy neighbour. I desire that thou shouldst walk not on one but two feet, and fly to heaven on two wings.'"[3] With trepidation St. Catherine prepared to obey and prayed for courage and guidance as she reentered the world.

In her brief thirty-three years on earth she was not only a Dominican sister but also a papal counselor and stigmatic. In 1970, Pope Paul VI declared her a Doctor of the Church.

April in the Garden

> The finest fertilizer on a gardener's ground is his own footprints.
>
> —Ancient Saying

Practical Gardening: Amending the Soil: Composting

Previously I wrote about how to identify the types of soils in your garden. This section will help you with composting as a way to amend the soil.

I must admit that when it came to composting, I was a reluctant participant. In several gardening circles I would hear others talk about their compost piles as of a special pet: feeding it greens, keeping it warm, and never adding junk food to its microbial digestion. My eyes would glaze over as temperatures and techniques were debated. There were several misconceptions I had to resolve before I could really embrace this activity.

Composting Is Complicated

Those who are into composting are, well, into it. They have read articles and books gleaning information, but you needn't worry about all that. Pile whatever composting materials you have, and it will decompose; as the saying goes, compost happens. Adding water now and then and turning it over will speed the process. If you tend to forget about your pile, as I often do, nature will still run its course.

The Yard Is Too Small for a Compost Pile

Think of it this way: if you have a large yard your compost pile is usually larger; with a small yard the pile will be smaller in proportion. If you have a garden apartment or condo, use a thirty-six-gallon black plastic garbage can with a tight-fitting lid. Drill half-inch holes around its sides and bottom for air movement. To "stir" the compost, lay the container on its side—with lid secured by bungee cords—and roll it around.

Compost Piles Stink and Attract Rodents

Most people have this misconception. Compost piles do not attract rodents or have a bad odor unless the wrong stuff is added. The rule here is no animal products: meats/bones, oils, dairy, or poo. Do not add sugary materials either. Add only vegetative materials from the kitchen or yard. Healthy compost smells like spring soil.

Compost Piles Are Ugly

Location is everything. Placing it in the middle of the yard or driveway will certainly create an eyesore. Locate it in an out-of-the-way place where it will receive sunlight. You can hide the pile by using fence panels or, again, black garbage cans. There are also commercial composting containers and bins available on the market.

I Don't Have the Time to Compost

This was a favorite myth of mine. I believed I was far too busy to focus on creating the healthy compost pile that gardeners bragged about. Once my compost pile was started, I discovered it took less than thirty minutes a month to flip the pile and maintain it.

Faith-Filled Gardening: Holy Week and Eastertide

Holy Thursday

Holy Thursday at noon marks the end of Lent,[4] and we now remember the Last Supper and the institution of the Eucharist. Jesus is bracing himself for the events to come.

Make this a quiet time in your garden. Set aside a portion of your day and plan on praying the Sorrowful Mysteries of the Rosary or reading pertinent Bible passages. There may be a new and deeper meaning behind your thoughts and prayers in the forty stones or sticks you collected during Lent, as mentioned in the March chapter.

As a reminder that our Lord was betrayed and denied, remove all but one chair from the prayer space. If you, as do I, speak as if Jesus were sitting there with you in the garden, the absence of a chair where he might sit will be profoundly felt. This simple act echoes the abandonment Jesus felt by the turning away of his followers. As you sit alone in your space, examine how you may have turned away from Jesus.

Good Friday

Good Friday is a day of deep remembering and, as such, a day of deep silence. I personally try to keep the time from noon to 3:00 p.m. as a period of silent contemplation and prayer. If you created a Stations of the Cross garden, this is a very good day to walk it slowly, with purpose in deep prayer.

Holy Saturday

Holy Saturday evening is the Easter Vigil when the alleluias return and the light of God shines forth.

Before you leave for the Vigil Mass, resurrect your outdoor prayer space. Remove the purple cloths and coverings from statues and benches. Pile the fronds that were laid on the path on Palm Sunday with the forty sticks to be burned. Place a statue of a lamb in your garden during the next fifty days.

And don't forget candles! After the Easter Vigil, gather in the garden and light candles to continue the paschal celebration. Every evening during the Easter season, continue to light the candles, offering prayers of gratitude, to honor the light of Christ.

Remember that basin of sand with the cross and sticks? You can now remove them and replace them with a forest of thin white tapers lit in celebration of the Light of the World.

Candles are prominent throughout the Easter season. Group candles together on a table, set them in low spots in your garden, or arrange them tiered among the plants. You can also put them inside hurricane glasses if you live in a windy area. To line a walkway of a night garden, use white lunch bags filled with two inches of sand and set a tea light or glassed votive candle inside each bag.

Easter Season

Easter Sunday! The Lord is risen; he is risen indeed! It is a day of new life and light, of breaking bread with God and family and friends.

The garden on Easter Sunday can be much more than a hunting ground for colorful hard-boiled eggs hidden around the lawn.

On Holy Saturday, before you went to Mass, you removed all of the reminders of Lent. For Easter, you can now decorate your garden with white and gold accents. Hang tiny white Christmas lights or white paper lanterns around your outdoor prayer space.

The holy women who came to the tomb of Jesus brought myrrh along with other herbs for anointing. Myrrh was also present at the birth of Jesus. If you purchased some of this resinous incense at Christmas, pull it out of storage and use it during Easter to make your garden fragrant.

You can make or buy a resurrection cross to add to your garden. Paint it white and adorn it with what brings you joy. Because Christ is risen, a crucifix with raised arms is more appropriate than the crucified corpus.

If you desire to create an Easter garden, use elements that remain true to the Easter season. White and gold colors are prominent. Include an assortment of white lilies that will bloom at different times as well as other white- and gold-flowering plants. You could also use plants that symbolize the theme of resurrection and ascension. Here is a list to help you get started:

Eastertide Garden Plants

Theme	Plant	Botanical
Adoration	Dwarf sunflower	*Helianthus annuus* (various species)
Ascension	Ascension flower, lilac	*Syringa vulgaris*
Confidence	Liverleaf	*Hepatica sp.*
Confidence in heaven	Flowering reed/rush	*Butomus umbellatus*
Consolation of hope	Snowdrops	*Galanthus*
Easter	Easter lily	*Lilium longiflorum*
Eternal life	Mums	*Chrysanthemum sp.*
	Holly	*Ilex sp.*
	Evergreens in general	
Eternal love	Globe amaranth	*Gomphrena globosa*
Eternity	Apple or olive trees	
Glory	Bay laurel	*Laurus nobilis*
	Daphne	*Daphne sp.*

Hope, watchfulness, and promise	Sweet almond tree	*Prunus dulcis*
	Calla lily	*Zantedeschia*
	Forget-me-not	*Myosotis*
	Hawthorn	*Crataegus*
	Jasmine	*Jasminum*
	Petunia	*Petunia*
	Plum	*Prunus*
	Snowdrops	*Galanthus*
I live for thee	Cedar	*Cedrus*
Immortality	Globe amaranth	*Gomphrena globosa*
Joy	Wood sorrel	*Oxalis sp.*
Love	There are more than thirty plants symbolizing love. Three are listed in the Divine Mercy table on page 87.	
Love returned	Ragweed	*Ambrosia*
Mystery	Crimson polyanthus	*Primula sp.*
Never-ceasing remembrance	Everlasting	*Helichrysum sp.*
Pure love	Single red pinks	*Dianthus sp.*
Radiance	Buttercup	*Ranunculus*
Remembrance	Rosemary	*Rosemarinus officinalis*

Resurrection	Resurrection lily	*Lycoris squamigera*
	Resurrection plant	*Curcuma sp.* and *Selaginella lepidophylla*
Return of happiness	Lily of the valley	*Convallaria majalis*
Transport of joy	Cape jasmine	*Gardenia jasminoides*
Triumph	Bay laurel	*Laurus nobilis*
	Oak	*Quercus sp.*
Victory	Ivy	*Hedra sp.*
	Palm trees	
	Parsley	*Petroselinum sp.*
	Purple columbine	*Aquilegea sp.*

Consider Easter Monday a day of rest from the previous day of devotion and celebration and a time to rejoice in the fifty days ahead. Read Luke 24:13–35, the story of the walk to Emmaus. Go for a walk in your own garden or along a woodland path. Reflect on the previous passage from Luke and ask yourself as you journey with nature: How often in my own life have I not recognized Jesus walking with me?

Divine Mercy

I am particularly fond of the Divine Mercy prayers brought to us through St. Faustina. For me they expound the fullness of the purpose of Jesus: our acceptance of forgiveness and mercy.

The most recognizable Divine Mercy image is of two rays coming from the heart of Jesus. A simple way to re-create this for the garden on a surface, such as wood or cement, is by drawing a heart with two obtuse triangles coming downward from it. You could add the word *Trust* underneath, abstracted from the phrase "Jesus, I trust in you."

A garden dedicated to the Divine Mercy could have red and white bicolor flowers depicting the rays that appear to flow from Jesus' heart. The most popular flower is bleeding heart, *Dicentra spectabilis*. Other bicolored flowers to consider are roses, dahlias, dianthus, tulips, impatiens, petunias, amaryllis, gloxinias, and columbines, just to name a few.

To add interest to the red and white flowers, bring in plants with symbolic meanings, such as the following:

Divine Mercy Garden Plants

Theme	Plant	Botanical
Eternal love	Globe amaranth	*Gomphrena globosa*
Love	Myrtle	*Vinca minor*
	Roses	*Rosa*
	Any evergreens	
Forgiveness	Daffodil	*Narcissus sp.*
	Baby blue eyes	*Nemophila sp.*
Mercy, compassion	Allspice	*Pimenta dioica*
	(also consider the Carolina allspice, aka sweetshrub)	*(Calycanthus sp.)*
	Rue	*Ruta sp.*

Patience	Chamomile	*Matricaria chamomilla*
	Fir tree	*Abies sp.*
	Oxeye daisy	*Leucanthemum vulgare Matricaria recutita* or *Anthemis sp.*
Trust, confidence	Hepatica, liverwort	*Hepatica sp.*
	Primrose, usually lilac	*Primula sp.*

Throughout this book you will find other plants with symbolic meanings that could be used in your garden or prayer space. Be sure to choose the ones that hold the most meaning for you when you think of Divine Mercy.

Biblical Reflections

"This land that was desolate has become like the garden of Eden; and the waste and desolate and ruined cities are now inhabited and fortified." Then the nations that are left round about you shall know that I, the LORD, have rebuilt the ruined places, and replanted that which was desolate.

—Ezekiel 36:35–36

I will rebuke the devourer for you, so that it will not destroy the fruits of your soil; and your vine in the field shall not fail to bear, says the LORD of hosts. Then all nations will call you blessed, for you will be a land of delight, says the LORD of hosts.

—Malachi 3:11–12

For as the earth brings forth its shoots, and as a garden causes what is sown in it to spring up, so the Lord GOD will cause righteousness and praise to spring forth.

—Isaiah 61:11

Whatever a man sows, that he will also reap. For he who sows to his own flesh will from the flesh reap corruption; but he who sows to the Spirit will from the Spirit reap eternal life.

—Galatians 6:7–8

Hear then the parable of the sower. When any one hears the word of the kingdom and does not understand it, the evil one comes and snatches away what is sown in his heart; this is what was sown along the path. As for what was sown on rocky ground, this is he who hears the word and immediately receives it with joy; yet he has no root in himself, but endures for a while, and when tribulation or persecution arises on account of the word, immediately he falls away. As for what was sown among thorns, this is he who hears the word, but the cares of the world and the delight in riches choke the word, and it proves unfruitful. As for what was sown on good soil, this is he who hears the word and understands it; he indeed bears fruit.

—Matthew 13:18–23

Prayer Focus for April

> We are made of earthen clay, the firmness of the soil of God, and in this we know there is no such thing as marginal land. Even deserts are productive.

Considering Palm Sunday, could you pull apart your life and lay it all down for the good of another? In what small ways have you done this? Do you recall a moment of conversion when your faith began to take root? What gave you the needed push to claim it? Have you had times of depression or hardness of heart? What did you believe or do during those times to maintain your faith? Develop it further? Seek new avenues? Finally, consider the terrain of your spirituality; we are not all the same, nor should we be. Consider how the diversity allows for differing growth.

May: **Beginning to Flower**

Bring flowers of the rarest
bring blossoms the fairest,
from garden and woodland and hillside and dale.

–"Bring Flowers of the Rarest" (hymn)

Entering late spring, the garden and the Catholic calendar move into an ordered time of development. Now we can fully realize the potential of our gardens as a vital element of our faith. The seeds that were planted have rooted, started growing, and are setting buds to become fruitful. The true beauty of a flower comes when it reaches full bloom, and that takes time. Our lives open up slowly in God's hands, and in time we too become a beautiful reflection of the Creator. The most beautiful example of this fullness is our Blessed Mother Mary.

The month of May is one of four months dedicated to the Blessed Mother. Her celebrations start with the May Crowning on May 1 and end with the Feast of the Visitation on May 31. Our Holy Mother was also with the apostles when Jesus ascended into heaven and when the Holy Spirit descended upon them.

During the month of May we often celebrate the Ascension, Pentecost, and Trinity Sunday. All three of these are movable feasts because their dates are based on Easter, and Easter is based on the varying seasonal cycles of the moon. Looking to these three Sundays (though the Ascension in many areas is still observed on Thursdays), we can see our Church begin to flower.

At the Ascension the apostles were told to go and wait for the Holy Spirit to come. Here the first novena of the Church was established; Jesus instructed the apostles to return to Jerusalem to pray (Acts 1:1–14). Their faith and prayers over those nine days maintained them until Pentecost when the Holy Spirit descended upon them.

The story of Pentecost is in Acts 2. Here the promise of Christ to send the Holy Spirit was fulfilled. The petals of faith started to unfold as "those who received [Peter's] word were baptized, and there were added that day about three thousand souls. And they devoted themselves to the apostles' teaching and fellowship, to the breaking of bread and the prayers" (Acts 2:41–42).

Trinity Sunday follows Pentecost, sometimes at the end of May but more frequently in June. It honors the most fundamental belief of our Catholic faith and, as with the Eucharist, is a mystery that we can never fully understand. The mystery of the Trinity is that God is three persons in one nature and all are equally God and cannot be divided.

We thrive and grow in our faith by developing a relational prayer life and accept in our hearts the Holy Three in One of the Trinity. We embrace the teachings of our Church that unfold the *what* and *why* of our beliefs, and we act upon those teachings.

Trinitarian Plants

Plants that symbolize the Trinity are the three-leaf clover, *Trifolium repens* (St. Patrick's favorite), or the shamrock, *Oxalis sp.*, and the *Viola tricolor* with its three-petaled "face." Also the *Trillium*, water poppy, *Hydrocleys* and *Hydrocharis sp.*, spiderwort, *Tradescantia sp.*, and Mexican shell flower, *Tigridia pavonia*, can be used.

Some accents to hold our focus on the Trinity in the garden could be a triangle with a heart inside, three interconnected circles, or a trefoil. With the popularity of candles, purchasing a larger one with three wicks will signify the Trinity and hold up better in the summer heat than three tapers.

Traditions and Feasts of May

> God has filled the whole of Creation with signs of his existence, signs that our senses can apprehend and that our minds can translate into knowledge of him.
> —Vigen Guroian, *The Fragrance of God*

May 1 isn't really a holy day, but it is certainly an occasion widely celebrated in the Catholic Church. And the crowning of the Blessed Mother couldn't be more closely tied to the garden; in fact, the crowning itself is usually done with flowers.

This is a special day to honor our Blessed Mother and recognize her contribution to salvation's history. A statue or image of Mary is adorned with a wreath of flowers, traditionally hawthorn or rose blossoms, to indicate Mary's virtues. A crown of any type of flowers will be perfectly fine.

There are customary practices when a May crowning is celebrated or commemorated in a parish. For your home garden, create your own crown of live or silk flowers and arrange them on your Marian statue. If you have an icon or Marian symbol in your garden instead of a statue, you can use a garland instead. As you place your floral piece honoring Mary, think about the virtues that our Holy Mother models for us. You might pray the Rosary, and instead of petitioning her for more wants and needs, why not express your gratitude and thanks to her? On May 1 we also celebrate St. Joseph the Worker. As we crown Mary, it is most fitting to remember how she and Joseph provided a loving home in which the child Jesus was nurtured and grew.

The apparition of Our Lady of Fatima is celebrated on May 13. In 1917, from May 13 to October 13, the Blessed Virgin appeared six times to three children, Francisco and Jacinta Marto, and Lucia Sabtos, in Fatima, Portugal. The Holy Mother earnestly encouraged that the Rosary be recited with devotion and asked that prayer, and whatever sufferings that may be experienced, be offered in reparation for sin, for the conversion of sinners, and for world peace.

A Rosary garden can be created to honor her request. To read more about doing so, go to the chapter for October, which is the month dedicated to the Holy Rosary and the archangels.

At one time there were two celebrations for Mother Mary taking place on May 31: the Queenship of Mary and the Visitation. The Feast of the Queenship of Mary, begun in 1954 by Pope Pius XII, was moved in 1969 to August 22 by Pope Paul VI (August is dedicated to the Immaculate Heart of Mary). The celebration of the Visitation of the Blessed Virgin Mary to her cousin Elizabeth remains.

The Feast of the Visitation was begun by St. Bonaventure among the Franciscans in 1263. It became a universal feast day in 1389 during the papacy of Urban VI. The Visitation is the second Joyful Mystery of the Rosary and reflects the story in Luke 1:39–56. We think of the Visitation as an event all about Mary, but it intimately involves two women.

A few verses earlier in Luke 1 we learned about Elizabeth's miraculous pregnancy. The aged Elizabeth had kept her pregnancy secret for the first five months. Was she so humbled by her miracle that she did not want to appear as if flaunting God's gift? Did she fear a miscarriage, possibly not her first? A friend once told me that by the sixth month, a woman feels secure of the viability of her unborn child and is glowing with the grace of life. I suspect that women two thousand years ago weren't much different, and in her sixth month Elizabeth probably felt confident enough to reveal herself with a noticeable belly. And it wasn't until this time that Gabriel was sent to Mary, who then became pregnant with Jesus.

Mary awoke in her first month of pregnancy with pressing thoughts of Elizabeth. I can image that dear young woman, really just an adolescent child, bolting upright in bed one morning when she realized the second half of what the archangel had said to her just weeks ago. Somewhere in the middle of her own foretelling was the casual angelic comment that . . . Oh, and by the way, your cousin also got a miracle pregnancy. It seems it took a few days for this to sink in, but when it did, Mary was off in great haste.

I have often thought about that line, "went with haste." What prompted Mary to pull her husband off work, disregard her own safety and comfort, and head out across rugged terrain to Elizabeth? Did she fear for Elizabeth that the older woman might not survive carrying her child to term, or that both her cousin and baby might perish in birthing? Did she realize that at Elizabeth's age, trying to run a household was tough enough, but with a pregnancy, exhausting? Was Mary compelled by God to confer on Elizabeth's unborn son the purpose of his life in the salvation story? I wonder about the humanness of this divine event. The Visitation is a story of two women intimately linked to each other and to God for our sake and our own journey of love.

Stargazing

Gazing at God's stars from a garden is a time-honored practice and allows for a deeper sense of amazement of the heavens and earth. There is a beautiful astronomical coincidence for this time of year. If you go outside early in May, face east, and look directly up overhead, you will see a relatively faint *L* in the sky. This is the constellation

Coma Berenices. It was named after a queen. The second brightest star in this constellation is called *Diadem*, crown of royalty. Take your children outside, point out the star *Diadem* to them, and think of Our Lady, crowned in heaven—our Holy Mother Mary who wants nothing more than for us to love her son.[1]

Blessing of Roses

O God, Creator and Preserver of mankind, deign to pour out Thy heavenly benediction upon these roses, which we offer to Thee through devotion and reverence for Our Lady of the Rosary. Grant that these roses which are made by Thy Providence to yield an agreeable perfume for the use of men and women may receive such a blessing by the sign of Thy holy cross that all the sick on whom they shall be laid and all who shall keep them in their houses may be cured of their ills; and that the devil may fly in terror from these dwellings, not daring to disturb Thy servants.[2]

May Saints for the Gardener

> Trying to pray is prayer, and it is very good prayer.
> —Cardinal Basil Hume

May 15: St. Isidore, ca. 1070-1130

Patron of Farmers

St. Isidore was married to Maria Torribia (later canonized as St. Mary de la Cabeza), and their only child, a son, died in infancy. Isidore and Maria felt it was the will of God that they not have children and instead devote their lives to charitable acts and prayer.

Isidore was a farm laborer who loved working the land. Because he attended Mass each day and took time to pray, he was often accused by fellow workers of shirking his duties. When confronted about his absences, Isidore claimed he had no choice but to follow the highest Master. The disgruntled coworkers, feeling they had to work harder because of Isidore's truancy, complained to the landowner.

One tale is told that the wealthy landowner, tired of the complaints, went one morning to chastise Isidore for skipping work for church. His frustration changed to amazement when he found angels plowing the fields in place of the missing Isidore.

Another legend tells that this same landowner, curious to know how Isidore accomplished so much work though frequently absent from the fields, clandestinely approached the site that Isidore was plowing. When the master peered through the brush, he was astonished to see angels on each side of the holy plowman. With the help of these heavenly beings Isidore was able to accomplish his work in a third of the time.

Besides the miracle of plowing and planting, there are also miracles of the multiplication of rye. One story tells of a cold winter's day when the saint carried rye to be ground at the mill. As he walked he came upon a flock of birds scratching in vain at the frozen ground in search of food. His love of animals led him to pity for the starving birds, and he shared half of his sack of rye to feed the hungry flock. Those who witnessed his action mocked him until he returned from the mill with twice the amount of flour than a whole sack of rye would have provided. Not only was the rye doubled in the sack, but also it increased again when it was ground.

Many miracles and cures have been reported at St. Isidore's burial site in Spain, where his body remains incorrupt. History records that the first time his body was exhumed from the church graveyard, the chapel's bell mysteriously began to toll and all of the townspeople were miraculously cured of every ailment. The bell continued to ring until his body was placed securely in the modest shrine prepared for it. More than 450 years later his body was exhumed again to be placed in a more elaborate tomb and was found to still be incorrupt.[3]

May 22: St. Rita of Cascia, 1381–1457

Patron of Desperate Causes, Association with Bees

In the parish church of Laarne, near Ghent, Belgium, there is a statue of St. Rita in which several bees are featured. This depiction originates from the story of albino bees, a unique gift from God, which drew near St. Rita as an infant and reappeared after her death.

On the day after her baptism, her family noticed a swarm of bees flying around her as she slept. The bees were unusual because they were white in color, and they peacefully entered and exited the baby's mouth without causing her any harm. Instead of being alarmed for her safety, her family was mystified by this sight. It is said that one of the farmers witnessing the event, whose arm had been deeply cut by a scythe, passed the injured arm over the child to shoo the bees away and his arm was miraculously healed.

Nearly two hundred years after her death, at the monastery St. Mary Magdalene of Cascia, where St. Rita had lived, the white bees appeared again. Then, as now, they come out of the wall during Holy Week—which we know varies from year to year—and remain about the gardens until St. Rita's feast day of May 22 when they return to the wall for their mystical hibernation until the next year. During more recent centuries the bees are no longer white, appearing as any other bee in yellow but without a stinger.

There is another miraculous story of this saint set near the end of her life. When St. Rita was bedridden at her convent, a cousin visited her and asked the saint if she desired anything from her old home in Rocca Porrena, Italy. St. Rita responded by asking for a rose and a fig from the garden. It was January, and her cousin did not expect to find anything at the garden. However, when she went to the homestead, a single blooming rose was found in the garden as well as a fully ripened and edible fig. Her cousin brought the rose and fig back to St. Rita at the convent. Legend has it that this rose bush is still alive today and is often in bloom.

May in the Garden

> He who cultivates a garden and brings to perfection flowers and fruits, cultivates and advances at the same time his own nature.
>
> –Ezra Weston

Practical Gardening: Increase Flowering

I'm like most gardeners; I like a lot of flowers all season. Searching for the few perennials that bloom all summer is one way to accomplish this. Another way to extend flowering is by deadheading.

Deadheading is the maintenance practice of removing spent flowers. By deadheading you keep the plants looking tidy, redirect the plants' energy from seed production to roots and top growth, minimize reseeding, and prolong the flowering period by several weeks for most perennials. Extending a blooming period is different than *remontant blooming,* where a cultivar is designed to "remount" with blossoms a second time in the season without our intervention, such as specific cultivars of daylilies or the yellow corydalis.

Deadheading can be a daily activity or done every couple of weeks depending on seasonal temperatures, rainfall, and the species. Often when I am wandering through my backyard in the morning, coffee cup in hand, I find myself snapping off spent flowers. I feel less overwhelmed by doing this task daily.

Your cue will be the overall appearance of the plant as flowers decline. But don't wait too long to deadhead, unless you are saving seeds. When spent flowers become seed heads, chemical changes occur that can halt flower production.

There are several perennials that produce flowers along their stems and on a spike that can have their blooming period extended by deadheading. To deadhead perennials that produce flowers along their stem, known as lateral blooming, cut just below the spent flower to the first set of leaves or next bud. A few common perennials with both terminal and lateral flowering are bee balm (*Monarda*), blanket flower (*Gaillardia*), coneflower (*Echinacea*), false sunflowers (*Heliopsis*), garden phlox (*Phlox paniculata*), Shasta daisy (*Leucanthemum*), and Stokes' aster (*Stokesia*).

There are several perennials that flower from the bottom up on single or multibranching spikes. The single-flowering spike should be deadheaded when about three quarters of the stem has finished blooming; cut it off at the same junction as mentioned above. A few common perennials with spiked flowers are Culver's root (*Veronicastrum*), delphinium, foxglove (*Digitalis*), hosta, lupine, and spiked speedwell (*Veronica*). In the case of multibranching spikes, such as globe thistle (*Echinops*) or hollyhock (*Alcea*), each flower head and its stem can be removed to the central spike.

Deadheading flowers of one-time bloomers keeps them looking good but does not prolong the flowering. Some of the more recognizable single-season bloomers are bergenia, bleeding heart (*Dicentra*), most coral bells (*Heuchera*), most daylilies (*Hemerocallis*), iris, lamb's ear (*Stachys*), and rose mallow (*Hibiscus*). Daylilies and iris can be groomed daily, but you will also need to remove the spent flowering stalks.

Another method of deadheading is shearing. This is done when masses of flowers die back all at once, as with thread leaf coreopsis.

With one hand gather up the spent blooms and with the other clip off the stems and part of the upper leaf cover using garden scissors. Perennial geranium, often called cransebill, and salvia can be cut back almost to the ground to produce a second flowering. This method may look messy at first but will look fine in a few days.

There are several books on caring for perennials. Here are two of my favorites: *The Perennial Care Manual* by Nancy Ondra and Rob Cardillo (2009) and *The Well-Tended Perennial Garden*, a detailed reference by Tracy DiSabato-Aust (2006, second edition).

We all love that colorful burst of life after the dreary days of winter and will plant winter hardy bulbs for spring color. Most of us dislike those ragtag leaves that spring bulbs leave behind after they're done blooming. It is necessary to let the leaves remain in order to rejuvenate the bulbs through photosynthesis, a chemical process where food is produced from sunlight. If you cut off the tops of the plants while they are still green, you prevent food from going to the bulb and reduce the chance of it flowering next year. The leaves over time will turn yellow and can then be cut down. While waiting for them to get to that stage, the garden often looks messy and unappealing.

Mix colorful bulbs with a variety of perennials to hide the yellowing leaves and create a sensational early season display. Cornell University did an enlightening study of what works well together.[4]

One thing to remember when mixing bulbs and perennials is that shade-loving perennials can be combined perfectly with many sun-loving bulbs. The reason is that the bulbs are at their best while the branches of deciduous trees are without leaves. This means that many wooded areas have the benefit of plenty of spring sunshine. By the time the early summer sun heats things up—and the spring-blooming bulbs are done for the season—the tree leaves have come out, providing plenty of shade for perennials.

Faith-Filled Gardening: Creating Marian Gardens

A Marian garden is the most popular Catholic garden. At one time a Marian garden was considered such only if it was enclosed by a fence or some other type of delineating structure. This tradition came from scripture in the Song of Solomon: "A garden locked is my sister, my bride" (4:12). The first garden known to be dedicated to Mary was planned by St. Fiacre in France during the seventh century. Today, this definition has broadened to include any garden dedicated to Mary. It can include a painted image or statue of Mary or even a small shrine to our Holy Mother.

If you decide to follow the tradition of "a garden enclosed," a simple wattle fence of woven twigs will look very sweet in a naturalistic setting, as would a low fieldstone wall. A small white picket fence is brighter and would look a bit neater in a suburban yard. In formal gardens an open weave of brickworks could form the walls. Living plants can also provide the enclosure. A line of ornamental grasses of all the same cultivars, such as *Calamagrostis Karl Foerster*, could provide a structure. For a larger Marian garden—provided you don't have deer—the evergreen arborvitae shrub *Thuja occidentalis*, 'Smaragd,' would form a rich and elegant hedge wall.

Flower meditations for Marian gardens are numerous, culturally based, and overlapping in symbolism. There are several books and websites dedicated to plants that symbolically represent some aspect of our Holy Mother.

If you are creating a Marian rose garden, there are four colors of roses that are used that match the traditional colors of the Mysteries of the Rosary. Red roses are used to meditate on her sorrows; white roses are for her joys; yellow roses are for her glories; and roses that are dark burgundy or deep magenta are the purples of the Luminous Mysteries.

Your Marian garden can also be an herb garden or a container garden.

Mary has been and still is a strong influence in the hearts of the faithful, and for this reason many plants and flowers are associated with her. A few of these plants have already been mentioned. The table below lists several more. Even though this list is extensive, it is by no means exhaustive.[5]

With so many options, you are sure to find a plant to suit your prayer space, whether your garden area is sunny or shady. If you have a plant that reminds you of Mary that is not on this list, by all means use it. The purpose of this garden is to lead you into a deeper appreciation of our Holy Mother.

Marian Garden Plants

Symbolic of Mary	Plant	Botanical
Annunciation	Garden angelica, archangel herb	*Angelica sp.*
	Madonna lily (aka St. Joseph's lily)	*Lilium candidum*
Beautiful lady	Regal geranium or Martha Washington geranium	*Pelargonium domesticum*
Herb of grace	Rue	*Ruta graveolens*
Lady's fingers	Honeysuckle, woodbine	*Lonicera sp.*
Lady's fringe	Starleaf begonia	*Begonia heracleifolia*

Lady's hair or maiden's hair	Maidenhair fern	*Adiantum tenerum*
	Asparagus fern	*Asparagus setaceus*
Madonna flower	African violet	*Saintpaulia ionantha*
Madonna's milk	Dead nettle	*Lamium sp.*
Mary-loves	English daisy	*Bellis perennis*
Mary's bed	Herb Robert	*Geranium robertianum*
Mary's bedstraw or Our Lady's bedstraw	Carthusian pink	*Dianthus carthusianorum*
	Creeping thyme	*Thymus praecox*
	Male fern	*Dryopteris filix-mas*
	Oregano or wild marjoram	*Origanum vulgare (Majorana onites)*
	Yellow clover	*Melilotus officinalis*
Mary's bitter sorrow	Dandelion	*Taraxacum officinale*
	Garden sorrel	*Rumex acetosa*
Mary's bouquet	Rosemary	*Rosmarinus officinalis*
Mary's crown	Bachelor's button	*Centauria cyannis*
Mary's drying plant	Lavender	*Lavandula officinalis*
Mary's eyes or Madonna's eyes	Bluets	*Houstonia caerulea*
	Forget-me-not	*Myosotis scorpioides*
Mary's flax	Toad flax	*Linaria vulgaris*

Mary's flower	Feverfew	*Tanacetum parthenium*
	Wallflower	*Cheiranthus cheiri (aka Erysimum cheiri)*
Mary's fruitfulness	Pear tree	*Pyrus communis*
Mary's gold	Marigolds	*Tangetes sp.*
	Pot marigold	*Calendula officinalis*
	Rosary plant	*Crassula rupestris*
	Sunflower	*Helianthus annuus*
Mary's hair, Our Lady's tresses, or Our Lady's hair	Solomon's seal	*Polygonatum multiflorum*
	Stonecrop	*Sedum acre*
	Strawberry begonia	*Saxifraga stolonifera*
Mary's heart (aka heart of Jesus)	Bleeding heart	*Dicentra spectabilis*
	Fuchsia begonia	*Begonia fuchsioides rosea*
Mary's herb	Balsam herb, bible leaf, costmary	*Tanacetum balsamita*
Mary's humility or the Virgin's humility	Violet	*Viola odoratoa*
	Thyme	*Thymus vulgaris*
Mary's nettle	Catnip, field balm	*Nepeta cataria*
	Horehound	*Marrubium vulgare*
Mary's plant	German chamomile	*Matricaria recutita*
Mary's prayer	Tulip	*Tulipa*
Mary's purity	Jasmine	*Jasminum officinale*

Mary's purse	Shepherd's purse	*Capsella bursa-pastoris*
Mary's rose or Our Lady's rose	Carnation	*Dianthus caryophyllus*
	Corncockle	*Agrostemma githago*
	English daisy	*Bellis perennis*
	Peony	*Paeonia officinalis*
	Pheasant's eye	*Adonis aestivalis*
	Poet's narcissus	*Narcissus poeticus*
	Rose campion	*Lychnis coronaria*
	Rose Daphne	*Daphne cneorum*
Mary's shawl	Sage	*Salvia officinalis*
Mary's shoes or Our Lady's slippers	Columbine	*Aquilegia vulgaris*
	Lady slipper	*Paphiopedilum sp.*
	Monkshood	*Aconitum napellus*
	Pocketbook flower	*Calceolaria herbeohybrida*
Mary's star	Lent lily or wild daffodil	*Narcissus pseudonarcissus*
	Oxeye daisy	*Leucanthemum vulgare*
Mary's sword of sorrows	Iris	*Iris*
Mary's tears or Our Lady's tears	Delphinium	*Delphinium sp.*
	Larkspur	*Consolida oreintalis*
	Lily of the valley	*Convallaria majalis*
	Star-of-Bethlehem	*Ornithogalum umbellatum*

Mary's thistle or Our Lady's thistle	Blessed thistle	*Cnicus benedictus*
	Milk thistle	*Silybum marianum*
	Scotch thistle, cotton thistle	*Onopordum acanthium*
Mary's thorn	Rose	*Rosa hyb.*
Mary's tree	Wormwood	*Artemisia absinthium*
Mother of God flower	Sweet marjoram	*Origanum majorana*
Mother of God's platter	Henbane	*Hyoscyamus niger*
Mother's love	Patient Lucy	*Impatiens walleriana*
Our Lady by the gate	Soapwort	*Saponaria officinalis*
Our Lady in the shade	Love-in-a-mist	*Nigella damascena*
Our Lady's balsam	Costmary	*Chrysanthemum balsamita*
Our Lady's bells	Water avens	*Geum rivale*
Our Lady's bowl	Creeping buttercup	*Ranunculus repens* (most *Ranunculus* species in general)
Our Lady's brushes	Fuller's teasel	*Dipsacus sativus*
Our Lady's candlestick or Mary's candle	Great mullein (aka Mary's flannel)	*Verbascum thapsus*
	Oxlip primrose	*Primula elatior*
Our Lady's cushion (flight into Egypt)	Thrift, sea pink	*Armeria maritima*

Our Lady's delight	Miniature pansy	*Viola tricolor* or *V. cornuta*
Our Lady's duster	Lovage	*Levisticum officinale*
Our Lady's earrings	Bush or hardy fuchsia	*Fuchsia magellanica*
	Rose balsam or touch-me-not	*Impatiens balsamina*
Our Lady's fennel	Fennel	*Foeniculum vulgare*
Our Lady's flavoring	Pennyroyal	*Mentha pulegium*
Our Lady's garleek	Chives	*Allium schoenoprasum*
Our Lady's keys	Cowslip	*Primula veris*
Our Lady's laurel	February Daphne	*Daphne mezereum*
Our Lady's leaf	Horsemint	*Mentha longifolia*
	Sweetbriar	*Rosa eglanteria*
Our Lady's little flower	Germander	*Teucrium chamaedrys*
Our Lady's little vine	Parsley	*Petroselinum crispum*
Our Lady's mantle	Blue morning glory	*Ipomea purpurea*
	Lady's mantle	*Alchemilla vulgaris*
Our Lady's Milkwort or Mary's milk drops	Bethlehem sage	*Pulmonaria saccharata*
	Lungwort	*Pulmonaria officinalis*
	Wall fern	*Polypodium vulgare*
Our Lady's mint or Mary's mint	Spearmint	*Mentha spicata*

Our Lady's needlework	Valerian	*Valeriana officinalis*
Our Lady's nightcap	Canterbury bells	*Campanula medium*
Our Lady's pincushion	Pincushion flower, morning bride, or sweet scabiosa	*Scabiosa atropurpurea*
Our Lady's praises	Petunia	*Petunia hybrida*
Our Lady's signet	Red bryony	*Bryonia dioica*
Our Lady's slipper	Dyer's greenwood	*Genista tinctoria*
Our Lady's sprig	Anise	*Pimpinella anisum*
Our Lady's tuft	Sweet William	*Dianthus barbatus*
Our Lady's vine	Ground ivy, hedgemaids	*Glechoma hederacea*
Our Lady's violet	Dame's rocket	*Hesperis matronalis*
Sweet Mary	Lemon balm	*Melissa officinalis*
The virgin	Common zinnia	*Zinnia elegens* or *Z. violacea*
Virginity	Myrtle	*Vinca minor*
Virgin's bread	Mallow	*Malva alcea*
Virgin's face	Borage	*Borago officinalis*
Virgin's glove	Foxglove	*Digitalis purpurea*
Virgin's milk	Caper spurge	*Euphorbia lathyris*

| Virgin's palm | Savin juniper | *Juniperus sabina* |

Your Marian garden, besides being a retreat space for prayer, can also be used for celebrating special days of devotion to Mary. Some of these special days are May Crowning, the Immaculate Conception, and Mary's birthday or dates of her apparitions. Often shrines are created as a devotion to a particular Marian apparition, as they are also created for devotions to saints.

Hail Holy Queen

Hail Holy Queen, mother of mercy, our life, our sweetness, and our hope. To thee do we cry, poor banished children of Eve. To thee do we send up our sighs, mourning and weeping in this valley of tears. Turn then, most gracious Advocate, thine eyes of mercy toward us. And after this our exile show unto us the blessed Fruit of thy womb, Jesus. O clement, O loving, O sweet Virgin Mary. (v. Pray for us O Holy Mother of God, R. That we may be made worthy of the promises of Christ.) Amen.

Biblical Reflections

Arise, my love, my fair one, and come away; for lo, the winter is past, the rain is over and gone. The flowers appear on the earth, the time of singing has come, and the voice of the turtledove is heard in our land. The fig tree puts forth its figs, and the vines are in blossom; they give forth fragrance. . . . My beloved is mine and I am his, he pastures his flock among the lilies.

—Song of Solomon 2:10–13, 16

Who shall ascend the hill of the LORD? And who shall stand in his holy place? He who has clean hands and a pure heart, who does not lift up his soul to what is false, and does not swear deceitfully. He will receive blessing from the LORD, and vindication from the God of his salvation.

—Psalm 24:3–5

As a father pities his children, so the LORD pities those who fear him. For he knows our frame; he remembers that we are dust. As for man, his days are like grass; he flourishes like a flower of the field; for the wind passes over it, and it is gone, and its place knows it no more. But the steadfast love of the LORD is from everlasting to everlasting.

—Psalm 103:13–17

For I know the plans I have for you, says the LORD, plans for welfare and not for evil, to give you a future and a hope. Then you will call upon me and come and pray to me, and I will hear you. You will seek me and find me; when you seek me with all your heart, I will be found by you, says the LORD.

—Jeremiah 29:11–14

Thus says the LORD of hosts, the God of Israel, to all the exiles. . . . Build houses and live in them; plant gardens and eat their produce. . . . But seek the welfare of the city where I have sent you into exile, and pray to the LORD on its behalf, for in its welfare you will find your welfare.

—Jeremiah 29:4–5, 7

Prayer Focus for May

No time is ever lost by prayer, for those who pray are workers together with God.

–St. Isidore

In what ways have you helped our Church to flourish? What does it mean for you to be in a relationship with the Holy Trinity? In our lives, if we are fortunate, we encounter others who live out their faith in courageous ways. How have their actions affected you?

What role does the Blessed Virgin Mary play in your life? How do you express your gratitude to her for the life of Jesus? How do you ask for Mary's intercession in your own life? In the lives of those near to you? We are challenged to stay on the "right path" and grow in wisdom. Do you ask her to make you a true child of God?

June: Transformation and New Life

And I am sure that he who began a good work in you will bring it to completion.

–Philippians 1:6

We are transformed through Christ's love and given the opportunity of new life in him. In June we honor the Sacred Heart of Jesus, recognizing his willingness to endure the passion of the Cross for the sake of all. It is during this month that we give our hearts to him in return.

Devotion to the Sacred Heart of Jesus was a localized and private practice when it began in the eleventh century. But after the visions of St. Margaret Mary Alacoque in 1675 it became universal.

Jesus appeared to St. Margaret Mary numerous times from December 1673 until June 1675 and urged her to spread devotion to his Sacred Heart. "The 'great apparition,' which took place on June 16, 1675, during the octave of the Feast of Corpus Christi, is the source of the modern Feast of the Sacred Heart. In that vision, Christ asked St. Margaret Mary to request that the Feast of the Sacred Heart be celebrated on the Friday after the octave (or eighth day) of the Feast of Corpus Christi, in reparation for the ingratitude of men for the sacrifice that Christ had made for them. The Sacred Heart of Jesus represents not simply His physical heart but His love for all mankind."[1]

Through St. Margaret Mary, Jesus conveyed the promises he would keep with those who practice the Sacred Heart devotion:

I will give them all the graces necessary in their state of life.

I will establish peace in their homes.

I will comfort them in all their afflictions.

I will be their secure refuge during life and, above all, in death.

I will bestow abundant blessings upon all their undertakings.

Sinners will find in my Heart the source and infinite ocean of mercy.

Lukewarm souls shall become fervent.

Fervent souls shall quickly mount to high perfection.

I will bless every place in which an image of my Heart is exposed and honored.

I will give to priests the gift of touching the most hardened hearts.

Those who shall promote this devotion shall have their names written in my Heart.

I promise you in the excessive mercy of my Heart that my all-powerful love will grant to all those who receive Holy Communion on the First Fridays in nine consecutive months the grace of final perseverance; they shall not die in my disgrace, nor without receiving their sacraments. My divine Heart shall be their safe refuge in this last moment.[2]

The Solemnity of the Sacred Heart takes place on the first Friday in June. If you are interested in adding this devotion to your prayer life, I recommend the book *A Heart on Fire: Rediscovering Devotion to the Sacred Heart of Jesus*, by James Kubicki, S.J. (2012).

Traditions and Feasts of June

> If we believe that the Eucharist is merely symbolic, we confine it to earth, we measure it in time, and we consign it to death. . . . It is a sacrament that does not end, because it is the sacrament of love.
>
> —Anthony Esolen, "Food for the Journey"

June is filled with solemnities, memorials, and feasts that exemplify God's loving ways in the heart of our world. The most significant event this month is the Solemnity of the Most Holy Body and Blood of Christ, also known as Corpus Christi. This is a movable celebration on the first Sunday after Trinity Sunday that can fall at the end of May or early in June.

Corpus Christi is often celebrated with a procession. Candles are placed in windows—the electric ones from Christmas are perfect—and those who live along the processional path decorate their homes with greenery and flowers much as they do at Yuletide.

You can celebrate a similar activity along your garden path. Since we cannot possess the Blessed Sacrament at home, why not plan to carry a sheaf of wheat to your garden cross, or maybe bring some bread for the birds. Think about how Christ's death brings a new and more abundant life, how he feeds his Church, or how not even a sparrow falls to the ground without God's knowing. We are worth so much more to him than a sparrow (Mt 10:29–31). It is a day to celebrate the light of Christ, so light those candles and give praise!

Meredith Gould, in her book *The Catholic Home*, suggests planting in the garden Michaelmas daisies (*Aster novae-anglie*) and, in the Scottish tradition, carrots. These plants have been used for decades to decorate the altars of Michaelmas (St. Michael the Archangel Mass) on September 29. What's the connection? St. Michael the Archangel defends our Church, the Body of Christ, and leads all souls to heaven, so it is fitting to anticipate his feast day. Wild carrots were ready for harvesting in Scotland by this date in September and were dug by making a triangular hole with a three-pronged tool. The hole represented his shield and the tool his trident. The carrots were then bundled with a red cord and shared as a blessing of St. Michael the Archangel.

The Saturday following Corpus Christi is the memorial of the Immaculate Heart of Mary. It's hard to imagine all that her heart contained. What would Mary have thought and felt as the holy child grew in her womb, as her child marked by God grew into an independent adolescent, and as her son walked away from her into the desert? Mary kept the Word of God in her heart by thought and by obedience, and she allowed that word to transform her life. There is an unmistakable resounding between the Immaculate Heart of Mary and the Sacred Heart of Jesus, one that echoes through our lives as well.

June 24 is the Solemnity of the Nativity of St. John the Baptist. It comes three months after the celebration of the annunciation and six months before Christmas in anticipation of the birth of Jesus. The purpose of these celebrations is not to establish the exact dates of these events but simply to commemorate them in an interrelated manner. The Nativity of St. John is one of the oldest Christian festivals, showing up in the recorded history of the sixth century and was similar to Christmas in that three Masses were celebrated.

The interlinking of Jesus and his cousin John helps us connect to Jesus' earthly life—there was extended family. When I reflect on all that surrounds the verse of Jesus' parents finding him in the Temple (Lk 2:41–52), I can imagine that the troop that the Holy Family was traveling with included neighbors and relatives. The adolescent John would more than likely have been journeying with aunts, uncles, and other teenage cousins as they made their way to Jerusalem for the

Passover. I can also imagine Mary, upon finding her son, keeping "all these things in her heart." Her son had graduated from childhood; the transformation of Jesus into manhood and his role as the Christ was beginning.

June Saints for the Gardener

> When we surrender our lives to God, the light and beauty
> that shines forth is as effortless as that of a wildflower–it
> is the work of God's hand alone.
>
> –Anonymous

June 5: St. Boniface (also known as St. Winfrid), ca. 672–754

Patron of Brewers

St. Boniface was an Anglo-Saxon Benedictine monk who evangelized the peoples of present-day Germany. Because plain water was often polluted, monks brewed beer for themselves as a source of nourishing drink. It was also the daily drink of the people St. Boniface came to evangelize; they had a common ground on which to begin. He took literally the monastic teaching "That in all things God may be glorified." He was known for his ability to perceive a local custom and convert it to reflect a Christian virtue.

Because of St. Boniface, the fir tree has had a long association with Christianity. The story relates how he came across a group of pagans worshipping an oak tree in the druidic tradition. In anger, he swung an ax, cutting down the oak tree to prove that the false god had no power over him.

To the amazement of the onlookers, a young fir tree immediately sprang up from the roots of the fallen oak. St. Boniface took this as a sign from God and began to teach the Christian faith saying,

"This humble tree's wood is used to build your homes: Let Christ be the center of your households. Its leaves remain evergreen in the darkest days. Let Christ be your constant light. Its boughs reach out to embrace and its top points towards heaven. Let Christ be your comfort and your guide."[3]

June 17: St. Botulph of Ikenhoe (Also Known as Boltulf), ca. 610–680

Patron of Agricultural Workers

Oftentimes building a monastery was challenging, not only spiritually, but practically as well.

In the year 654 St. Botulph had attracted enough brothers and hermits to begin work on the Benedictine monastery on Ox-Island (Ikenhoe) in England. It is said that he was often assaulted and his efforts thwarted by evil spirits who occupied the desolate swampy island and wanted to keep that piece of land from him and his holy men. Through faith and hard work the monastery grew in population and turned the large scrubby marshland into productive farming and grazing lands.

Botulph became a favorite saint in Scandinavia beginning at the end of the tenth century. Many churches and hundreds of baby boys were named after this beloved farming saint. There are several theories surrounding the development of his cult. One is that evangelizing monks came across the sea from his monastery in eastern England. Another possible reason was the date of his feast day. In Scandinavia his feast day fell at the approach of midsummer when it was appropriate to plant root crops. The familiar appellation for this saint was *rov grubben*, the turnip chap. There were Botulph fairs for trade and to celebrate the time of planting root crops.[4] These included plants in the *Brassica* and *Beta* families such as turnips and beets.

Try this simple recipe for a thick Norwegian soup similar to what the monks may have shared with the people in Scandinavia. When selecting your turnips, pick the younger, smaller root. The older turnip is stronger, can be bitter, and takes longer to cook.

North Seas Turnip Soup

(*Makes enough for a crowd!*)
6–8 tbs. butter (do not substitute)
3 large sweet onions
1½ lbs. baking potatoes, peeled if desired
3 lbs. small turnips, peeled
6 c. chicken stock (if using bouillon paste, reduce salt by half)
½ tsp. salt
¼ tsp. nutmeg
fresh parsley, diced

Very thinly slice onions, potatoes, and turnips. In large stockpot, melt butter and sauté onions until translucent. Add potatoes and turnips and stir together until covered with butter. Add salt, reduce heat to low, and slowly cook for about 20 minutes until vegetables are tender, stirring occasionally. Add stock and bring to a boil, reduce heat, and simmer for about another 10 minutes. Puree soup, add nutmeg, and serve with fresh parsley sprinkled on top.

Botulph and Boston

The city of Boston, Massachusetts, is named after the city of Boston in Lincolnshire. The name Boston is a contraction of Anglo-Saxon origin and translates as "Botulph's stone"; it indicates the foundation of the church dedicated to St. Botulph's in Lincolnshire. The contraction changed stone to ston/tun (town) and further to Boston. Boston/Botulphston was not the origin of the saint's monastery.

June 29: Solemnity of the Apostles, Sts. Peter and Paul

There is a tradition either that Peter and Paul died on this date in different years or that perhaps the translation of their relics occurred on this date.

Jesus placed the responsibility to develop the Church with Peter. He strengthened the other apostles. It was Peter who "took the lead in deciding what should be done: he designated a successor to Judas; he preached authoritatively at Pentecost; he was the first apostle to work a miracle and soon became the most notable miracle-worker; he justified the apostles' teachings to the Sanhedrin, condemned Ananias and Sapphira, admitted Gentiles into the church with Cornelius; later he took a prominent part in the council at Jerusalem."[5]

The Conversion of St. Paul, on January 25, helps us remember how even the hardest of hearts can be brought to new life through Christ. The other apostles and new followers of Christ were wary about where Paul's loyalties were truly placed, and it took St. Barnabas (whose feast day also happens to be this month on June 11) to calm the community of followers about the truth of Saul's conversion to Paul.

This solemnity focuses on the persecution and martyrdom of these two great saints. In the language of flowers, the checkered fritillary, *Fritillaria meleagris*, represents persecution, and when you see the nodding, dark blood-red flower, its name seems well suited. A spring-flowering bulb, it can represent in your garden the many men and women martyred for our faith.

June in the Garden

God cannot inspire unrealized desires.

–St. Thérèse of Lisieux

Practical Gardening: Enhancing the Garden, Encouraging Plants to Grow

The gardening season is well underway. The daffodils and orange poppies are done, and midsummer has arrived.

It's at this time of year when bare spots show up in the garden. Not only are there bare spots where the bulbs and poppies use to be, but also you may have an area of winter-killed perennials, or maybe the transplanted seedlings you started never took.

There are several ways of transforming bare spots to eliminate the holes. A container garden can be placed in the location or maybe a shrub if you decide to add more structure to your landscape.

Another consideration is planting fast-growing annuals. Flats, cell packs, and pots of annuals are usually on sale this time of year. Local greenhouses often have a nice selection still available, as do some big-box stores.

There are a few tricks to remember about filling in bare spots when planting annuals late in the season. Plant the annuals closer together by one-third than what the tag says. The growing season is shortened so you will not get the full spread (or height) as indicated on the tag. Even though the selection may be minimal, look for bigger, beefier plants.

In late June when purchasing packs or a flat of annuals, especially the taller varieties, the plants will probably be root bound. Using your fingers to tease the roots apart before planting will do more harm than good. What I found works best is to take a pair of garden scissors and nip off the very bottom of the root mass by about a quarter inch.

With potted plants that are severely root bound, cut an X with scissors across the bottom of the root mass and one-quarter of the way up the sides. In both cases cutting and not tearing the roots apart will allow new roots to develop without too much trauma to the plant.

Remember to keep your new plants evenly moist if the weather is hot and dry, and before long that bare spot will have disappeared.

Faith-Filled Gardening: Creating a Stations of the Cross Garden at Home

The fourteen Stations of the Cross as we know them were not fully established until the mid-eighteenth century. During the years from Jesus' death until then, there were observances with varying inclusions of his passion. One form was the labyrinth, which will be discussed in appendix D.

The fourteen Stations of the Cross that Catholics observe are as follows:

I.   Jesus is condemned.

II.   Jesus carries his cross.

III.   Jesus falls the first time.

IV.   Jesus meets his mother.

V.   Simon of Cyrene helps carry the cross.

VI.   Veronica wipes Jesus' face.

VII.   Jesus falls a second time.

VIII. Jesus meets the women of Jerusalem.

IX.   Jesus falls a third time.

X.   Jesus is stripped of his garments.

XI.   Jesus is nailed to the cross.

XII.   Jesus dies on the cross.

XIII. Jesus' body is taken down from the cross.

XIV.   Jesus' body is laid in the tomb.

In presenting the stations in an outdoor prayer space they will naturally be placed in order from one to fourteen. This can be done in either a linear or circular manner.

Depending on your personal preferences, a simple Way of the Cross can be handcrafted or a more elaborate one can be constructed with purchased plaques that are permanently set in a designed landscape.

The simplest method of representing the Stations would be to use Roman numerals applied to various surfaces. I have seen beautifully weathered wooden planks that had the numerals traced into the wood with a wood burner. These were then mounted on trees along a woodland path. With fallen leaves that caught on the corners or moss eventually growing, their contemplative purpose was enhanced and made the visitor feel at one with nature.

Another form for the Stations used large tree trunks cut into fifteen two-foot-long logs. The logs were placed on end in a circle with one log secured at the center to sit on. The Roman numerals were routered out on the angle-cut top of the logs, but numbers could also be painted on them if the surface was planed and smoothed. The power of the sheer mass of logs brings me to marvel at how their weight could have ever been carried on the back of our Lord.

Logs can also be cut into discs and then placed along a walking path as stepping-stones. If you already have a garden path, consider adding something like this on the path's edge. You could also plant a specific flower that corresponds to a particular station, such as lamb's ear where Jesus is condemned, or maybe marigolds where he meets his mother.

You may wish to create your own stepping-stones from cement, imprinting them with the Roman numeral and including found objects that represent one of the Stations. Some possible objects that could be embedded in the cement for each station are as follows:

I.   A rope for his tied hands

II.   An upright cross that he was to carry

III.   A cross at an angle with a single piece of glass placed near it for the first fall

IV.   A heart outlined for the heart of his Mother, Mary

V.   The sandals of Simon of Cyrene represented by embedded leather straps or possibly imprinting the soles of shoes

VI.   Drawing tear drops for the tears Veronica shed as she wiped the tears and blood from the face of Jesus

VII.   A cross at an angle with two pieces of glass placed near it for the second time he fell

VIII.   Three or five colorful vertical elements to represent the upright figures of the women standing along the road

IX.   A cross at an angle with three pieces of glass placed near it for the third time he fell

X.   A lamb for the meekness of Jesus as he was stripped naked

XI.   Three large nails

XII.   A black horizontal object, or possibly a black circle; its color reminding the viewer of the netherworld where our Lord went before his resurrection. The circle also represents completeness.

XIII.   The letters IHS are Greek monograms for the name of Jesus and are often seen on depictions of the cross; this sign was all that remained once he was taken down from the cross. INRI were the letters for "Jesus, King of the Jews" and could also be used.

XIV.   A circular stone or maybe a representation of a gate for the
        closing of the tomb

Formal settings on the grounds of religious institutions for the
stations are often stark and unadorned; the sheer mass of the stations
is sufficient in the public landscape. For the home or small church,
an outdoor Way of the Cross can be a beautiful garden space.

There are several plants that can be grown for meditative purposes to represent the Stations of the Cross. Two plants that are used
to teach about the Crucifixion are the dogwood and the passion
flower.

Dogwood

The legend of the dogwood is a familiar children's story. It is told
that at the time of the Crucifixion the dogwood was comparable in
size to the oak tree. Because its wood was firm and strong, it was
selected as the timber for the cross, but to be put to such a cruel
purpose greatly distressed the tree. The crucified Jesus, sensing the
beautiful tree's sorrow at his suffering, said to it, "Because of your
sorrow and pity for my sufferings, never again will the dogwood
tree grow large enough to be used as a gibbet. Henceforth it will be
slender, bent and twisted, and its blossoms will be in the form of a
cross—two long and two short petals. In the center of the outer edge
of each petal there will be nail prints—brown with rust and stained
with red—and in the center of the flower will be a crown of thorns,
and all who see this will remember."[6]

Passion Flower

The flowering vine *Passiflora incarnate* is one of the few plants that
can be traced back to preliterary times as a teaching tool for religious
practices. The passion flower has the following meanings:

1. Ten petals represent the ten of the twelve apostles that did not betray Jesus (Judas) or deny him (Peter).

2. The three topmost stigmas as attached to their styles (tiny little stems) recall the three nails that impaled our Lord to the cross.[7]

3. The five stamens that hold the anthers together signify the five wounds of our Lord.[8]

4. The anthers alone represent the sponge used to moisten Jesus' lips.

5. The central column of the three stigmas and five anthers signifies both the post to which Jesus was scourged and also the cross on which he was hung.

6. The seventy-two radial filaments are for the number of lashes Jesus received throughout his passion. They are also said to represent the crown of thorns.

7. The leaves of most species are shaped like a lance and represent the spear thrust into Jesus' side.

8. The red stain on the corona at the base of the central column and the red speckling on the style holding the stigma is a reminder of the blood Jesus shed.

9. The fruit of most passion flowers is round and signifies the world that Jesus came to save.

10. The tendrils symbolize Jesus holding firmly to his purpose and being supported by God's love.

11. The wonderful fragrance is said to represent the spices that the holy women brought with them on the day of the Resurrection.

12. The duration of the flower's life is three days: the time elapsed before the resurrection of our Lord.

The passion flower is an amazing plant rich in symbolism. When we feel ourselves faltering in our faith, we can reflect on this flower and, in its beauty, find confidence in the greatest love story ever lived.

Other plants that can be used for the Stations of the Cross are ones associated with a particular station.

I. Jesus is condemned.

- Lamb's ear, *Stachys byzantina*. Jesus stood meek as a lamb as he was condemned.
- Lily of the valley, *Convallaria majalis*, "Our Lady's tears." As Mary wept at the sentencing of her son, her tears struck the ground, and this flower is said to have sprouted there.
- Morning glory family, *Convolvulus sp.*, symbolizes extinguished hopes, being bound.
- White campion, or catchfly, *Silene latifolia*, symbolizes betrayal.
- White English daisy, *Bellis perennis*, conveys innocence.

II. Jesus carries his cross.

- Oak, *Quercus sp.*, is symbolic of bravery and steadfastness.
- Willow tree, *Salix sp.*, and more specifically the almond willow, *Salix triandra*, are symbolic of tenacity and also bravery.
- Yarrow, *Achillea millefolia*, "Our Lord's back." The red flowers are reminders of the welts on Jesus' back.

III. Jesus falls the first time.

- Checkered fritillary or leper's lily, *Fritillaria meleagris*, denotes persecution.
- Holly, *Ilex sp.* It is said the holly's berries were stained red by drops of blood as Jesus walked by; can be used at any of the three falls.

IV. Jesus meets his mother.

- Harebell, *Campanula rotundifolia*, has been associated with grief since the middle ages.

- *Iris sp.*, "Mary's sword." Its sword-like foliage recalls the prophesy of Simeon when he said to Mary that "a sword will pierce through your own soul also" (Lk 2:35).

- Lungwort or Bethlehem sage, *Pulmonaria saccharata*, "the Virgin Mary's tears." Legend tells us that the flower's blue color turned red as the plant witnessed Mary's tears at the suffering to come for her son. It is also known as "Our Lady's milk" for it is said when she stopped to nurse the Holy Infant, some of her milk spilled upon the plant. This plant, as with the herb rosemary, was said to be present at both the beginning and the end of Jesus' life.

- Pot marigold, *Calendula sp.*, symbolizes a mother's grief and despair.

- Scarlet geranium, *Pelargonium sp.*, refers to gentility and comforting.

V. Simon of Cyrene helps carry the cross.

- Balm of Gilead, *Commiphora opobalsamum*, signifies relief. The modern balm of Gilead is made from *Populus candicans*, the balsam poplar.

- Ground ivy, *Nepeta glechoma*, has been named "Where God Walked." It grows in patches and is considered a weed, but there is a variegated cultivar that is ornamental.

VI. Veronica wipes Jesus' face.

- Costmary or allspice, *Tanacetum balsamita*, was associated with compassion (it was also used to treat a broad range of illnesses).

- Crown of thorns, *Euphorbia splendens*, is a thorny plant bearing red flowers denoting the blood of Christ. There is also *Paliurus spina-christi*, crown of thorns or Jerusalem thorn, native to the

Mediterranean. It was the blood from the crown of thorns that Veronica wiped away.

VII. Jesus falls a second time.

- Chamomile, *Anthemis nobilis* or *Chamaemelum nobile*, is indicative of persistence in adversity.
- St. John's wort, *Hypericum perforatum*, is sometimes called "Christ's sweat" because when the flower buds (not the opened yellow flower itself) or the seedpods are crushed, a dark red liquid is produced.

VIII. Jesus meets the women of Jerusalem.

- Butterfly weed, *Asclepias sp.* In the modern language of flowers, it is indicative of letting go. (It could also be used in a garden dedicated to St. Mary Magdalene, for Jesus told her "do not cling to me" when she saw him at the tomb.)
- Maidenhair (or lady's hair) fern, *Adiantum* or *Asplenium*, recalls the woman who washed Jesus' feet with her tears and dried them with her hair. The plant is also used in Europe for the feast of Corpus Christi honoring the Eucharist.
- Red columbine, *Aquilegia sp.* and, more specifically, *Aquilegia vulgaris*, is said to represent the act of being anxious or trembling.

IX. Jesus falls a third time.

- Fennel, *Foeniculum vulgare*, calls to mind enduring strength.
- Again, St. John's wort, *Hypericum perforatum*, is sometimes called "Christ's sweat."

X. Jesus is stripped of his garments.

- Ornamental grasses signify submission because they offer very little resistance as they move and bend in the wind.

- Rush, *Juncus effuses* or *J. communis*, is considered to represent docility.

XI. Jesus is nailed to the cross.

- Greater stitchwort, *Stellaria holostea*, "tears of Mary." As Mary wept, her tears struck the ground, and this flower is said to have sprouted.
- Red poppy, *Papaver rhoeas* (or most any red poppy), is representative of the blood of Christ.

XII. Jesus dies on the cross.

- Jacob's ladder, *Polemonium reptans*, is referenced in the Bible: "And he [Jacob] dreamed that there was a ladder set up on the earth, and the top of it reached to heaven; and behold, the angels of God were ascending and descending on it!" (Gn 28:12). In the language of flowers, it indicates "to come down" (as in God came down). It can also be used in a Nativity garden.
- The violet, *Viola odorata*, according to legend, is one of the flowers upon which the shadow of the cross fell, and, in acknowledgment of the event, the violet dropped its head in sorrow. Its purple bloom is reminiscent of the Church in mourning.
- White heliotrope, *Heliotropium europaeum*, indicates faithfulness to the end because its leaves follow the sun from its rising to its setting. There is also a deep blue cultivar *Heliotropium peruvianum*.

XIII. Jesus' body is taken down from the cross.

- Bleeding heart, *Dicentra spectabilis*, reminds us of the mixture of blood and water, the red and white of the heart-shaped flower, from our Lord's pierced side.

- The use of any plant whose flowers are both red and white, for instance, carnations. This color combination is also used for gardens dedicated to the Divine Mercy.

XIV. Jesus' body is laid in the tomb.

- Forget-me-nots, *Myosotis*. There are many legends associated with this little weedy flower, but its common name suffices for the fourteenth station.
- Morning glory, *Convolvulaceae sp.*, represents death and rebirth because its flowers die at the end of each day.
- Rosemary, *Rosmarinus officinalis*, was strewn in the tombs of the departed (and is said to have been laid on the straw in Jesus' manger).
- Snowdrops, *Galanthus*, usually the first flower to bloom in early spring, are indicative of hope, death, and resurrection.
- White rose, *Rosa sp.*, signifies a martyr's death.

Contemplating the final days of Jesus through the Stations of the Cross has been done for centuries. It is a powerful and sometimes daunting meditation. We can also focus on joy by turning our attention on his life.

You can contemplate the life of Christ through found objects in nature. This is a very personal form of contemplative prayer. The more obvious items mentioned throughout the Bible, such as vines, branches, and water, easily stir our thoughts to prayer. Listed here are other objects found in nature that evoke a sense of the holy.

- **Feathers**: This brings to mind God's concern and caring for us, more than for a sparrow of the field.
- **Leaves**: The color green represents hope and new growth. Sometimes I think of palm fronds or olive trees.

- **Mud**: This was used to help a blind man see. The dirt of our lives mingles with the waters of eternal life. I think also of how we all wrestle in the mud of humanity.
- **Ornamental grasses**: These make me think of gentleness; he would not bruise a reed of grass. Often I think of the breath of God and its gentle movement in my life.
- **Rocks**: I think of a solid foundation, or sometimes of the tomb in which our Lord was laid.
- **Seeds**: Numerous parables are found throughout the Bible. For me, a whole book could be written on contemplating a single seed!
- **Shell of bird's egg**: This could symbolize rebirth, new life, or breaking free.
- **Thorny plants**: The Bible mentions how these choked out the good seed, or recall the crown of thorns.

You can also meditate on the wonders of the night: the enormity of creation in stars, planets, and our world so securely placed within this space of eternity. If you are a night watcher, a white garden would be a perfect place for meditation.

The Unpretentious Egg

We often associate an egg with the Resurrection, but it is also symbolic of the creation of the world and all its elements. The shell represents the vault of the sky where the stars lie; the thin membrane indicates air; the white symbolizes waters; and the yolk represents the earth. I like the way this symbol is so relevant; after all, an egg really is the beginning of new life.

Biblical Reflections

I do as the Father has commanded me, so that the world may know that I love the Father.

—John 14:31

And we all, with unveiled face, beholding the glory of the Lord, are being changed into his likeness from one degree of glory to another; for this comes from the Lord who is the Spirit.

—2 Corinthians 3:18

A new heart I will give you, and a new spirit I will put within you; and I will take out of your flesh the heart of stone and give you a heart of flesh. And I will put my spirit within you, and cause you to walk in my statutes and be careful to observe my ordinances.

—Ezekiel 36:26–27

Be still, and know that I am God. I am exalted among the nations, I am exalted in the earth!

—Psalm 46:10

Prayer Focus for June

> There are two things that must always be meditated on together in the devotion to the Sacred Heart of Jesus: Christ's heart of flesh and Christ's love for us.
> —"The Sacred Heart of Jesus"

Was there a moment in your life when a shift occurred in your heart, a change in circumstances unexpectedly took place, or a particular grace was given? Reflect on how your heart encountered the Sacred Heart of Jesus in that situation. Do you attend Adoration, praying before the exposed Blessed Sacrament? What do you experience there? Why do you not go? Pope Benedict XVI indicated that *adoratio* was to share a kiss with God. How do you feel about such a close, personal relationship with our Lord?

July: Storms

By asking for the Precious Blood to be poured out on souls we prevent its being, as it were, spilled out on the ground in vain. . . . God has put the salvation of others in our hands.

–Venerable Mother Mary Potter

Storms. We all face them, and they can fill us with doubts and fears. Sometimes we anticipate their arrival and brace ourselves as best we can. There are good storms that bring a needed darkness and a refreshing rain to cleanse us. But there are also other storms that are unexpected, hit hard, and bring devastation. The storms that are most challenging to endure are those that threaten us physically, our very bodies and blood.

The month of July is dedicated to the Precious Blood of Jesus. This dedication brings home the nearness of Jesus' humanity. I often want to draw back emotionally when I realize the demanding truth of what he endured in offering his very body and blood for my salvation. The terrible beauty of it all brings me to tears.

I am deeply challenged by this devotion—the shedding of his blood during his passion is a horrific image for meditation and prayer. My tender heart cannot endure this reality for very long. What I have learned from this devotion is that we are called to be

pray-ers for the salvation of souls and that salvation was at the cost
of every drop of blood shed by Jesus to his death.

One of the many prayer offerings of the Precious Blood comes
from the vision of St. Gertrude the Great:

> Eternal Father, I offer you the most Precious Blood of your Divine
> Son, Jesus, in union with the Masses said throughout the world
> today for all the holy souls in purgatory, for sinners everywhere, for
> sinners in the universal Church, those in my own home, and within
> my family. Amen.[1]

I offer this short prayer often throughout the day as a way of
offering my awareness of his gift. The immensity and implications
of our Lord's passion is more than I can understand. How much can
any of us fully understand it this side of eternity?

The gospels reveal to us that Jesus knew this storm was coming.
I wonder if he knew of its approach on the day his cousin John
baptized him, and I wonder too if that is why he immediately went
off into the desert—to allow his humanity to grapple with his God-
ness and destiny. I wonder how he (or we) through prayer learn to
come to grip with the inescapable.

Whether the tears, doubts, and fears are for us or a loved one,
we are often at first confounded by the approaching darkness. A
spiritual director once advised me, when I faced a crisis of my own,
not to cry out to God how great is the storm but to cry into the storm
how great is our God. There was a significant paradigm shift in my
prayer life after her words.

All storms end eventually, and after the big ones there is usually
the debris of broken branches littering the street and lawns. The
weakest limbs, those that have declined from lack of nourishment,
have snapped off during the turbulence. It is usually the branches
that had grown farthest away from the trunk that have fallen away.

When sufficient energy is not drawn up from the root, the branch becomes weak and it no longer has enough life within it to withstand the storms. This offers a pretty clear analogy of how I should live: drawing life from God's strong roots and developing a living faith, thus keeping me strong so I won't break apart in the turbulent storms that come.

Storms come; storms pass. While we are often left with debris about our feet, the light of God shines before us. The cleanup begins, and we move on with faith.

Traditions and Feasts of July

> Discouragement is never from God because it clouds faith and hope.
>
> —St. Ignatius of Loyola

Sts. Anna and Joachim were Mary's parents and are remembered on July 26. For most of their lives these saints faced the sadness and shame of infertility. But another storm would brew when their only child, still unwed, told them she was pregnant. In considering their lives, it occurred to me that there may have been a lot of doubts in this little family.

The elderly Anna and Joachim were childless. Legend tells us that on one particular day the sadness of this situation overwhelmed Joachim. He left the Temple and set off to the mountains to be alone with God. He wandered and lamented, doubting he would ever know the joy of playing with a child whom he and Anna had conceived.

Anna heard about her husband's tears. As his wife she would have spoken of her barrenness with him and her doubt that in their advanced years they would ever have a son or daughter. Anna too went off by herself to pray. Would God answer her plea this time?

Would he bring her beloved Joachim down from the mountains and into her empty arms? She doubted that her husband could endure the shame of childlessness much longer.

I can imagine despair and hope colliding as they prayed. Hopelessness and trust were equally present in their hearts, reality nurturing one and faith the other.

The legend continues that on that day God sent an angel to each of them. Anna was told she would conceive and the fruit of her womb would bless the world. A similar promise was made to Joachim. Did an angel really say they would have a child? They each had to see the other to share what they had been told. Falling into each other's arms, they knew by the joy in the other's face that a miracle would take place and a child like no other would be born.

Anna bore a daughter and named her Mary. She and Joachim reared their beautiful child with awe and wonder at her grace and ability to grasp the roots of their faith.

Then one day their daughter, now a young woman, stood before them flushed with apprehension. How could they believe her fanciful story—that she was pregnant but not by Joseph, her betrothed, not by a man; she was *impregnated by God*?

This was their daughter, and they knew her heart. God had whispered into this child a purity of soul. Very soon Anna and Joachim understood the magnitude of Mary's claim.

Soon Joseph too learned his young bride was pregnant. What would he have thought? How could he focus on his work? Imagine that poor man wandering the countryside looking for building materials, stopping to sit under a shade tree, and weeping about the sexual betrayal of his beloved. If there had been violence against her he would have known. To sleep with another man was so far beyond what this young woman would do. It was an action wholly incongruent with Mary's nature, and yet she was with child and it wasn't his.

Anna and Joachim would have known that Joseph needed to believe in a truth that they could not explain. He would have to come to know, on his own terms with God, a truth that never existed before. There was nothing they could say to remove the apprehension in Joseph. But they could give him time to nurture the seed of faith.

During this stormy time Joseph wrestled with his doubts and prayed with an aching and weary heart. In his despair God came to him through an angel who appeared in a dream. God enlightened him of a truth so preposterous and outrageous that only God could have created it. So Joseph too came to understand the magnitude of Mary's claim. Joachim and Anna rejoiced knowing Joseph believed what they had known for months.

All of Mary and Joseph's relatives heard of the child Jesus. How many of them counted the months from marriage to birth? Did they have faith enough to believe that the angels had repeatedly come to Mary and Joseph? Not all of the relatives accepted what they heard. A seed of growing disbelief prevailed among the relatives. They knew Joseph, the carpenter; they knew that Mary had grown up like any of the other girls. The seeds of doubt grew so much that Jesus was blocked from sharing his gift of healing with them. As Jesus said, "A prophet is not without honor except in his own country and in his own house" (Mt 13:57).

It is hard to imagine a woman bearing a normal, healthy child when she is in her seventies, as Anna might have been. It is hard to imagine talking with angels and not suspect mental illness, and yet many times across three generations, the angels did speak.

If there is anything we can learn from the events before Jesus' birth, it is that doubt is a part of human nature. We must and will wrestle with it because a seed of doubt is the same size as a seed of faith; the greater growth is in which we nurture. God entrusted us to nurture faith.

The month of July is also notable because on July 22 we celebrate St. Mary Magdalene, the second-most significant woman with a role in the story of our redemption. She is acknowledged not only on the Catholic calendar but also in Orthodox, Anglican, and Lutheran Churches as a true female heroine. She was a woman of great courage and perseverance in her support of Jesus before and after his death.

St. Mary Magdalene was the first to come to Jesus' tomb in the garden owned by Joseph of Arimathea. We know the story well, that through her tears at the empty tomb she mistook the risen Lord for the gardener. And when Jesus revealed himself to her, she ran to announce the news to the apostles.

There is a wonderful legend about Mary Magdalene and an egg. The legend tells that she went to Rome to meet with Emperor Tiberius to share with him the story of Jesus' resurrection. The emperor mocked her when she told of Christ's rising, so she held out an egg as a metaphor for the event. Tiberius said that a man could no more rise from the dead than the egg in her hand could turn red. At that very moment the egg held out to him turned a deep scarlet. This story may have given rise to the practice of coloring eggs at Easter, originally only in red. Historical records tell us that Tiberius acknowledged Christianity, and I like to think St. Mary Magdalene had a hand in this—through God. Though the emperor acknowledged Christians, there is no evidence that he was ever converted.

July Saints for the Gardener

> Hope teaches us not to scorn the struggle. . . . It reframes
> present struggles–not by denying them–by placing them

in a larger, truer, context. It yields courage to keep inching forward.

–Pat Gohn

July 2: St. Swithin, ca. 800–862

Patron of Rain or against Drought

St. Swithin was a well-loved English monk (possibly a follower of St. Benedict) who lived during the latter part of the ninth century. He guided the king, the king's son, and all the people of the region to holiness, and as a result their land was prosperous. He became the bishop of Hampshire in 852 and was known for his efforts in restoring the churches during his episcopate.

Before his death he had requested that his body be buried outside and not be enshrined in a cathedral. He wanted the "raindrops pouring from on high" to wash over his grave. This was the humblest of acts before God for his people to see, instead of the pomp so often associated with a bishop. For this reason he was often prayed to when it came to rain.

Another story comes from the day that his body was exhumed to be moved to a shrine in the cathedral. Records indicate that on that day, July 15, 971, incessant rain delayed and nearly halted the activities. Picking up on the story of Noah, the following rhyme came about:

> St. Swithin's day if thou dost rain
> For forty days it will remain
> St. Swithin's day if thou be fair
> For forty days 'twill rain nae mair.[2]

During the Middle Ages peasant farmers were the backbone of society. It was the peasants and not the lords who kept their country fed and prosperous. It was essential for the health of the kingdom that the peasants were successful in managing the land and the livestock. The food they grew maintained the urban areas, and their livestock provided goods for weaving and tanning as well as meat.

The farmers often prayed to a range of patron saints and may have offered a prayer of intercession, similar to this Irish prayer, as a blessing over their labor.

> From the orchards of Armagh
> to the fields of Wicklow,
> may God bless the farmer's work
> and help his crops to grow.
> And St. Swithin intercede
> that whether rain or shine
> his labors are rewarded
> this coming harvest time.[3]

July 4: St. Ulric, 890-973

Patron against Rodents

The Benedictines were noted for their knowledge of nature. They documented this in beautifully illustrated texts. With this wealth of information readily at hand, they were often sought to educate the children of royalty. Ulric was one such child and at age seven was sent to study at the Benedictine monastery in St. Gall.

The rules of the Benedictines were carefully defined and required discipline in all levels of faith and work. Ulric embraced the exacting obligations, and through the years he eventually became a priest. He was noted for being very gentle in his ways and yet unfaltering in the faith. In time he became a beloved bishop.

Earth from his grave is said to repel rodents, and over the centuries a lot of the soil has been carried away. This is attributed to the manner of his death. When he knew the time was near for his soul's passage from this world, he made a special request of his brothers. He asked that they take the ashes from the chapel and draw a cross with them on the ground. Then he asked to be placed upon this cross. Shortly after they had laid St. Ulric upon the powdery cross he passed away. The ground upon which he died was said to have become holy, and no vermin were seen to ever scurry across it.

St. Ulric was the first saint to be officially canonized by a pope rather than solely through popular acclaim.

July 11: St. Benedict of Nursia, ca. 480-547

Multiple Patronages; Horticulture

St. Benedict is a well-known and beloved saint, and there are volumes written about him. His guidance to other monks encouraged them to not fear, for all storms pass, to be humble, to trust in God, to receive all visitors as they would Christ, and to work and pray always.

Though St. Benedict did not intend to establish a religious order, he did intend for communities of monks to develop in specific and holy ways. St. Benedict also encouraged his followers to understand the relational nature of humans to each other, their neighbors, and the natural world. Part of his discipline for the monks was that all necessities for their living and providing for those in need should be supplied by the work of their own community. From within the monastery walls would come vegetables, fruit, dairy, fowl, fish, and provisions of medicinal and utilitarian herbs.

Because they were also scribes and illustrators, the Benedictines helped to preserve formulas for medicinal herbals and advanced horticultural gardening techniques.

The Cistercians are another group of monks that developed from the Benedictines. This order expanded horticultural knowledge in the area of agriculture. Because the Cistercians desired to revert back to the original intent of St. Benedict that a monastery should be self-sustaining, they became the main force of agriculture throughout Europe for the advancements of farming.

Throughout the centuries of working a garden with the humus of earth, the enormity of sky, and the labor of prayer, the monks of both orders were led into a harmonious and full life—a life of living and eating within the rhythm of nature.

St. Benedict did not develop his monasteries without opposition. He faced resistance from other groups of monks who did not appreciate the challenges he proposed to their somewhat privileged way of life. For this reason, several attempts were made against his life, all of which were miraculously averted.

Being unable to deter St. Benedict with murderous efforts, an attempt was made to draw shame on his brothers as they tended to their gardens. From the book *The Golden Legend,* this story is told of a priest named Florentine who had often tried unsuccessfully to murder Benedict. Father Florentine then attempted to "slay spiritually the souls of his disciples." He took seven maidens and sent them naked into the monastery garden to dance and sing "to move the monks to temptation."[4]

St. Benedict knew that his monks were only mortal men and, fearing for their souls, immediately led them away from the monastery. When Florentine saw Benedict and his monks fleeing in great haste, he ecstatically joined the dancing maidens, rejoicing in his success. The celebration was short lived however, for very suddenly, and to the horror of the young women, the tower's upper chamber collapsed upon the corrupt priest and sent him into eternity.

July 23: St. Phocas, ca. 303

Patron of Gardeners and Gravediggers

St. Phocas the Gardener lived near Sinope, Turkey, during the third century and used the crops of his garden to feed persecuted Christians and the poor. He was known for his impressive skills at gardening, his hospitality, and his generous nature. Phocas even provided hospitality to the soldiers who were sent to execute him during the persecutions of the Roman emperor Diocletian.

Legend tells us that St. Phocas lived just outside the gates of the city. Roman soldiers had been sent by order of their emperor to find and kill the Christian, Phocas. They knew he lived near Sinope. When they arrived late to the city, they found the gates had been secured for the night. Seeking shelter, they soon came to the home of Phocas, where he generously offered them lodging.

The soldiers, not knowing that their host was their intended victim, agreed to his hospitality and enjoyed the fresh produce he set before them with their meal. From the mealtime conversation the saint realized that his life was soon to end—he was to be martyred for his faith. As the soldiers slept, Phocas dug his own grave and also prayed fervently for the men. In the morning, when the soldiers awoke, Phocas revealed his identity. The soldiers hesitated and offered to report to their commander that their search had been fruitless. Phocas refused this offer, knowing the danger the soldiers would be placing themselves in. He was then killed, and the soldiers buried him in the grave that he had dug for himself.

There is some confusion about this third-century saint. According to *The Oxford Dictionary of Saints*, the St. Phocas who died in 303 was not a bishop: "It seems probable that hagiographers have made one saint into three: Phocas of Antioch, Phocas the Bishop of Sinope and Phocas the Gardener. Only the last seems authentic."[5] There is a St. Phocas in the Eastern Orthodox Church who was a bishop in Sinope and was martyred in 117 with twenty-six other holy men.

Here is a short prayer from the *Book of Blessings* for the blessing of cemeteries. This prayer has often been said by gravediggers who prepare the final resting place.

> May the bodies buried here sleep in your peace,
> to rise immortal at the coming of your Son.
> May this place be a comfort to the living,
> a sign of their hope for unending life.
> May prayers be offered here continually in supplication
> for those who sleep in Christ and in constant praise of your mercy.[6]

July in the Garden

> We come to know both ourselves and God better in times
> of struggle and when our spirit is all dried up.
>
> –St. Catherine of Siena

Practical Gardening: Recovering the Garden after a Downed Tree

I live in an area of the Midwest where tornadoes, electrical storms, and wind shears take place during the summer. The intensity of these storms can bring down limbs and at times a whole tree. Losing a mature tree changes the landscape significantly and exposes a shade garden to damage from full sun. Dealing with the problem can be a challenge.

After removing the fallen limbs and raking up debris you will need to remove the remaining trunk. If the remaining stump is ground down, rake up the chippings too. If the chips are left to mix into the ground, these pieces will create a loose and unstable soil, preventing good root development of replacement plants. The other option for the stump is to cut it as close to ground level as possible and let nature take its course.

The shade plants that grew protected by the tree are now fully exposed. These plants will need to be relocated. If there are a lot of plants to move, you may need to protect them from the sun for a short time while you work. Construct around the exposed garden a shade screen on the south and west sides: use metal garden posts pounded into the ground and a painter's drop cloth or old white sheets attached to them with wire. Remember to keep the plants evenly moist to help reduce stress.

Any well-established tree will use up soil nutrients around its roots. You will need to take this into consideration when selecting replacement plants.

Woody plants that will grow in poor soils and full sun are locusts, junipers, barberry, black currants, and shrub roses to name a few. Ornamental grasses will also tolerate depleted soils. Use a noninvasive ground cover to hide the stump as it decomposes.

Plant a replacement hardwood a few feet from the stump in an open pocket of soil between the roots. Do not plant a new tree over the top of the existing ground-out stump area; the soil will be unstable, and the high carbon ratio from the sawdust will compromise nitrogen uptake.

As the old roots decompose, available nitrogen in the soil will decrease. Remember to fertilize to maintain plant health.

Another option is to construct a raised bed over the top of the stump for herbaceous plants such as perennials, annuals, and smaller ornamental grasses. Make the area at least twice the size of the stump. Should you plan to enclose the area inside a frame, do not use treated lumber if you plan to grow edible plants in it (cedar planks are best).

Use composted material mixed with topsoil. Toss in a few worms and some organic fertilizer, and your new flower bed will flourish.

Faith-Filled Gardening: Memorial and Healing Gardens

Memorial and healing gardens are garden spaces specifically constructed to reflect or honor an individual, group, or issue. Memorial gardens are meditative simply by their very purpose of focusing our attention on an individual or event.

Memorial and healing gardens can be grouped together because in both situations we are approaching God through prayers of petition. We want a space that encourages us to pray especially for something or someone. The intent of the garden is personal and could include a statue or other elements from other types of gardens.

In the case of a memorial garden, this could include items that remind you of a loved one who passed into eternal life. Maybe this was someone who was a carpenter, loved birds, and had a special devotion to St. Joseph. It is easy to see what elements would be included in this garden.

A memorial garden is a healing garden, and a healing garden can be a garden for physical healing as well as mental health and spiritual well-being. The lines between garden concepts blur here. You may have a patron saint to which you are praying, or maybe the Rosary has taken on a deeper meaning for you. Possibly you are dealing with your own mortality and delving more deeply into the Way of the Cross.

For a healing garden that includes an angel, St. Raphael is a good choice. St. Raphael the Archangel's name is *God is my health*, and he is the angel in the Bible who brought sight to the wealthy Israelite Tobit. Raphael's colors are bright yellow or gray, and he is represented by a fish. The two-lined Christian symbol of a fish, the ichthys, is a mark of the healing of the soul. Any area of your garden could be devoted to him if you used yellow flowers. Adding a statue or some stepping-stones with the two-lined fish drawn in them or even buying an ornamental metal fish would be appropriate.

There are several saints associated with good health or healing, including the Infant Jesus of Prague. Some patron saints are associated with a certain affliction, disorder, or disease. An excellent resource on the Internet for learning more about saints for healing purposes is http://saints.sqpn.com.

Flowers of the Shroud of Turin

The Shroud of Turin was wrapped around the body of Jesus after it was taken down from the cross. Experts in the natural sciences began examining the shroud toward the end of the nineteenth century. Botanical experts on the research team found the imprints of plants and grains of pollen that can serve as seasonal calendar and geographic indicators.

Four plants on the shroud are significant because as researchers Avinoam Danin and Uri Baruch reported, "The assemblage . . . occurs in only one rather small spot on earth, this being the Judean mountains and the Judean Desert of Israel, in the vicinity of Jerusalem."[7]

These experts succeeded in identifying thirty-six species of plants on the shroud.[8] They discovered that almost all of the flower images remaining on the cloth and the highest concentration of pollens were where the head of the corpus would have been lying; plant parts and pollens were also located throughout the rest of the shroud.

Plants Found on the Shroud of Turin

Botanical name	Common name (English)
Acacia albida	Acacia
Anabasis aphylla	Anabasis
Artemisia herba-alba	White wormwood
Atraphaxis spinosa	Atraphaxis
Capparis ovata	Caper
Carduus	Carduus thistle
Cedrus libanoticus	Cedar
Echinops glaberrimus	Echinops
Fagonia mollis	Fagonia
Gundelia tournefortii	Tumble thistle
Haplophyllum tuberculatum	Haplophyllum
Hyoscyamus reticulatus	Henbane
Linum mucronatum	Armenian flax
Paliurus spina-christi	Jerusalem thorn, garland thorn, or crown of thorns
Prosopis farcta	Dwarf mesquite, Syrian mesquite

Reaumuria hirtella	Reaumuria
Ricinus communis	Castor oil plant
Scabiosa prolifera	Carmel daisy
Scirpus	Scirpus
Secale	Rye
Suaeda	Seepweed
Tamarix	Salt cedar[9]

The botanists found several factors of particular interest to those studying, even doubting, the authenticity of the shroud. These are some of their findings:

1. All the plants are ones that grow in Israel. Of these, twenty are known to grow in Jerusalem itself, and eight others grow in the vicinity in the Judean desert or the Dead Sea area.
2. Although some of these plants are found in Europe, fourteen plants grow only in the Middle East.
3. Twenty-seven of the plants bloom in the springtime at the same time as the Jewish Passover.
4. *Zygophyllum dumosum* has both pollen as well as an image on the shroud and grows only in Israel, Jordan, and the Sinai region.
5. *Gundelia tournefortii* (most frequent of the pollens found by the scientist on the shroud and indicative of season) is the plant material found where the crown of thorns was imprinted around the head on the cloth.

Tale of Three Trees

This is a wonderful children's story of how when dreams seem to be cut down we later find them fulfilled beyond our imagining.

There were three young cedar trees on a hillside in Jerusalem, each proud in its own way. The first tree looked at the stars and wanted to hold a treasure; the second looked at a flowing stream and desired to be a great ship that carried powerful kings; and the third little tree simply wanted to grow tall so that when people looked at it their eyes would follow its limbs upward, looking to heaven and thinking of God.

Many years passed, and the three trees grew large and stout. Then a woodcutter came and felled the first tree. It did not become the finely crafted treasure chest it wanted to be but ended up as roughly hewn feedboxes for animals. The woodcutter returned with his ax and felled the second tree, but instead of a mighty ship, it was made into small fishing boats. Too small for an ocean voyage, the boats were intended for use in calmer waters.

The third tree grew awhile longer, thinking proudly of its stature. But then the woodcutter came once more and felled this tree, too. It was milled into large timbers and then left alone for many years.

All the trees were humbled, their prideful plans left behind. One evening the first tree found itself being dragged into a stable where it was filled with fresh straw. And then, of all things, a baby was placed within. The tree soon realized that it was holding the greatest treasure of all.

Several years later, the second tree was put out upon the lake packed with so many weary travelers that it was in danger of capsizing. As a storm rose and the boat struggled against the crashing waves, one man stood up and raised his arms and yelled "Peace" into the night, and the waters and all became quiet. The tree realized its dream had been fulfilled in that it was carrying the King of Kings.

Not so long thereafter, the third tree was dragged from the woodpile, and its beams were bound together. It was frightened of the yelling crowds and even more terrified as soldiers pounded nails through a man's hands and feet and into its wood. The tree felt ugly, so harsh and cruel, even after the body had been removed, until the following Sunday morning when a great light shone. The earth trembled in joy, and the tree knew that it would forever direct man's heart to see God's great love.

Biblical Reflections

He will yet fill your mouth with laughter, and your lips with shouting.

—Job 8:21

For [you, O Lord, have] been a stronghold to the poor, a stronghold to the needy in his distress, a shelter from the storm and a shade from the heat. . . . [The Lord] will swallow up death for ever, and the Lord GOD will wipe away tears from all faces.

—Isaiah 25:4, 8

I will rejoice in Jerusalem, and be glad in my people; no more shall be heard in it the sound of weeping and the cry of distress. . . . They shall build houses and inhabit them; they shall plant vineyards and eat their fruit . . . and my chosen shall long enjoy the work of their hands. They shall not labor in vain, or bear children for calamity; for they shall be the offspring of the blessed of the LORD, and their children with them. Before they call I will answer, while they are yet speaking I will hear.

—Isaiah 65:19, 21–24

May those who sow in tears reap with shouts of joy! He that goes forth weeping, bearing the seed for sowing, shall come home with shouts of joy, bringing his sheaves with him.

—Psalm 126:5–6

Through many tribulations we must enter the kingdom of God.

—Acts 14:22

Prayer Focus for July

All suffering prepares the soul for vision.

–Martin Buber

Dear Lord, I thank you for the storms that move through life. Though there is darkness, there is assurance of its passing. You send the rain to cleanse, the thunder to make us attentive, and the wind to remind us that all things move according to your plan.

Although I do not like the darkness, I love that your storms draw me down and away from the often-consuming blaze of this world. And with every storm that moves across my heart, I embrace the time to patiently watch for your return. I pray to have grown strong enough to hold fast when storms become intense and if I grow weary to call out for others to shore me up.

I praise you, Lord, for dark nights and stormy days that deepen my desire for you. Amen.

August: **Fruitfulness**

Growth in selfless love is not natural to fallen human beings. Only the power of God's Spirit and our surrender to it can explain a steady growth in charity.

–Anonymous

August is one of four months dedicated to the Blessed Mother. During this month we honor her Immaculate Heart. Just as the Sacred Heart of Jesus represents Christ's love for all people, the Immaculate Heart of Mary represents the Blessed Virgin's desire to lead all to Christ. They are often venerated together to deepen our love of God. "Love is more the result than the object of the [Immaculate Heart] devotion, the object being rather to love God, and Jesus better, by uniting ourselves to Mary for this purpose and by imitating her virtues."[1] Just as Jesus came to us through Mary, we come to Jesus through Mary, who magnifies her son.

When I think about Mary's Immaculate Heart, it is easy to see how her life exemplified the perfection of the fruits of the Spirit. The Catholic Church lists twelve fruits of the Spirit, nine of them found in the Bible, in Galatians 5:22–23. The twelve fruits of the Spirit are charity (love), joy, peace, patience, kindness, goodness, generosity, gentleness, faithfulness, modesty, self-control, and chastity (*CCC*, 1832). We learn through imitating Mary's virtues how these spiritual fruits can mature in us and that they do not develop individually but are mutually dependent; it's a daily endeavor to grow toward God.

The first and most important of the fruits is *love,* or charity (from the Latin *caritas*). Our Church teaches that it is from this stance of loving that all other virtues grow. We read in the *Catechism of the Catholic Church,* "The practice of all the virtues is animated and inspired by charity [love], which binds everything together in perfect harmony" (1827).

Pope Francis stated in *Lumen Fidei,* "Faith transforms the whole person precisely to the extent that he or she becomes open to love."[2] Mary's complete love of God and deep trust in his care of her allowed her to transcend the implications of being chosen to carry the incarnation. Mary was able to transcend the sufferings that she and her son were to face during his passion into a love for all mankind.

Joy is sometimes confused with happiness. Happiness comes from things of this earth. True joy is a thing of eternity and exists whether we are happy or not. It too is relational to the extent that we are open to love. Joy comes from the confidence in recognizing utter dependence to the Creator (*CCC,* 301). Throughout the Bible, Mary, along with St. Joseph, displays the confidence that brings a quiet joy. I'm sure they were not happy about the situation in Bethlehem, or fleeing into Egypt, and yet I can imagine there was joy in their hearts knowing God would take care of them. Joy liberates peace.

We hear at Mass and read in the Bible that we are to be free from all anxieties and that we are to be at *peace.* Jesus said, "Peace I leave with you; my peace I give to you; not as the world gives do I give to you. Let not your hearts be troubled, neither let them be afraid" (Jn 14:27). I find that being free from anxieties is a challenge, and I must often rein myself in when the "what ifs" start and I lose my grip on peace.

Peace comes from doing what needs to be done as it needs doing and not fretting about future or past events. In her Immaculate Heart, Mary modeled the peace of "doing" within God's love. Even where the Bible does not reveal it, we can assume that she was present in the daily moments: with St. Joseph in rearing Jesus, as they taught him Mosaic Law, in her accompanying Jesus in his ministry, and in attending to his domestic needs during that time. It was in her constancy that she displayed the way of peace, again, rooted in the joyful confidence of holy love.

To be *patient* in all things is a tall order, certainly for us and probably at times for Mary. Patience is about trust, not tolerance, though tolerating a situation demands a lot of patience at times. For years Mary was patiently waiting for Jesus to begin his ministry as the Christ. We are told she "kept all things in her heart," knowing who her child was, and trusted God to reveal the incarnation in due season.

As with all good mothers, she encouraged her child to develop God-given gifts, but in her situation it was the gift of God himself. After Jesus had been baptized, we read the story of the marriage feast at Cana. Here, Mary's patient prompting of Jesus was fulfilled. His first recorded miracle was water to wine.

Mary was the essence of *kindness*, *goodness*, and *generosity*. These are fruits of the Spirit that have within them a great desire to do good for others. It is in the fulfilling, as well as in the desiring to give, that fruitfulness grows. This thread runs throughout the Bible, and we first read of it in Genesis 18 when Abraham saw three men in the hot sun and "ran from the tent door" begging them for the favor to serve them.

We see this same yearning to assist when Mary went in "great haste" to pregnant Elizabeth to assist the aged woman through the months ahead. I don't imagine it was easy for Mary, during her own pregnancy, to manage Elizabeth's household, to wait on her cousin, and to be present through the suffering and pain of delivery.

When we think of being generous and kind, we often associate this with giving to others. We should also keep in mind being generous and kind with ourselves. We are going to make mistakes, some serious with hurtful consequences, and we may condemn ourselves for having done so. Imagine how Joseph and Mary would have felt when they lost track of their son. Their one job was to watch over God's child, and they blew it. The boy was gone! I suspect there were a lot of frantic prayers being said as they headed back to town, trying—as does any parent—not to fear the worst. It took a lot of faith to maintain confidence that Jesus was safe.

When I've messed up and have already done my best to atone, I recall what St. Francis de Sales wrote: "If you happen to do something that you regret, be neither astonished nor upset, but, having acknowledged your failing, humble yourself quietly before God and try to regain your gentle composure. Say to your soul: 'There, we have made a mistake, but let's go on now and be more careful.'"[3] This simple act of self-kindness allows for a heart, constricted by self-deprecation, to more fully reopen to the flow of grace.

The fruit of *gentleness*, apparent in Mary's conduct, grew from an interior seed. She first had to be gentle in her thoughts, words, and deeds to be able to express gentleness in her acts of kindness and generosity.

Faithfulness is a lifestyle that develops all other fruits of the Spirit. There are subtle but distinct differences between having faith, believing in something, or trusting something to be as it is. When we trust, it is in something tangible. We trust a person who has been educated in an area we are not, such as a doctor or a contractor. We trust that turning a key will open a door or start an engine. To believe is to embrace something intangible. Belief in love and the love of God, and belief in the Incarnation, is not verifiable. It is in our believing Jesus and in Jesus that faithfulness flourishes.[4]

There is no greater example of faithfulness than the Blessed Virgin Mary. In each phase of her life—as a child of God, as spouse to the Holy Spirit, and as the mother of Jesus the Christ—she was faithful. Mary trusted in her child and believed that, no matter what, God's will would be done. She journeyed in ever-increasing love.

The last three fruits of the Spirit perfected in Mary's Immaculate Heart are *modesty*, *self-control*, and *chastity*. I've grouped these fruits together because for me they focus on keeping things in balance.

Many Christians relate the perfection of these fruits with sexuality, and discerning our physical natures and desires is important. When I think of Mary and her chaste spouse, Joseph, the full weight of self-control is revealed. But modesty and self-control include more than chastity—though a chaste life demands the other two.

What Mary helps us to understand is that a holy life is a balanced life. There is the modesty of how we use our resources, the self-control needed when we start to focus on acquiring—more things, more food, and more thrills—and the self-control with emotions. Imagine Mary's tears and emotional state as she watched the Passion start to unfold and how deeply she was called to believe in God's plan and keep things in balance.

The virtue of chastity is required in all states of life, whether one is single, married, widowed, ordained, or in religious life. According to the glossary of the *Catechism of the Catholic Church*, chastity "provides for the successful integration of sexuality within the person leading to the inner unity of the bodily and spiritual being."[5] Developing this fruit helps us find ways of expressing love beyond physical gratification. This brings us full circle, in that love goes beyond the physical body. Joy and peace develop through patience and faithfulness and are expressed in a kind and generous heart that reflects gentleness. All of these are present in the Immaculate Heart of Mary.

Traditions and Feasts of August

> Faith is born of an encounter with the living God who calls us and reveals his love, a love which precedes us and upon which we can lean for security and for building our lives.
>
> –Pope Francis

There's a lot going on in August. The Feast of the Transfiguration of the Lord is on the sixth, Solemnity of the Assumption of the Blessed Virgin Mary is on the fifteenth, the memorial of the Queenship of the Blessed Virgin Mary falls on the twenty-second, and a whole slew of memorials for saints also take place. This is indeed a prayerful month for us!

The Transfiguration holds a special place in my heart. The definition of transfigure is to transform in appearance or change so as to glorify or exalt. That last part—to change so as to glorify—is something that many of us experience. It's sometimes called conversion.

An insight into the Transfiguration of the Lord came one August day while I was out in the gardens. It had been a cool summer, and most of the perennials were flowering later than usual. I was cleaning up a small bed along the driveway and gingerly pulling the neighbor's intrusive blue-flowering vinca vine from between rose canes and lance-shaped leaves of the yucca. Kneeling on a pad in the driveway, I reached in repeatedly to remove the vine from between the yucca leaves. Absentmindedly I stabbed my arm on one of the tips. I pulled back with a low murmur of pain, looked up at the massive flowering stalk, and intended to have a short disgruntled conversation with God. Instead he decided to have a moment with me.

There, three feet over my head, against a clear bright-blue sky, was a glowing white oblong shape of flowers. I imagined I could almost see Jesus wearing his luminous white robes in the Transfiguration as it was told in the Bible. I was captivated, not unlike the apostles, I'm sure.

The incongruity of the radiant flowers rising from the earthly whorl of piercing lance-shaped leaves reminded me of Jesus' brief life. How his presence was wholly incongruent with this world. How he too would be pierced by a lance and would rise past the violence and pain.

Through all this—the Transfiguration and the Passion—we were shown by our Lord a way to be "of God" and not just for God. We were shown how to live in a world of piercing sharpness that is discordant and not in harmony with the soul's desire to be illuminated and illuminating.

I studied the yucca for a moment longer, knowing my soul had become a little brighter from the small revelation. I knew on that day I would never see the yucca in the same way again.

Intending to return to my task of clearing vinca from the lance-shaped leaves, I noticed the flowering stalk was shading my face, a nice touch to end the lesson. The transfigured Jesus stands between me and the hot-white light of God.

The Solemnity of the Assumption of the Blessed Virgin Mary on August 15 is a holy day of obligation and commemorates her death and bodily assumption into eternal life. This took place before her physical body could begin to decay. But did you know that Mary's tomb was not found empty? In 451 it was noted by St. Juvenal, bishop of Jerusalem, at the Council of Chalcedon, that the apostle St. Thomas was said to have found beautiful roses and lilies where her body once laid.[6] In your garden, you can grow these two plants together around the base of your statue of Mary as a reminder of her assumption and our own bodily resurrection to take place at the end of time.

This holy feast day is also associated with celebrating the summer's harvest. The Roman Ritual includes the Assumption Day Blessing of Produce, Fields, Gardens, and Orchards. A portion of that ritual includes this prayer:

> Let us ever praise and extol God's all-embracing providence, who gives us food from the fruits of the earth. Blessed be God for ever. The Lord has bestowed the fruits of the earth for the benefit of all the world's people. May we share with all in need and so be good stewards of God's earth and its abundance. We remember the words Mary speaks in the gospel story of the visitation: "The hungry he has filled with good things."[7]

There is also a wonderful tradition on this day of giving baskets of fruits and herbs to friends. In this way we can imitate Mother Mary by bringing comfort to others.

August Saints for the Gardener

> Life is not the product of non-being or chance, but the fruit of a personal call and a personal love.
>
> –Pope Francis

August 11: St. Clare of Assisi, 1194–1253

Patronage for Good Weather

St. Clare of Assisi, St. Francis's companion, was fond of creating specialized gardens. She grew unique dedicated gardens of prayer and meditation at the San Damiano convent. Her favorite flowers were violets that symbolized humility, white lilies for purity, and red roses that were at the time tokens of love for God and his love for us.

The members of the Poor Order of Ladies, who were later renamed the Poor Clares, were known for their joyousness and austere lifestyle that included being vegetarians. They relied heavily on their gardens to provide the food they needed for their community as well as the flowers for the altar and the necessary medicinal and household herbs. These gardens were displays of beauty even in their functionality, for Clare and her sisters understood well how the Creator was revealed in the beauty of his world. And typical of the monastic traditions, manual labor was seen as a deep and unifying prayer.

As the order of monastic women grew and other monasteries developed, this dedication to gardens that were both functional and places of meditation and prayer continued.

St. Clare is not listed as a patron of gardens but, among other things, as a patron for fair weather. This patronage starts with her name. While she was still in her mother's womb, her mother, Orlata, prayerfully begged at the foot of the cross for the safe birth of her child. While she prayed she heard a voice say, "Be not afraid, woman, since you will joyfully shine a light that will illumine with greater clarity the entire world." When the child was born, she was given the name of Clare—from Latin *clarus*, meaning luminous or clear.

This simple etymological root extends itself into other languages, including—for our purposes here—Castilian (Spain). In Castile, *clara* means "a short interval of fair weather on a rainy day."

Many of those who pray to St. Clare for nice weather will often set eggs at the foot of her statues in addition to flowers. The egg was used by St. Mary Magdalene to describe the creation of the heavens and earth, where the egg whites signified the air and sky; in Spanish, the albumen or whites of eggs are the *claras*. It is a logical form of veneration for most.

August 14: St. Werenfrid, ca. 690-780

Patron of Vegetable Gardeners

St. Werenfrid was a Benedictine monk born in England who traveled to Ireland as a missionary and died in the Netherlands. As with most Benedictines, he worked the monastery gardens so as to feed the community and the poor. He was well known for his holy nature and service to the poor; he nourished not only their bodies but their spirit as well.

The care of monastery gardens during the early Middle Ages continued to develop the rule of self-sufficiency to reduce the reliance on secular provisions. This can be traced back to St. Benedict of Nursia, who taught not only specific religious rules but also that from within the monastery walls would come all the necessary foods and medicinal and utilitarian herbs.

The cellarer was the leading monastic official in charge of maintaining provisions. He was responsible for feeding the entire monastic community, including lay workers and peasants in need, as well as a steady stream of guests who visited the monastery on a journey or pilgrimage. This official would have managed all the gardens, apiaries, ponds, and herds. It is he who would have assigned the work for St. Werenfrid to perform.

This beloved saint performed his duties well and for many decades. He lived into his late eighties, which at that time would have been considered miraculous. He died in Arnhem, the Netherlands, and many reported that at the site of his death the scent of heaven was emitted; some of those present sensed the fragrance of roses and others of lilies. A dispute arose between the inhabitants of Estervoost and Elst near Arnhem for the honor of possessing his sacred remains.

To settle the dispute, his coffin was set afloat upstream and floated until it came to rest . . . on the shore at Elst.[8] This incident is still commemorated on the provincial coat of arms.

August 20: St. Bernard of Clairvaux, 1090–1153

Patron of Apiarists

St. Bernard was a Cistercian monk who was noted as being one of the most influential men of his age. He was an educated man of eloquence and great wit and is a Doctor of the Church. His renowned ability to preach and debate for a cause earned him the reputation, and moniker, of being honey-tongued.

Though he did not have direct beekeeper's responsibilities, he became the patron saint of apiarists because of his speaking ability. Not only did St. Bernard use his communication skills to spread the Word of God, but he also used them in an endeavor to advance farming techniques. In his desire and deep involvement in feeding those in need, he committed himself to the advancement of agriculture in Europe.

One of the ways that agrarian practices were advanced by the Cistercian order was with the location of their monasteries. Bernard was quoted to say that "our fathers built their monasteries in damp, unwholesome places, so that monks might have the uncertainty of life more sharply before their eyes." Through this uncertainty, knowledge was gained about how to transform unproductive land into fertile fields and pastures.

A particularly challenging site was a house he founded in the Valley of Wormwood in the diocese of Langres, France. The transformation of the site included not only the reclamation of the land but also the reversal of its notoriety; the site had been the home of robbers and other unsavory individuals. The land was particularly poor, and during their first few years the religious community experienced severe hardships and survived only by foraging for wild herbs and leaves. Their evangelizing efforts were no easier as they worked to convert the people of the region. Steadily their efforts bore fruit and the coarse meals and hardened souls changed.

During the life of St. Bernard, France was experiencing not only the start of the Crusades but also a time of widespread famine and plagues. It was against this backdrop that St. Bernard's largesse was displayed in concern for God's people. One well-recorded event of his generosity was during a time of famine near his monastery of Clairvaux. The monks there distributed free meals that fed more than three thousand individuals, and all this from their now-improved farmlands.

A familiar saying by St. Bernard speaks of how he encouraged and assured his followers that they would find God more in the woods than in his words: trees and stones will teach that which one can never learn from master teachers.

August 23: St. Rose of Lima, 1586-1617

Patron of Florists and Gardeners, Roses

St. Rose is the first saint born in the Americas. Her birth name was Isabel, but she was called Rose because of two occurrences:

> The very circumstances of the birth of our blessed Rose were mi-raculous. Her mother had been frequently in danger of death at her former confinements [pregnancies]; but not only did she suffer nothing with Rose, but the child herself was born enwrapped in a double cuticle, like a goodly rosebud peeping from its covering of bright green leaves. She was baptized Isabel, which might perhaps have continued henceforth her name, had it not pleased God about three months after her birth, to cause her mother to perceive on the face of her infant daughter sleeping in her cradle, the figure of a

lovely rose. Thus admonished, she called her by the name of that flower.[9]

Initially the name of Rose caused a great deal of distress for the child, who feared it was a path to vanity. One day the Blessed Virgin Mary spoke to Rose when the girl had cried in exasperation to the statue in the Chapel of the Rosary. The Blessed Virgin comforted Rose, assuring her that this was the name that her son chose for her and that she would from then on be known as Rose of Saint Mary. Comforted by this encounter, she took the name of Rose when confirmed, assured that this was the will of God. Another story mentions a butterfly being attracted to this flower of God. She was perplexed about what religious order to follow as a nun, and a black-and-white butterfly fluttered about her until she recognized its representative colors as that of the Dominicans. Looking further into the native butterflies of Peru, it is very likely that the butterfly that St. Rose saw was the lovely *Battus* species, being mostly black with lovely cream markings on wings that can span more than three inches.

St. Rose did fine needlework and grew beautiful flowers and abundant produce that she would take to market and sell to help her family and the poor. During the day she was industrious in caring for others, tending her gardens, and making exquisite lace and embroidery. Her nights were devoted to prayer and penance in a little grotto she had built with the help of her brother. She eventually became a recluse, leaving the grotto only for her visits to the Blessed Sacrament. It is said that her living area was a small cell attached to the grotto that she had built.

August in the Garden

It is the actions of small things each day that show the fruit of true conversion.

Practical Gardening: Keeping Productivity Going

I love August! It is the month when the fruits of my labor are realized. Everything is ripening. Eating tomatoes or cucumbers still warm from the sun is one of my secret delights. Meals are made up of freshly harvested produce—fresh, grilled, or roasted.

The tomato harvest begins for me in USDA Zone 5 in early August and rapidly picks up speed. A habit I have developed while picking tomatoes after midmonth is to remove any new flowers from the vines. The flowers that open that late in the season will usually not produce green tomatoes mature enough to ripen indoors. By removing the flowers, more energy will be diverted to the ripening fruits.

This is also the month for daily harvesting of cucumbers, summer squash, pole beans, and blueberries. Depending on the cultivar and how wet the growing season, you could be picking a lot of raspberries too. And let's not forget about the melons—if you had room to grow the vines!

The growing season doesn't end in August. Replanting fall crops is a common practice. By late summer, garlic, onions, and most other root vegetables including potatoes have been dug out. These cleared beds can be reseeded for autumn harvesting. Crops that do well when direct seeded in August are short-root carrots, bush beans, summer squash, leafy greens, and peas. Be attentive to watering since August tends to be dry.

At the beginning of the month, direct seed summer squashes such as bush zucchini, yellow crookneck, and patty-pan. They all come up quickly with the warm soil and often bear fruit within four weeks. And, being out in the garden so often, you'll remember to pick them before they get too big.

I enjoy late-season beans. As with carrots, the cooler nights of September seem to make them a bit sweeter. Be sure to plant bush beans, and you'll be able to pick until frost.

Faith-Filled Gardening: The Fruits of the Holy Spirit

Fruiting is a purposeful development. To grow from a seed, flower, and ripen, fruits depend on sound roots and secure branches for nourishment. It doesn't happen by chance.

God has planted seeds of faith in us so we too may develop in fruitfulness. These seeds grow to maturity as the fruits of the Holy Spirit. Each fruit does not develop in isolation from the others. As we saw in reflecting on the Immaculate Heart of Mary, they are interdependent and interrelated.

Pope emeritus Benedict XVI tells us that "the fruits of the Holy Spirit are perfections formed in us as the first fruits of eternal glory."[10] To repeat, the twelve fruits of the Spirit are charity (love), joy, peace, patience, kindness, goodness, generosity, gentleness, faithfulness, modesty, self-control, and chastity.

I've mentioned before about creating stepping-stones or wooden markers that are embedded with a verse or image to reflect a particular theme in the garden. Here again, this craft works well.

When I think of fruits, whether spiritual or physical, I think of trees and vines. Expanding on this concept, creating a garden for the spiritual fruits could include that imagery. A series of paths that branch out from a central walkway could be laid out to represent a tree or arbor. At the tip of each branch a symbolic representation or plant of each spiritual fruit can be placed. If you are blessed with a mature tree in your yard, consider placing markers under its shade with small paths, symbolizing a different spiritual subject, radiating outward into the light and the bordering garden.

Another alternative would be steps or pavers placed in sequence. You could order them as they are listed in the *Catechism* (*CCC*, 1832). They can also be arranged in a circle. At the center place a circular bench, a statue or symbol, or white flowers that signify the Holy Spirit, with blue ones for eternity.

The fruits of the Spirit are interior developments, an unseen perfecting toward eternity. We can learn from the blind about trust and developing confidence in finding our way when we cannot see what lies ahead. Those with visual impairments are often gifted with or develop keener perceptions than you or I as sighted persons. With this in mind, consider incorporating Braille to "feel" your way along the journey.

The following table offers suggestions for representations in a garden dedicated to the fruits of the Spirit. Throughout this book, the representative meanings of plants have been given, and a few are repeated here.

Fruits of the Spirit Garden

Fruit of the Spirit	Symbol		Plants	Braille[11]
Love/charity		Celtic	Irish moss *Sagina subulata*	
Joy		Japanese	Wood sorrel *Oxalis spp.*	

Peace	Christian dove	Olive *Olea sp.* (or fine-leaved mock olive)	
Patience	Acorn	Oxeye daisy *Leucanthemum vulgare* (or oak tree!)	
Kindness	Heart in hand	Blue flax *Linum lewisii*	
Goodness	Support	White zinnia *Zinnia elegans*	
Generosity	Basket of plenty	*Gladiolus spp.*	
Gentleness	Lamb of God	Ornamental grasses	
Faithfulness	Chi Rho	White heliotrope *Heliotropium europaeum*	
Modesty	Ghana fabric design	*Viola spp.*	
Self-control	Balance	Blue hyacinth	

Chastity Fig leaf   Rose, peach
                                           colored

Apples

Apples are wonderful fruit to use to teach the youngest of children. When you cut an apple in half along the equatorial plane, the cross section in the core looks like a star. The five seeds inside the five-pointed star stand for the five wounds of Christ.

There is another apple story used to teach about the Trinity. Cut an apple in half from top to bottom and note the three parts: skin, meat, and seeds. The outer skin represents the Father, who encompasses all; Jesus is the meat of the fruit that feeds us; and the seeds are the Holy Spirit that when planted will bring new life. An apple wouldn't be an apple if any one of these elements was missing—so too with the Trinity.

Biblical Reflections

Blessed is the man who[se] . . . delight is in the law of the Lord, and on his law he meditates day and night. He is like a tree planted by streams of water, that yields its fruit in its season. . . . In all that he does, he prospers.

—Psalm 1:1–3

From the fruit of his words a man is satisfied with good, and the work of a man's hand comes back to him.

—Proverbs 12:14

He who tends a fig tree will eat its fruit, and he who guards his master will be honored. As in water face answers to face, so the mind of man reflects the man.

—Proverbs 27:18–19

Fear not, O land; be glad and rejoice, for the LORD has done great things! Fear not, you beasts of the field, for the pastures of the wilderness are green; the tree bears its fruit, the fig tree and vine give their full yield. Be glad . . . and rejoice in the LORD, your God; for he has given the early rain for your vindication, he has poured down for you abundant rain. . . . You shall eat in plenty and be satisfied, and praise the name of the LORD your God, who has dealt wondrously with you.

—Joel 2:21–23, 26

You did not choose me, but I chose you and appointed you that you should go and bear fruit and that your fruit should abide; so that whatever you ask the Father in my name, he may give it to you. This I command you, to love one another.

—John 15:16–17

You will know them by their fruits. Are grapes gathered from thorns, or figs from thistles? So, every sound tree bears good fruit, but the bad tree bears evil fruit. A sound tree cannot bear evil fruit, nor can a bad tree bear good fruit. Every tree that does not bear good fruit is cut down and thrown into the fire. Thus you will know them by their fruits.

—Matthew 7:16–20

Prayer Focus for August

The fruit of silence is prayer.
The fruit of prayer is faith.

The fruit of faith is love.
The fruit of love is service.
The fruit of service is peace.

–Blessed Teresa of Calcutta

St. Basil wrote, "Virtues become our possession when they are, through practice, woven into our nature."[12] Our nature as Christians is to strive to live a holy life. Consider these questions as you work toward imitating the holy life of Mary and her Immaculate Heart.

How often have I run from my comforts and gone "in great haste" to others in need? What does it mean that they "bless me" by allowing me to be of service? Do I willingly accept help, allowing them to be blessed?

It is not always easy, but do I strive to be gentle in my thoughts as well as in my words and deeds?

Who in my life has helped me to transform my faith? Have I been a presence to others, helping them develop their faith?

September: **Harvesting**

We cannot produce or give any other fruit but the fruit we have taken from the Tree of Life.

–St. Catherine of Siena

September is dedicated to the Seven Sorrows of Mary, also known as the Seven Dolors. Not so very long ago, this devotion was also seen as a prayer for religious orders—to increase laborers to help our Lord with the harvest (Lk 10:2).

In the beauty and wisdom of the Church, this month's focus on the Seven Sorrows of Mary follows last month's devotion to Mary's Immaculate Heart. Having previously reflected on her interior life of virtue and joy last month, we now reflect on the relational or exterior part of her life—her work alongside her son and her witness to sufferings.

The Seven Sorrows of Mary are taken from the gospels and are reflective of several Mysteries of the Rosary. Much like the inclusion of meditating on the Immaculate Heart of Mary with the Sacred Heart of Jesus, the meditation on Christ's passion often included contemplation on Our Lady of Sorrows; they developed side by side. The Church has placed these two events, Jesus' passion and Mary's sorrows, one after the other in the liturgical calendar; the Exultation of the Cross is on September 14 and Our Lady of Sorrows on September 15.

Three of Mary's sorrows took place during the childhood of Jesus, the first occurring shortly after his birth. The last four culminate at the Cross, with her heart being martyred with her son's. The Seven Dolors of Mary are as follows:

I.   The prophecy of Simeon (Lk 2:25–35)

II.   The flight into Egypt (Mt 2:13–15)

III.   Loss of the Child Jesus for three days, later found in the Temple (Lk 2:46–47)

IV.   Witnessing Jesus carrying his cross

V.   The crucifixion of Jesus

VI.   Taking Jesus down from the cross

VII.   The burial of Jesus

The fruit of Mary's womb, Jesus, was harvested on the Cross—the Tree of Life. To persevere through these trials she relied upon her faith in God. She accepted his will with courage, reflecting the obedience of Jesus.

When I meditate on her Seven Sorrows, I pray that in my weakness I am never called to endure such sorrows, but if I am called to this level of suffering, that God will favor me enough to help me endure it with some modicum of grace.

Our Lady's Birds

Ladybugs were named for the Virgin Mary and originally called Our Lady's birds, then lady beetles. According to a medieval legend, one time when their crops were being devastated by aphids the farmers prayed fervently to Our Lady to protect the plants and save the harvest. A miracle occurred. Millions of the little red beetles swarmed into the area and devoured the infesting aphids. Legend has it that the red color of the ladybug's body represents Mary's red cloak, and the seven spots of the European species are indicative of her Seven Sorrows.

Traditions and Feasts of September

> May God deliver us from living in illusion and make us live in truth–the truth of our destiny and the truth of his love and mercy.
>
> –St. Teresa of Avila

We gather additional insights into our faith through several significant liturgical events in September. On the eighth is the Feast of the Nativity of the Blessed Virgin Mary—her birthday.

I have a sweet memory that helps me celebrate it. Several years ago, directly across the street from my house lived a loving (and growing) Catholic family. I remember the day when they moved into the brownstone ranch; at that time they were only a family of four, and the mother was pregnant. After many years of the single-story house being vacant, it would once more become a home. I was delighted when the young couple asked if I was Catholic and what churches were in the area. They decided to become parishioners at my home parish, and we became good neighbors as their family grew.

One pleasant September day I was in the front yard gardening and heard the laughter of children. Looking up I saw the small crowd across the road with the oldest daughter carrying a birthday cake. They were headed for the picnic table under the big oak tree.

I stared at the gaggle of kids and for the life of me couldn't recall which of the children's birthday it was. I also wondered if I had a card in the desk drawer that I could sign and hurry over to the appropriate child—once I remembered which one it was. I headed for the house, but before I even got across the lawn, the mother waved at me to come join them.

I was delighted by the children's boisterous greeting and amazed at the vivid-blue frosted cake. The children excitedly told me it was the Blessed Mother's birthday. Now, this was a cause for celebration!

Before the cake was cut, each child offered the Blessed Virgin a gift: a sincere and heartfelt prayer of gratitude. What a lovely birthday bouquet our Mother Mary received.

The Feast of Greenery

On September 8 is the Polish Feast of Greenery. The farm families bring to church large bouquets, cut from their fields and gardens, of herbs, vegetables, corn, and a few flowers. These bouquets are blessed by the priest, carried home, and kept until the same day of the following year. Throughout the year if there is sickness in the household, the herbs are brewed and used for medicinal purposes— not only for the people but for the livestock as well.

We continue to honor our Holy Mother four days later on the twelfth, the memorial of the Holy Name of Mary. The memorial originated in Spain and was approved by the Holy See in 1513. Pope Innocent XI extended its observance to the whole Church in 1683 in thanksgiving to our Holy Mother for answered prayers for the Polish king John Sobieski's victory over the Turks on September 12, 1683. This day was commemorated in Vienna by creating a special pastry shaped in the form of the Turkish half moon. It was eaten along with coffee, which was part of the booty from the Turks.[1]

September 14 is the Exultation of the Cross. We read from the book of Numbers (21:4–9) how the Israelites fell into sin, were plagued by snakes, and had to look upon that which harmed them in order to be healed. We too are harmed by our sins, and that which harmed us is mirrored in the wounds of Jesus. It is to the crucified Christ we must look to be healed.

Only through believing in what lies beyond this world, through the truths of our faith, are we able to endure the horrific image of Jesus' tortured body upon the cross. At times the truth of his suffering makes me shudder, and I wonder how Mary could endure watching her son being killed. I imagine the angels themselves would have been at her side to help her through his passion—it doesn't seem humanly possible to go through that without heavenly support.

Angels are our invisible companions who, unlike us, are not imprisoned in corruptible bodies. The archangels are a significant part of salvation history, as they are in Judaism and Islam as well. They are honored this month in the Catholic tradition with a feast day on the twenty-ninth, also called Michaelmas. The word *angel* means messengers of God. The last syllable of each archangel's name is *el*, a Hebrew name for God. There are three archangels celebrated this day: Michael, Gabriel, and Raphael. Michael means "One who is like God," Gabriel means "God is my strength," and Raphael means "God is my health." A fourth archangel not named in scripture but acknowledged in Catholic traditions is Uriel, "God is my light," who guarded Jesus' tomb and stands at the gate of Eden. These are four of the nine archangels mentioned in the book of Revelation who will rule the earth at the Apocalypse.

In June we discussed planting Michaelmas daisies, *Aster novae-anglie*. This aster flowers when daylight hours shorten. It is associated with the commemoration of St. Michael the Archangel because he is celebrated as a protector from evil and darkness, just as the aster fights against the advancing gloom of winter—with gay color in our otherwise declining gardens.

Traditionally, Michaelmas celebrations were early harvest festivals that included dancing, costumes, games, and of course lots of food prepared from what grew in the fields and gardens. One of those foods prepared in abundance was anything that included blackberries, which were ripe by the end of September. And every good Christian in Europe knew the berries had to be harvested by this day lest the fiery effects of Lucifer destroyed the fruits sent by God. The story told is that St. Michael cast Lucifer from heaven and, during the battle, the devil landed on earth, where he fell into a brier of blackberry canes. The devil spat on those canes, cursed the fruit, and scorched them with his fiery breath—all before St. Michael could finish the job of sending the devil into hell.

A Healing Herb

Angelica, *Angelica archangelica*, was named for the archangels who brought protection. This herb has many healing properties. Its healing nature was revealed during the terrible Black Plague of the Middle Ages that destroyed one-third of the people of Europe. It is said that one of the archangels revealed the healing properties of this plant to a monk who began using it in preparations to heal the sick.

September Saints for the Gardener

> God's blessing is true light in the mind's darkness, true rain for the soul's earth, true life for the seed of everlasting life that lies buried in the soil of the human heart. With God's blessing, the earth yields a rich harvest of generous thoughts, kind words, and good deeds. For today's harvest, we give thanks and praise.
>
> —Peter John Cameron, O.P.

September 1: St. Fiacre, d. 670

Patron of Vegetable Gardens

St. Fiacre is the patron saint of gardeners, especially of those who grow vegetables and herbs. He was a seventh-century Benedictine monk who was filled with that unique joy and humor so often seen in the Irish. He is becoming a very popular saint today as more community gardens are created to serve neighborhoods and the poor.

At the monastery in Kilkenny, Ireland, he learned a great deal about horticulture. He became very skilled in the use of healing herbs and, because of his doctoring skill, had many followers. With so many people seeking his help, he was unable to practice the sacred solitude he desired. With the hope to once again live in solitude, he went to France and for a while lived in a cave near a spring.

Eventually he went to the bishop of Meaux, St. Faro, and asked for land to establish a hermitage and to grow healing herbs and vegetables for himself and those in need. From his own inheritance in nearby Breuil, the bishop gave Fiacre a dwelling place in the forest. Faro also told Fiacre that he could have as much land as he could fallow in one day. Legend has it that the next morning after Fiacre prayed, he walked around the perimeter of the land dragging his spade (or, as one story claims, the tip of his staff) behind him. Wherever the spade touched, trees were toppled, bushes were uprooted, and the soil was entrenched.

Witnessing the event was one of the ever-watchful church ladies who adored St. Faro and felt it was her duty to protect the bishop's holdings. She immediately scurried off to tell Faro that this hermit he was so overly fond of was betraying him with witchcraft. What she did not realize until the bishop set her straight was that he had developed a friendship with the monk and St. Faro recognized the occurrence for what it was: an act of God.

This garden, miraculously obtained, became a place of pilgrimage over the centuries for those seeking healing. It was said that animals never ate from this garden. "It was as if his unwalled garden was spiritually enclosed."[2]

There are legends about Fiacre's garden that relate to an odd patronage to this saint: hemorrhoids. This unfortunate condition, called "Saint Fiacre's illness" during the Middle Ages, was at times fatal back then. Its association with the saint may be due to the following story: One day after St. Fiacre had worked long in the gardens, he was suffering with this affliction. Sorrowfully he sat upon a large cold stone and prayed to God for a cure, and that stone softened, curing the hermit and apparently leaving a very specific imprint! People still journey to his garden to sit upon this healing stone and pray that their ailment will also be remedied.

Christian scholars debate the actual date of St. Fiacre's feast day. Checking several reliable sources I found that in Ireland it is on September 1; elsewhere it varies from August 18 (the date of his death) or August 30 (also thought to be the date of his death). August 1 and August 11 are also being debated. Regardless of the date, it is during the harvest season for most countries in the northern hemisphere, and that is what has meaning for us here.

September 2: St. Agricola, ca. 625-700

Patronage for Good Weather and against Storks

St. Agricola, whose name literally means "farmer" in Latin, is another saint for the young, especially if they are aspiring gardeners or agriculturalists. Agricola knew of his calling at a very young age and at sixteen became a monk. Following in his father's footsteps (celibacy was not yet required), he became bishop of Avignon. He was a gifted preacher and known well beyond his diocese for his charity and care of the poor.

It is believed that his blessing ended an invasion of storks in the countryside of Avignon, France. The migration of storks takes place during the time of harvest, about mid-August. The storks with their young are returning to Africa for the winter and need the high-energy food produced by grains for their journey.

The residents of Avignon, seeing thousands of storks flocking into their fields, knew that their own food supply would be seriously diminished. Unable to frighten off the storks, they went to St. Agricola and pleaded with him to save them from the imminent starvation that would surely come that winter. The bishop, following the farmers back to their fields, raised his arms to heaven and prayed that God would find it in his mercy to protect these fields from the marauding storks. The flocks immediately rose up like a giant cloud and departed, and the fields were left untouched throughout the remaining migration.

This phenomenon lead to his patronage of storks, which is why stained glass and icons of this saint are accompanied by these birds as his emblem. He is sometimes called upon to avert other misfortunes related to agriculture; his prayers were said to produce rain, good weather, and fine harvests for farmers.

September 5: Blessed Teresa of Calcutta, 1910-1997

Patron of the Poorest of the Poor

Blessed Teresa of Calcutta holds a special place in my heart. Against all odds she tried to listen for that still, small voice of God and to follow what she discerned was his will, even through the dark nights of her soul. As a Benedictine oblate, I too try to listen for that soft whisper from the Holy Spirit that trains my words to the will of God.

The Missionaries of Charity, the religious order begun by Blessed Teresa's efforts, has grown exponentially since established in 1950 and is found in more than 130 countries. It includes not only active sisters but also brothers, priests, and a contemplative branch of nuns and brothers. There are also lay groups consisting of the Coworkers of Mother Teresa, the Sick and Suffering Coworkers, the Lay Missionaries of Charity, as well as thousands of volunteers.

There are several books written about Blessed Teresa and many stories shared about personal encounters with her. She understood, as Pope Francis has made clear, that to serve God is to serve him in the poor—to return to the very basics of our faith and bear fruit in the vineyard of our Lord. Through Blessed Teresa's example we learn that to teach our religion is second to the modeling of our faith in service to those in need. These words of hers are especially relevant for us as gardeners:

> The fruit of silence is prayer.
>
> The fruit of prayer is faith.
>
> The fruit of faith is love.
>
> The fruit of love is service.
>
> The fruit of service is peace.

September 9: St. Ciaran, ca. 512–545

Patron of Oat Growers

At an early age St. Ciaran showed a love for learning. He came by this naturally through his maternal grandfather who was a historian and a poet. As a boy, while studying his lessons, he worked as a herdsman watching over the family cattle. Within this pastoral setting he developed a deep sense of kindness and wisdom well beyond his years. Eventually, as an adult, he established several monasteries and a school.

When he was of age he entered the monastery at Clonard, where his miraculous gifts became known. His first miracle occurred while he traveled to Clonard. He asked his family for a cow to take with him as a gift to the monks, but they refused. At this he went to the herd he had tended to for so long and blessed it. As he departed for the monastery, a cow and her calf followed not far behind. When he discovered his bovine companions, he was delighted at the cow's loyalty but dismayed that two animals had left his family's herd. While offering a prayer for the cow's safe return home, he drew a line in the ground instructing the cow that she should travel no farther. The cow refused to cross the line and turned back, but the calf continued her pursuit of Ciaran. This calf, when mature, miraculously provided enough milk for all of the monastery and its guests.

There are many recorded miracles performed by St. Ciaran, one being that of the holy oats. Ireland has seen its share of famines, and one recorded in the Gaelic Irish annals took place from 536 to 539 when unusually cold temperatures caused widespread crop failures. One day Ciaran was carrying a small sack of recently harvested oats to be milled in order to provide a little food for the monks. He prayed in gratitude for the oats that managed to grow when the fine wheat for bread had failed. As he prayed and sang the Psalms, the single sack of oats became much heavier and was miraculously transformed into the equivalent of four sacks of purest wheat. After the wheat was milled, Ciaran returned home and baked many loaves of bread with this holy flour. The older monks said the bread was the best they had ever tasted. These loaves not only satisfied their hunger but also were said to heal every sick person in the monastery who ate them.

September in the Garden

> Thine was the first and holiest grain
> to die and quicken and increase;

and then came these, and died again,
that spring and harvest should not cease.

–Walter H. Shewring

Practical Gardening: Harvesting the Fruits of Our Labor

The work we have put forth in our gardens brings us to harvesting—a simple analogy to how we have labored in faith to glean fruits of the Spirit. When we think of harvesting we think of food and nourishment. Historically this was a time to prepare for the lean months ahead. For many who subsist on what they grow, this still holds true.

For years I took part in the frenzy of preserving God's bounty through canning and freezing and making hundreds of jars of pickles and jams. I enjoyed sharing from the garden. Whether fresh picked in summer or canned and shared in December, the gift was just as much fun to give.

If you're a gardener on a property with little space for growing vegetables but still want to take part in putting up food, there are a couple of options. Check your state's listing of farm markets and for a centrally based farmers' market in town. Pick-your-own farms are a great activity for the food-loving family, and the cost per bushel is lower. Read your state's crop availability calendar, found through the local county extension office or online, to find out what's ready for harvest in your region.

I find September to be as busy a month in the garden as is May; there is a lot to do. We cling to lingering summer days, warm and bright, but there is no denying that autumn is upon us. Soon the gardening season will draw to a close. A large part of our labors will be putting the garden to rest and cleaning up declining plants.

Pull out annual plants as they fade or are damaged by frost. As you harvest your vegetables, remove those plants as well. If you added vegetable plants in August they will have begun producing by now; within a few weeks those plants can be removed too. Do not compost diseased plant materials, especially tomatoes that carry late-season blights and fungus.

Collecting and saving seeds from one season to the next is simple and allows you to keep growing the plants you love best. Here are a few tips and techniques to guide you.

1. First of all you'll need to have planted open-pollinated varieties, those pollinated by birds, insects, or wind. They'll come back true to the species, whereas hybrid cultivars and crosses won't. Hybrid seeds can't be saved; the majority of seeds turn out to be infertile with a less than 20 percent germination rate, and those that do germinate rarely grow well.

2. To gather seeds of flowering plants, first allow blooms to dry on the stem. Deadhead into a small paper bag (or plastic container). Write the name of the plant on a bag with a permanent marker. Gently crush the flower head with your fingers to release the seeds and discard the chaff. For vegetables, let fruit fully ripen, harvest, wash produce, and then remove seeds from the flesh.

3. Spread the seeds on black (only) ink newspaper, parchment paper, paper towels, or a paper bag, and let them air dry for about a week. Write seed names on the paper so there's no mix-up. To save space, place sheets of seeds on large wire cooling racks, stacked one atop another and secured with twist ties at the little v-foot risers. Before laying seeds on paper to dry, cut paper to size and notch in from edge for risers.

4. You can dry vegetable seeds on unprinted paper towels, but they'll stick to the towels when dry. The benefit is that you can roll them up right in the towel to store them. When you're ready

to plant, unfurl and tear off bits of the towel, a few seeds at a time, and plant seed and towel into the soil.

5. Gather dried seeds into envelopes. You can make your own envelopes from the pattern provided. Once labeled, place seeds in center of largest area and fold over the biggest flap (with leaf pattern). Use a glue stick on edges of smaller flaps, fold over, and press to seal.

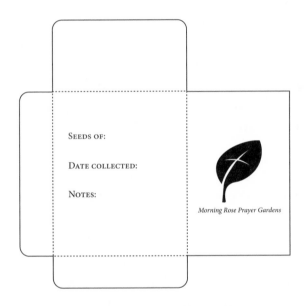

SEEDS OF:

DATE COLLECTED:

NOTES:

Morning Rose Prayer Gardens

6. Use clean storage containers that are airtight. Place seed packets in plastic food-storage bags, glass jars with tight-fitting lids (wide-mouth quart canning jars work great), or glass canisters with gasket under lids.

7. To keep seeds dry, wrap two heaping tablespoons of unflavored powdered milk in four layers of plain, untreated facial tissue, fold over, and tape corner. Put the milk packet inside the storage container with the seed packets. Replace milk packet every six

months if you keep the seeds past the next planting season. You could use silica gel packets, too.

8. Humidity and warmth shorten a seed's shelf life, so think cool, dark, and dry. A corner of the basement or semiheated garage will work, but keep seeds from freezing. The refrigerator is generally the best place to store seeds. When it's time to plant, remove seed containers from the fridge; keep them closed until the seeds warm to room temperature, otherwise moisture in the air will condense on the seeds.

9. Keep each year's seed harvest together by date. Properly stored, most seeds last about three seasons—some only two. A glance at the dates will tell you if the seeds are past their prime for planting.

10. When planting season comes, test a small group of seeds for germination rate. Even with careful collecting and storage, a certain number of seeds will not germinate. By checking first, you'll know how many seeds to sow to get the number of plants you'll want in the garden.

God has placed within the seed all it needs for its future; we need only to gather and grow.

Quarter Days

"There are traditionally four 'quarter days' in a year: Lady Day (March 25), Midsummer (June 24), Michaelmas (September 29), and Christmas (December 25). They are spaced three months apart, on religious festivals, usually close to the solstices or equinoxes. They were the four dates on which servants were hired, rents collected or leases begun, and debts paid. It used to be said that harvesting had to be completed by Michaelmas, marking the end of the productive season and the beginning of the next cycle of farming."[3]

Faith-Filled Gardening: Potagers and Archangel Gardens

St. Benedict and St. Fiacre planted gardens to feed the poor. Certain religious orders, such as the Benedictines and Cistercians, had attached to their hermitages small plots called *le jardin potager*, translated as "garden for the [soup] pots."

These gardens, whether the large cellarer's gardens or small *potagers* that were tended by a single monk, all contained many of the same elements. There were vegetables and fruits, medicinal and utilitarian plants, herbs for cooking, and flowers for the altar. The smaller potagers were often beautifully laid out with flowers and edibles growing together in a visually appealing manner conducive to prayer.

Many people think they need to have a plot for their vegetables and herbs. This may be true if you need to fence it off from marauding deer and other wildlife (such as your children and their hungry friends).

Transforming the landscape into a potager is easier than you think. Envision vegetables where you usually plant annuals. What about adapting the gardens along the sidewalk to the garage as a kitchen garden? As for cucumbers, my 'Straight Eights' grew on an eight-foot-high arching arbor. The leaves were dramatic, the flowers were bold yellow, and the dangling fruits—a delight to see hanging overhead—were easier to harvest. As an added bonus, I'd found the cucumbers were better pollinated in my area if they were not lying on the ground.

If you have the space, grow an abundance of produce to take to the local food bank and shelters. Freshly sliced vegetables and newly picked fruits bring delight to even the most desperate of the homeless—not to mention the delight in your own soul at being able to share.

Community, neighborhood, and school gardens have become very popular in recent years. How about putting a twist on this concept and create a St. Fiacre garden where you and your friends keep 10 percent for yourselves and give away the other 90? Now that's tithing! Add a statue of St. Fiacre at the center or entrance for that little something extra.

The three archangels we honor as Catholics each have their own symbolism and colors. St. Michael, hero of God, is often symbolized by a spear and the colors gold or orange. St. Gabriel, messenger of God, is depicted with lilies or a scroll, and his colors are often silver or blue. St. Raphael, healer from God, is represented with a fish and the colors yellow or gray.

If you can afford it, purchase three different angel statues (not fairies!) for your garden and then plant flowers of the symbolic color around each statue.

You could also create one large or three individual cement pavers embedded with the angels' symbols, mosaic wings in each of their colors, or an image of each angel with the tunic painted in the angel's color.

There is a blessing of our homes that uses the initials of the Magi. We can use the initials of the archangels, M-G-R, in a similar way to adorn our garden. Another way to display their initials is by purchasing wooden letters from a craft store and painting or decorating them in a manner that reminds you of each archangel. It will help if the paint and materials you use are weatherproof.

Biblical Reflections

If you walk in my statutes and observe my commandments and do them, then I will give you your rains in their season, and the land shall yield its increase, and the trees of the field shall yield their fruit.

And your threshing shall last to the time of vintage, and the vintage shall last to the time for sowing; and you shall eat your bread to the full, and dwell in your land securely.

—Leviticus 26:3–5

Jesus said to them, "My food is to do the will of him who sent me, and to accomplish his work."

—John 4:34

He that goes forth weeping, bearing the seed for sowing, shall come home with shouts of joy, bringing his sheaves with him.

—Psalm 126:6

And he will give rain for the seed with which you sow the ground, and grain, the produce of the ground, which will be rich and plenteous.

—Isaiah 30:23

Behold, the eye of the LORD is on those who fear him, on those who hope in his steadfast love, that he may deliver their soul from death, and keep them alive in famine.

—Psalm 33:18–19

For thus the LORD said to me: "I will quietly look from my dwelling like clear heat in sunshine, like a cloud of dew in the heat of harvest."

—Isaiah 18:4

Blessed is the man who walks not in the counsel of the wicked . . . his delight is in the law of the LORD, and on his law he meditates day and night. He is like a tree planted by streams of water, that yields its fruit in its season.

—Psalm 1:1–3

Do not be deceived; God is not mocked, for whatever a man sows, that he will also reap. For he who sows to his own flesh will from the flesh reap corruption; but he who sows to the Spirit will from the Spirit reap eternal life.

—Galatians 6:7–8

Prayer Focus for September

> I have perfect confidence that if I am faithful the will of God will be accomplished not only in spite of the obstacles but because of them.
>
> —Blessed Charles de Foucauld

Fruitfulness is not an event unto itself; it is durational. From the time of planted seed to the fulfillment of promised fruit, a lot can happen. The promised fruit of Mother Mary's womb was the Christ and the redemption of humanity. She suffered, shed tears while maintaining hope, faced fears, and stood fast in faith. We too face fears and suffering and at times may feel hopeless. What is it you can do, or have done, to move through challenging situations? Did you pray? With whom? To whom? What was it about those with whom you prayed that allowed you to feel it would be a fruitful endeavor?

Look to the poor who are not only lacking in food, clothing, and shelter but also challenged mentally, spiritually, and physically. Can you be supportive by volunteering, educating, assisting financially, or being an advocate? There is a saying that it is easier to embrace religion than it is to encounter God. Do you find it challenging to see Jesus, to encounter God, in the poor? What is it that prevents you from being of service?

October: **Preparing for Winter**

As long as matters are really hopeful, hope is a mere flattery or platitude; it is only when everything is hopeless that hope begins to be a strength at all. Like all the Christian virtues, it is as unreasonable as it is indispensable.

–G. K. Chesterton

October is filled with the excitement of transition. Those of us who live in the northern United States experience this with the familiar flame of colorful leaves. I have always loved the cooler days of autumn and bundling up in a sweater and vest to walk along a woodland trail—often praying a Rosary. When I pray the Rosary, daily distractions fall like leaves along the path of the Joyful, Sorrowful, Luminous, or Glorious Mysteries.

This month is devoted to the Holy Rosary and, less formally, the holy angels that guard and guide us on earth and into our eternity. I like how the two fit together through our Blessed Mother: she is Our Lady of the Rosary and the Queen of Angels.

We draw strength from the Rosary and other devotions when we face decline in our lives—and we all face diminishments. It is often in the "autumn of our lives" that we rely more fully on faith as we prepare for winter. We come to rely more on the help of others through each transition, especially if mobility becomes an issue.

The autumn experience of decline can sometimes include more than natural aging. An auto accident left me with trauma-induced arthritis in my neck and spine, and somewhat disabled by the time I was fifty. A friend in his thirties with pancreatic cancer progressed through his autumn experience rapidly and journeyed to his eternity with a Rosary constantly in hand. The economic downfall in 2008 forced millions into unexpected dependencies on friends and families. All of these experiences, and many I'm sure you can identify in your own life, call us into a deeper spirituality where faith remains even when difficult situations are not resolved.

We all move through the seasons of life until finally we are given eternity—a new life with the angels and saints.

Traditions and Feasts of October

> Angels remind us that there is more to the created order
> than what we actually see, feel, hear, and taste.
>
> —Richard McBrien

On October 2 we celebrate the Feast of the Guardian Angels. This is a relatively modern feast day that was acknowledged in the 1500s and fully implemented by the 1800s, even though guardian angels were reverenced in the early Church.

Angels are a significant part of God's arsenal for us against evil. Not only do we have the archangels, but also each of us has our own personal guardians. Many of us are taught from childhood that these heavenly beings protect us from harm both spiritually and physically. All we need to do is be prayerfully mindful to their urgings.

One of the earliest references to these protectors and guides is found in the readings for their feast day. In Exodus 23:20–23, God tells us we are to be attentive to their promptings, for it is they who will guide us "to the place which I have prepared," and his authority resides in them.

On October 7 we celebrate the memorial of Our Lady of the Rosary to whom this month is dedicated. The beauty of meditating on the Mysteries of the Rosary is that they teach us the lessons of a faith-filled life.

A Rosary garden is something that can be enjoyed and used all year. The last half of this chapter is about creating a Rosary garden with elements personalized to your desires for an outdoor prayer space.

You can also make a temporary Rosary garden by using smaller stones, bricks, or any number of objects assembled in the traditional fifty-nine-bead pattern. Ponder the life of Our Blessed Mother from her birthday to her assumption into heaven while you assemble your garden Rosary. Plan to remove your temporary Rosary at the end of October, on All Hallows' Eve, giving praise for how she and all the saints in heaven pray with and for us.

We've come to know October 31 as Halloween. It is also called Hallowtide, All Hallows' Eve, and, liturgically, the Vigil of the Solemnity of All Saints.

The holy night of All Hallows' Eve and the following day, November 1, is a celebration for all the deceased now in heaven. The day after, November 2, is when we remember the souls in purgatory.

In the nineteenth century, secularization took over All Hallows' Eve, which was a religious remembrance of all those who have died. It is distressing how the religious significance of this special time of year has descended into the grotesque and frightening aspects of Halloween, even though the night itself recalls the souls of the damned and should frighten us into grasping the reality of hell.

I prefer to focus on the love and mercy of God and the strength he gave to so many holy men and women who are saints. Most of us have patron saints that we petition for various reasons. Imagine adding to your garden a small shrine to your patron saint, or maybe a statue or other element symbolizing him or her. Almost any book on the saints will indicate what symbol is appropriate; for example, St. Joseph, foster-father and carpenter, is often shown with a carpenter's square and tools in his hands.

This would also be a good day to design or create a memorial garden for a loved one.

October Saints for the Gardener

> To dwell in time is to live by change . . . all exist only by
> tending toward their demise.
>
> —Anthony Esolen, "Food for the Journey"

October 1: St. Thérèse of the Child Jesus (of Lisieux), 1873–1897

Extensive Patronage; Roses

As a young girl of fifteen, Thérèse became a Carmelite nun and devoted herself to the infant Jesus. She is known for her simple, childlike way of praying to God and being holy. Her autobiography, *The Story of a Soul*, is well known to Catholics and non-Catholics alike.

She is often depicted holding a bouquet of roses. The significance of the rose is taken from two statements she had made. One assertion was that her little sacrifices were like flowers offered to God. The other was when Thérèse told her sister, also a Carmelite nun, that "after my death I will let fall a shower of roses. I will spend my heaven doing good on earth."[1]

There are many stories of those who pray to her and then finding a rose, an illustration of one, or even the fragrance of a rose, indicating that their prayer has been heard.

If you would like to offer a novena to St. Thérèse, this one is quite popular, and you may enjoy praying it in your garden.

O Little Thérèse of the Child Jesus,
please pick for me a rose
from the heavenly gardens
and send it to me as a message of love.
O Little Flower of Jesus,
ask God today to grant the favors
I now place with confidence in your hands . . .
(Mention your intentions.)
Saint Thérèse,
help me to always believe as you did,
in God's great love for me,
so that I might imitate your "Little Way" each day.
Amen.[2]

In 1931 a tea rose was named after her: *Rosa 'Soeur Thérèse'* (*Soeur* means sister). The color of the bloom is described as a deep golden yellow shaded with orange carmine. It was bred by a Frenchman, Francis Gillot, in honor of St. Thérèse. Typical of a tea rose, it is a very large semidouble flower of about twenty-five petals with a cupped bloom form and slightly fragrant; it is hardy to Zone 6b and warmer.

October 4: St. Francis of Assisi, 1181-1226

Patron of Ecology and Animals

St. Francis is probably the best-known saint associated with animals and nature. Though not listed as a patron saint of gardens, he loved all of God's creation, especially small animals such as those found in a garden. He is the patron saint of ecology, and all good gardeners are ecologists in some way when they attend to the safety and health of bees and birds.

There is a wonderful story about St. Francis and an apple tree. While Francis was walking down a farm lane one early winter day, he was deeply frustrated about his inability to reach the souls of many townspeople. As he approached a leafless apple tree, he raised his arm, grabbed a barren limb, and shook it in frustration shouting, "Teach me of God!" As the miracle was recorded, the tree immediately burst into bloom.

Francis was always, it seemed, preaching the love of Jesus. He taught that the world was created in beauty and goodness from the bosom of God and that it was the duty of all living things to praise God in return. Because of this belief, Francis preached to both man and beast. He always emphasized the duty to protect nature and be good stewards.

In being a good steward, St. Francis was often heard thanking the animals for their contribution to his life. Legend has it that he had a special fondness for donkeys and treated them with tenderness.

This loyal beast of burden has a special place in the Bible and throughout salvation history. In Genesis we read that they are an integral part of the life of the Jewish people. In the book of Numbers, one of these little asses speaks. The donkey sees an angel seeking to harm her master, Balaam, and continually averts these encounters, only to be repeatedly beaten by her owner. Fed up with the whole misunderstanding, the little donkey has her "mouth opened" by the Lord and speaks to her master in protest, demanding to know why he has taken such abusive action against her (Nm 22:21–29).

Few animals were as present throughout Jesus' life as was the donkey. In the salvation story, the docile beast carried Mary while she was pregnant with Jesus, and at the Nativity it was present in the stable. Sadly, it was the donkey that carried our Lord into Jerusalem as he prepared to face his passion.

St. Francis knew of all these Bible incidences and so treated his own little beast with much gentleness. As Francis aged, he was forced to ride his donkey. The story is told that on his deathbed the loyal donkey placed its head inside Francis's window, where the sickly monk petted his muzzle, thanking his little companion, and the donkey cried.

The First Crèche

Our present-day tradition of displaying Nativity sets was originated by St. Francis, who built the first one in Greccio, Italy, one Christmas a few years before his death. Francis desired to celebrate Mass and to pay homage to Christ's birth in a way that was as close as possible to what the child of Bethlehem knew when he entered our world. St. Francis's first crèche included hay, livestock, and Mass celebrated around the manger.[3]

October 15: St. Teresa of Avila, 1515–1582

Extensive Patronage

St. Teresa of Avila was a Spanish Carmelite nun and mystic who was an affectionate extrovert of great joy and determination. Often sick in her early years, she did not labor in gardens as required of the other sisters, but she did convalesce in them and found them a source of meditation and insight. It wasn't until she was around forty and had regained her health that her spiritual development really began to take root, and at forty-seven she began writing about the practice of prayer.

Part of her early writings on spiritual doctrine depicts different stages or grades, known as the "four waters," of a life in prayer; these stages are described in metaphorical terms, taken from watering a garden. The water represents how God reaches the soul, and the soul is the garden to be grown for his delight. A very simple description of prayer is that God plants the garden that we grow through prayer, which is equated with different ways of irrigation:

- We draw the water from a well using a rope and then carry the water to our garden; this is an active form of praying, using one's faculties and reaping what benefits one can through one's own efforts.
- Next, to simplify the flow, a waterwheel with dippers is used. As the wheel turns, the water is poured into a trough that hydrates our garden. St. Teresa described this stage as a point when the soul begins to learn how to recollect itself, and this enjoyment brings greater delight.
- The flow of irrigation is then expanded by means of a stream. This form of prayer is more mystical, requiring little human effort, with all the faculties focused on God.
- In the final method of watering our garden we accept the rain God sends without our own effort. This is called the prayer of union and is totally infused by God, a mystical action taking place in varying degrees.

In her book *The Way of Perfection*, St. Teresa gave a much more expansive and beautiful explanation of the gardens of our souls. The book also tells, by her own admission, of her exploits as a teenager with a great attraction to fashion, perfume, and boys. Her poor widowed father in exasperation and fear for her virtue sent her to an Augustinian nunnery, and once there her life found a different kind of fertile soil.

There is an endearing story about a friend of St. Teresa who was scandalized to find her gorging herself on a partridge. She asked

Teresa, "What would people think?" "Let them think whatever they want," said Teresa. "There's a time for penance, and there's a time for partridge." Heaven invaded her heart, but she never lost her head in the clouds.[4]

She became a Doctor of the Church and is one of the incorrupt whose body remains intact.

October 23: St. Oda of Scotland, ca. 680–726

Patron of Visually Impaired, Association with Magpies

St. Oda was a beautiful young woman who was born blind. Her family sent her to Liege, Belgium, on a pilgrimage, and while praying at the graveside of St. Lambert she miraculously gained her sight. After she returned to Scotland, her father, now confident that he could marry off his lovely daughter, sought a suitor for her. Instead of obedience he found her filled with resistance; after her wondrous healing she wanted only to serve the Lord.

St. Oda eventually left Scotland and her family to reside in the Netherlands. Sixth-century records describe how Oda prayed in various villages in the Netherlands and Belgium only to be continually disturbed by magpies. She was not aware that these persistent little creatures were on a mission from God.

One day while she was trying to flee from the birds, they herded her to an open space in the forest. She saw how perfect the space would be for prayer and made plans to live in this protected expanse of woods. Eventually a convent was built, and a village developed around the monastery. This municipality in the Netherlands became known as Sint-Oedenrode; in Dutch a small man-made open space in the woods is called a *rode* with the village named after the saint.

The magpie associated with St. Oda is the Eurasian species *Pica pica*. This startlingly beautiful bird is a member of the crow family. It is a sizable bird at about eighteen inches long (with half of that being its tail!) and a wingspan of up to twenty-four inches. This breed of magpies is considered the most intelligent of birds, and possibly of all animals except for humans. They work as a team—or more colloquially called a gang—in deterring intruders, hunting, and creatively solving problems using tools. They observe social rituals including expressions of grief and can recognize themselves in a mirror.

There are many superstitions throughout Europe and the British Isles pertaining to this bird. Legends have it that if the bird is seen singularly, it is an omen of bad luck. When seen in groups, it is a bearer of goodness and foretells of good weather. Farmers considered themselves well blessed if these birds nested in nearby trees, and they often fed the birds throughout the winter to keep them from leaving the farm.[5]

October in the Garden

> Hope is inherently paradoxical. It is our answer to the
> seeming silence of God, an act of supreme confidence.
>
> –Susan Muto

Practical Gardening: Preparing the Garden for Winter

Autumn is the season of decline. It is a time of turning from outward activity to a slower interior pace. There is less sunlight and less time to be outdoors; the color once vivid in early October fades to muted browns.

Before you settle in for the winter, there are a few more things to do in your garden. By now you have probably considered any number of Catholic garden themes. October is a great month for planting your outdoor prayer space. Hardwoods (trees and shrubs), perennials, and hardy bulbs can all be added during the autumn months.

When planting hardy bulbs, the soil temperature needs to be sixty degrees or cooler. Six weeks before the ground freezes is usually when the soil has cooled enough. If you purchased bulbs for fall but can't plant right away, keep them dormant by storing in a refrigerator or some place where the temperature stays around forty degrees. A trick I have learned is to wait on cleaning up the perennials that have died down. With their leaves still showing you will know where to plant your bulbs to avoid disturbing the roots of established plants and which plants will help conceal the declining bulbs' leaves next summer. After each group of bulbs is planted, I then remove the spent foliage and debris from the garden.

When adding perennials to your landscape this late in the season, plant only those that are hardy one cold zone lower (farther north) than where you live. There is a better chance of these plants surviving the winter under a layer of mulch, even without an established root system.

Trees and shrubs often fare well when planted this time of year. Their larger root mass is planted deeper and resists frost heave. If you are purchasing small, container-grown hardwoods, put down a heavy layer of mulch to help prevent frost heave, but be sure to pull it away in early spring. Leaving mulch piled up the trunk like a volcano is bad. You want the skirt of the trunk to be exposed to air. A good rule of thumb is literally your thumb—place it perpendicular against the tree trunk at soil level and spread your fingers apart. The tip of your pinky finger is as close as mulch should come to the tree or shrub during the growing season.

Do not fertilize your new plantings. Watering should also be kept to a minimum since days are cooler and autumn rains keep the soil wet longer.

Faith-Filled Gardening: Creating a Rosary Garden or a Garden Dedicated to the Angels

The Rosary is a familiar devotion that evokes a sense of peace as we meditate through the Mysteries. This sense of peace and quiet reflection can be re-created in a Rosary garden.

I love the origins of the word *rosary*. *Rosary* comes from the Latin word *rosarium*, meaning "rose garden." In the mid-1500s, *rosaire* came to mean "a garden of prayers" from the medieval concept of compiling a collection of items, which could include flowers, into bouquets. This apparently originated in the late 1400s with the printing of a prayer book, *hortulus animæ*, that literally meant "little garden of the soul." Creating a bouquet of prayers eventually led to a string of knots or beads to track one's praying. It was during the fifteenth century that the Rosary evolved into its present form.

When it comes to creating a Rosary garden, the options are nearly endless. It can be as big as a winding path through woodlands or as small as a single stepping-stone with inset glass cabochons. It is your garden, and its design is dependent on what leads you into the mystery of this type of prayer.

There are some established customs for creating a public Rosary garden, however. Usually a prominent statue of our Holy Mother Mary is placed in the center of the Rosary walk with a cross at the entrance to the garden. Stepping-stones or rocks laid into a path are a simple and common way to represent a Rosary in a garden. Quite often square stones are used for the *pater* (Our Father) beads and round ones for the *mater* (Hail Mary) beads. The path of stones can be laid in a linear or circular pattern and can be as large or as small as your area permits.

For the home garden, all you really need to do is follow the basic form of a Rosary: six pater and fifty-three mater beads with a cross and a Marian symbol or statue. Be sure to include someplace to sit, preferably in the shade, if you intend to pray the Rosary while in your garden. Let your imagination run as you consider what will work best for you.

One suggestion for forming a cross at the entrance to the Rosary garden is to lay a walkway with square pavers singly set, four pavers long and, near the top, three wide. You could also make your own stepping-stone with a cross made of shells, pebbles, or stained glass embedded in it.

If you have very limited space, you could put a small statue of Mary in the garden and surround the base with items representing the Rosary beads and a small cross. This is different from a Marian garden, which is always enclosed with a fence. A stepping-stone with a larger Rosary (that has not been blessed) set into it is also an option and looks very natural at the edge of a path, especially if a bench is set on the opposite side.

Another decorative way to display the prayer beads is to use plastic Christmas ornaments and bamboo or metal stakes. This arrangement makes the prayer garden look as if it is lighted by tiny gazing balls. Hammer the stakes in the garden so that a decade of "beads" is grouped together. Take the cap for the hook off the end of the plastic ornament, turn the ornament upside down, and slide it onto the stake. My favorite arrangement mimics a Missionary Rosary, where each decade is a different color for each continent: green for Africa, red for the Americas, white for Europe, blue for Oceana, and yellow for Asia. The five beads that start the Rosary are one of each color and arranged in the same order as the decades. The pater beads are usually slightly larger and matched to the decades, but I prefer to use purple, being the traditional color of the Luminous Mysteries and representing purpose.

Installing objects in the garden that physically evoke the life of Mary and Jesus is one way to meditate on the Mysteries. Another meditative prayer practice, mentioned earlier with the Stations of the Cross, uses plants.

Creating a quadrant garden, one having equal portions representing the Mysteries, is only one of many options. The garden could be divided to represent each set of Mysteries: Joyful, Sorrowful, Luminous, and Glorious. An easy way to distinguish each quadrant is by a distinctive and monochromatic color scheme. Historically there were specific colors associated with each set of Mysteries: Joyful, white; Sorrowful, red; Glorious, yellow; and for the most recent Mystery, Luminous, purple.

You could use newer color associations that elicit the feeling of the Mystery being contemplated. Scientific research shows that particular colors stimulate certain feelings and emotions. For a newer color scheme, consider the following: Joyful, oranges and gold; Sorrowful, purple and burgundies; Glorious, shades of blue; and Luminous, yellows and whites.

I feel a sense of joy when I see the colors gold and orange. Gold represents riches, prosperity, and like green, hope, while oranges remind me of cheerfulness, change, and fruition. Imagine the hope of both Mary and Elizabeth as they carried their unborn sons and the richness of faith in their God as their promised children prospered. Imagine the cheerfulness of the young mother Mary as she reared the child Jesus, all the while knowing that he was destined to make great changes in their nation.

Sorrow is often associated with darker hues, ones that are more saturated. For the Sorrowful Mysteries, consider using deep purples, burgundies, dark reds, and violets. Purple is strongly associated with spirituality and the mystical and is also used to convey authority and purpose. Dark burgundies often imply mystery. Meditate here on the darkness surrounding Jesus as he entered into his passion and the single mystical purpose of God. Consider also the scarlet military cloak placed on his shoulders as he was mocked and the blood that was spilled as he suffered.

We look toward heaven, toward the sky, and toward all that the Holy Spirit reveals to us in the Glorious Mysteries. Blues lead us to the infinite world beyond. They direct our perspective outward, are used to calm us, and encourage openness, communication, and prayer. When we pray the Glorious Mysteries, we are reassured of our own eventual rise home to God and Mother Mary.

The colors white and yellow stimulate our visual sense and are associated with the Luminous Mysteries. White is the color of the Holy Spirit, of truth and sanctity. It represents purity, innocence, and kindness. I wrote in a previous book that white teaches us about relationships because, in our perceptions of colors, white tints how we see. White in itself is not a color but the completely revealed energy (manifestation) of all the colors—a very nice explanation of the completeness of the Holy Spirit!

Yellow is pure, bright, and the easiest of all colors to see. It is full of intellectual energy, symbolizing wisdom, joy, happiness, attentiveness, and illumination. The color yellow brings awareness and clarity to the mind. In the Luminous Mysteries the light of God shines through each meditation, and interestingly enough, each Mystery is about relationship and being attentive, bringing us to a deeper understanding of the purpose of Christ.

You can begin your plant selection based on color using traditional or more modern schemes. But selecting a plant for its symbolic representation may suit you better.

There are a few plants whose seeds are used for making Rosaries. The *Canna* plant is known as the Rosary beads plant because of its hard black seeds. Another plant is Job's tears, *Coix lacryma-jobi*, a grain plant that produces hard white seedlike structures. The seeds of both plants are also used for jewelry making.

My suggestions for particular plants that enhance a Mystery are only one or two of several options. You will notice that a few plants can be used in more than one meditation garden, for instance, Stations, Rosary, Marian, or Bible gardens. These duplicate symbolic meanings make it easier for you to select which ones suit you best.

Now let's look at individual flowers and plants and how they are associated with each of the Joyful, Sorrowful, Glorious, and Luminous Mysteries.

Joyful Mysteries

Annunciation of Our Lord; Humility

- Bluebells, *Hyacinthoides italica*, represent humility, constancy, and gratitude; you could also use spring-blooming Virginia bluebells, *Mertensia virginica*.
- Japanese camellia, *Camellia japonica* 'Alba Plena,' signifies purity. An interesting note: the genus *Camellia* was named after the Jesuit priest George Kamel, who was also a botanist.

The Visitation; Charity

- Fuchsia begonia, *Begonia fuchsioides rosea*, heart of Mary is also known in Spanish as the heart of Jesus, *Begonia corazon-de-jesus*.
- Irish moss (aka Scotch moss), *Sagina subulata*, represents charitable love in the language of flowers.

Nativity of Jesus; Love of God

- Baby's breath, *Gypsophila paniculata*.

- Clove pinks, *Dianthus caryophyllus,* have a genus name that literally means "flower of God," representing Mary and the Incarnation of Jesus.

Presentation in the Temple; Spirit of Sacrifice

- Bearded iris, *Iris germanica,* Mary's sword of sorrows.
- Bleeding heart, *Dicentra sp.,* represents Mary's heart ("and she held all these things in her heart").
- Snowdrops or Candlemas bells, *Galanthus nivalis,* are said to have bloomed when Mary and Joseph took Jesus to the Temple on Candlemas.

Finding in the Temple; Witnessing

- The ash tree, *Fraxinus sp.,* is associated with sacrifice and spiritual awareness.
- Hyssop, *Hyssopus sp.,* symbolizes clean or pure and sacrificial.

Sorrowful Mysteries

Agony in the Garden; Repentance

- *Cyclamen sp.* symbolizes acceptance or resignation.
- Spotted meadow orchid or monk orchid, *Orchis maculata,* is common at Gethsemane and throughout Europe and is usually considered a weed.

Scourging at the Pillar; Emptying Oneself (Mortification)

- *Fuchsia speciosa,* Christ's blood drops.
- Yarrow, *Achillea millefolium,* Christ's back, was carried into battle and used to stop the bleeding of wounded soldiers.

Crowning with Thorns; Moral Courage

- A'kub, *Gundelia tournefortii*, has pollen that is found on the Shroud of Turin. It is also a food source in the Holy Land, much like an artichoke.
- Sea holly, *Eryngium planum*, or globe thistle, *Echinops sp.*, are similar-appearing plants with spiny textures.

Carrying of the Cross; Patience

- *Aster sp.* symbolizes patience.
- Sweet autumn clematis, *Clematis terniflora* (Virgin's bower, *C. flammula*), has a narrow four-petal flower that forms a cross and is very fragrant.

Crucifixion and Death; Final Perseverance

- Garland mum, *Leucanthemum coronarium* (formerly named *Chrysanthemum coronarium*), is very common in Israel. Legend has it that it was growing when Jesus was laid in the tomb. As a result, the chrysanthemum genus has been a part of funerals and decorations for graves for centuries.
- The Oriental poppy, *Papaver orientale*, according to legends, grew where drops of Jesus' blood fell at the foot of the cross.

Glorious Mysteries

Resurrection of Our Lord; Faith

- Easter lily, *Lilium longiflorum*.
- Resurrection plant, *Selaginella lepidophylla*, comes back to life even though it appears dead. It is more often grown indoors as an oddity or specimen plant.

Ascension into Heaven; Hope

- Lilac, ascension flower, *Syringa vulgaris*.
- Snowdrops, *Galanthus*, signify the consolation that comes to those who are filled with hope.
- The sweet almond tree, *Prunus dulcis*, symbolizes hope, watchfulness, and promise.

Descent of the Holy Spirit; Zeal

- Columbine, *Aquilegia sp.*, has petals shaped like a dove (*columba* is Latin for dove).
- Pentecost rose, peony, *Paeonia officinalis*.

Assumption of Mary; Happy Death

- The assumption lily, *Hosta plantaginea*, in most regions blooms around mid-August—and the bonus is its fragrance is similar to Easter lilies.
- Belladonna lily, *Amaryllis belladonna*, whose name literally means "beautiful lady," leafs out in spring, dies back, and then sends up single stalks of flowers in mid-August.

Coronation of Mary; Love of Mary

- Cornflower, *Centaurea cyanus*, Mary's crown.
- Yellow flag iris, *Iris pseudacorus*, Mary as queen (becomes invasive in some regions).

Luminous Mysteries

Baptism in the Jordon; Gratitude for Faith

- *Bougainvillea sp.* is known as the Trinitarian flower because of its repeating sets of threes in the flower's construction.

- Heartsease or wild pansy, *Viola tricolor*, trinity flower, symbolizes reflective thought.

Wedding at Cana; Fidelity

- Speedwell, *Veronica sp.*, symbolizes fidelity.
- Woodland phlox, *Phlox divaricata*, dubbed lady's wedding flower, implies the uniting of souls.

Proclamation of the Kingdom of God; Desire for Holiness

- Common ivy, *Hedera helix*, meaning "where God has walked," symbolizes fidelity. It is interesting to note that the plant's symbolic meaning "fidelity of love" is used to signify humans to each other, humans to God, and God toward his people.

Transfiguration; Spiritual Courage

- Edelweiss, *Leontopodium alpinum*, symbolizes courage and purity; its name literally means "white and noble."
- The herb thyme, *Thymus vulgaris*, represents strength and courage.

Institution of the Eucharist; Love of Eucharistic Jesus

- Basil, *Ocimum basilicum*, Holy Communion plant, has a name that comes from the Greek word for king, *basileios*. It was often strewn at the foot of a cross as well as strung on Communion rails on holy days. *Basilicum* is also the root word for *basilica*, which is the heart of Catholic Church architecture.

Don't hesitate to use other plants having personal meanings, being certain that they are suitable for the hardiness zone in your area. In my own garden is the *Yucca filamentosa*, regionally called the Lord's candlestick and historically St. John's palm, because it reminds me of the Transfiguration. (The story of why is told in the August chapter.)

Biblical Reflections

No temptation has overtaken you that is not common to man. God is faithful, and he will not let you be tempted beyond your strength, but with the temptation will also provide the way of escape, that you may be able to endure it.

—1 Corinthians 10:13

Behold, God is my salvation; I will trust, and will not be afraid; for the Lord God is my strength and my song, and he has become my salvation.

—Isaiah 12:2

And the rain fell, and the floods came, and the winds blew and beat upon that house, but it did not fall, because it had been founded on the rock.

—Matthew 7:25

Behold, I am with you and will keep you wherever you go, and will bring you back to this land; for I will not leave you until I have done that of which I have spoken to you.

—Genesis 28:15

If thou triest my heart, if thou visitest me by night, if thou testest me, thou wilt find no wickedness in me; my mouth does not transgress. . . . As for me, I shall behold thy face in righteousness; when I awake, I shall be satisfied with beholding thy form.

—Psalm 17:3, 15

He will swallow up death for ever, and the Lord GOD will wipe away tears from all faces, and the reproach of his people he will take away from all the earth; for the LORD has spoken.

—Isaiah 25:8

Prayer Focus for October

> The believer, even if his faith is weak, is never completely alone, never completely without help.
> —Servant of God Madeleine Delbrél

Change can be expected, where we may eagerly await the event, or unexpected and companioned by anxiety. Jesus is with us in whatever the nature of change. How do you seek him when change is hard and demanding? It's easy to show gratitude when things go well. How do you thank Jesus for the grace to endure what is difficult?

The Rosary is filled with lessons of virtue and faith. What is your devotional life like when you pray the Mysteries of the Rosary with Mother Mary? Often one of the Mysteries resonates with me relative to an event in my life. When you've prayed with Mary, was there a moment when one of the Mysteries touched your heart? What was that occasion?

November: **Dormancy and Rest**

We have come to see our death as a loss or rupture rather than a passing from one existence to another . . . a transition of a known life to the next.

–H. T. Obbink, D.D.

November is a difficult month to describe—not quite past autumn and not yet winter. Skies are often filled with heavy, dark gray clouds that suddenly break into glorious sunlight, illuminating the few yellow leaves that remain on the trees. The business of outdoor activities is ending, and the bustle of holiday celebrations is waiting to begin. This is the month when nature goes dormant, a time to be wrapped in restfulness.

It is a time for drawing down at home, in heavy sweaters, loose pants, and warm slippers. With hands encircling steaming cups, we slow our pace and reflect. This is when the true purpose of dormancy develops in our lives. Dormancy is when roots expand, when the overt activities of life decrease and we become grounded in the soil of purpose.

By definition, dormancy is a state of rest. As with hibernation, it is a time of minimal activity. Many organisms require this cycle of rest. Without it the future holds reduced productivity and impaired vitality: plants don't flower, animals become obese, and people become distraught.

November once was a time of harvest festivals, when merriment and gratitude were expressed within communities. Farming was for the most part finished, and food had been stored. Farm animals, especially horses, were blessed to protect them through the coming winter. We delight in a similar celebration on Thanksgiving Day, expressing gratitude for the fruitfulness in our lives. The Solemnity of Christ the King at the end of November is centered on the final judgment: the harvesting of fruitful souls.

In the Catholic tradition, we dedicate the month of November to the dead, to the precious souls in purgatory, and to the communion of saints in heaven. Throughout the Bible we are called to pray for the living and the dead. "From the beginning the Church has honored the memory of the dead and offered prayers . . . that they may attain the beatific vision of God" (CCC, 1032). We all come to a final resting of our outward bodies and enter eventually into eternal peace. If we are so blessed, in this eternity, we, as with other saints, will be allowed to help grow fruitfulness in those still on earth.

This month, during the quiet moments of our days, as we think about the celebrations to come, let us remember the generations that have come before us and shaped our present day.

Traditions and Feasts of November

> Just as the farmer, when he goes to till the ground, must take the proper tools and clothing for cultivating, so Christ the King, the heavenly and true farmer, in coming to humanity made barren by evil, put on the body and carried the cross as his tool and worked the barren soil of the soul . . . and planted the fairest paradise of the Spirit.
>
> —Pseudo-Macarius

November 1 is the Solemnity of All Saints and a holy day of obligation. It is a day to acknowledge the trust we have in the intercessors of heaven who pray with us—from our Blessed Mother to the lesser-known saints who touch our hearts. This communion of saints helps us realize that we are not alone in our challenges to be a holy people. Father Larry Delaney of the St. Francis Retreat Center in DeWitt, Michigan, often spoke of saints as "sinners who kept on trying"—encouraging words! The saints model for us how we, with all our shortcomings, can be an instrument for guiding others to redemption through Jesus.

November 2 is the Commemoration of All the Faithful Departed, formerly known as All Souls' Day. There are many customs on this day where candles are lit to symbolize helping souls find their way home to God. Re-create this in your garden by clustering votive lights, luminaries, or fine-tapered candles in an area to light the way to a cross, religious statue, or image. Several candles can be arranged in an area protected from the wind. Set them on top of a collection of stones or insert fine tapers in a sand-filled basin resting on a birdbath stand. What a beautiful prayer offering this would make in the gloaming of the day.

A similar practice using candles is found in the Jewish religion; the *Yartzeit* (anniversary of the date of passing) is very significant. "Kabbalah teaches that all the spiritual achievements of one's life . . . are revealed in the world and in the Heavens on that day . . . the soul is at its greatest strength and in its fullest glory. With each ensuing year, this radiance again shines forth in the world and in the Heavens, as the soul is elevated to a higher spiritual level and drawn even closer to G-d."[1]

An amazing and beautiful tradition in the Hispanic culture is to celebrate the Day of the Dead in cemeteries. After a day of picnicking, the night is aglow with candles surrounded by flowers. Consider sitting in the garden with a family photo album on All Souls' Day. Don't forget, praying for the souls in purgatory need not be limited to one day a year.

The Feast of Christ the King is celebrated on the last Sunday in November before Advent. On this day we pray for the conversion of all to embrace the teachings of peace through Christ. "It is Christ's eyes on us, and our eyes turned toward him . . . that brings about our participation and understanding" of our desire to serve the Lord of Lords.[2] We pray for those in power to recognize Jesus as King and adjust how they operate to conform to his teachings. It is a time of prayer for peace in our souls and in the souls of others. By embracing this peace we will be at peace within governments and there will be peace between nations.

November Saints for the Gardener

There, look, see—in the place where the wind blew the brush fire through . . . a phoenix of color rising from the ashes, a faith that flowers through the flames.

—Sally Clark

November 3: St. Martin de Porres, 1579-1639

Extensive Patronage, Association with Farm and Domesticated Animals

St. Martin is often depicted holding a broom in one hand while a dog, bird, cat, and mouse are eating in peace from the same dish near his feet.

He is another saint who had a special love for animals and remained a strict vegetarian because of this. Since he was of mixed parentage from an African slave mother and a Spanish nobleman, he was initially permitted to be only a lay brother at the Dominican Friary of the Rosary in Lima, Peru. There he served as a farmer, barber, infirmarian, and almoner. During the sixteenth century, the almoner was the person who distributed alms to the poor for the religious house.

Because of his comprehensive understanding of nature, he was very in tune with the healing properties of plants and learned their medicinal applications quickly. St. Martin's knowledge seemed almost supernatural in the speed at which he grasped their broad use for treatments. With his knowledge as an herbalist, he soon became known as a great healer.

St. Martin's tenderness and healing skills were shown equally to humans and animals, including vermin and beasts of the field. Besides his duties in the monastery infirmary, he maintained a small animal hospital for cats and dogs at his sister's house. He had the ability to communicate with animals, though he was somewhat shy with his brothers.

There is a delightful story about mice in the infirmary. Hundreds of mice had invaded the linens of the wardrobe room, and the other friars wanted to poison them. St. Martin asked his brothers not to harm the little animals. He was able to catch one of the vermin, and holding it in his hands he spoke to the mouse, telling it that if it led all the mice to the garden, he would bring them food every day. When he set the little rodent on the floor, a great scratching sound was heard throughout the buildings. As all the mice scurried from the monastery walls, they followed St. Martin across the lawn to the far gardens, where he kept his end of the bargain.

In addition to the miraculous gift of healing, St. Martin was given the gift of bilocation and levitation. Eventually the superiors of the order saw his piety and miraculous gifts and lifted the racial limits of their order, allowing him to become a full Dominican brother.

St. Martin was a close friend of St. Rose of Lima, also a Dominican and a sister. The two of them labored to serve the poor. Their miracles of healing the sick were most prevalent during a malaria epidemic of the 1600s. This epidemic eventually took St. Martin's life; he died in his sixties.

November 9: St. Benignus, d. 467

Patron of Connaught, Ireland, and Meadow Flowers

Benignus was a dedicated disciple of St. Patrick, eventually following in his footsteps. He sang for St. Patrick and while traveling with him sang at all of his Masses. Eventually St. Benignus was made a bishop and took St. Patrick's place.

When Benignus was a boy, St. Patrick came to the home of his parents in County Meath, where his father, Sechnan, was a chieftain. The story is told that shortly after Patrick's arrival, the family converted to Christianity and were baptized. Benignus was very fond of Patrick, and after his baptism, he would watch over the older man while he slept on clover in the shade of the garden. Benignus noticed that insects were being attracted to the dust from the road on Patrick's clothes. To help Patrick rest, the young boy picked strongly scented plants from the garden and field and placed them around the sleeping Patrick to keep the flies and bugs away.

Native plants the boy could have used would have included meadow rue and mint. The meadow rue was probably *Thalictrum minus*, a perennial—with foliage similar to maidenhair fern—that grows in stony lakeshores and moist rocky grounds. There are several mints in Ireland, and most likely the corn mint, *Mentha arvensis*, would have grown in that region.

There are other plants in Ireland that grow in County Meath whose leaves or flowers have been used to discourage insects. Some of them are lady's bedstraw, *Galium verum*; hairy bitter-cress,

Cardamine hirsute; lesser burdock, *Arctium minus*; Herb Robert, *Geranium robertianum*; Smith's pepperwort, *Lepidium heterophyllum*; wood sage, *Teucrium scorodonia*; and yarrow, *Achillea millefolium*.

Young Benignus was chastised by his family for stealing the herbs from the garden and, because of their shame, wanted him out of their sight. Knowing the true reason for the child's actions, St. Patrick responded, "Don't send him away. He's a good boy. It may be that he will yet do wonderful things for the Church."[3] From that moment on, Benignus was ever at the beloved saint's side.

Benignus and Patrick traveled extensively throughout Ireland and would have had to prepare meals along the way. A common food for encamped travelers and shepherds was stew. During that time a stew would have been made from the neck of mutton, onion, and water seasoned with salt and whatever wild cooking herbs could be found. This is a stew that few of us today would be able to appreciate. Since sheep were valued more for their wool and milk than for their meat, the only sheep in shepherd's stew would have been old. The mutton was tough, requiring hours of slow boiling. It would have had quite a distinct flavor. It wasn't until centuries later that the potato found its way into the land and then soup.

November 10: St. Tryphon, ca. 225–250

Patron of Young Farmers and Gardeners

St. Tryphon, a farmer himself, is recognized as a patron of fields and plants. He is often depicted holding a lily or stalk of crop plant. As a young indentured farm boy, he tended to geese as a herder. It is told that God, seeing Tryphon's purity of heart and love for the birds that he tended, gave him the special gift of healing, and this gift also applied to animals.

From the time he was a young boy until his death, assumed to have occurred in his early twenties, he was able to cure illnesses and expel evil spirits. One of his earliest recorded healings was when he was only seventeen and freed a young girl possessed by a demon. He never accepted payment for his services as a healer and so earned the moniker of Holy Unmercenary.

I wonder if in later centuries other patron saints of farming called upon St. Tryphon in prayers for blessings of their holdings. Here is a farmer's prayer to this young and gifted saint that comes to us from the Eastern Orthodox Church:

> Beloved St. Tryphon,
> whose name alone means gentleness,
>
> we pray to you for your protection of our crops, herds and all we do as farmers.
>
> We ask that you intercede in our behalf to Almighty God, creator and ruler of the seasons,
>
> that our fields are kept safe from pests and favored by the weather.
>
> That our crops and herds may be abundant, allowing us to supply the wants of life for ourselves and others in need.
>
> Pray for us that we are freed from earthly worries and focus our thoughts toward our heavenly home.
>
> We ask too that you pray to instill a love of the land into the hearts of the young and for their unity in Christ so, like you, they too will experience the same joy and peace on earth confident in the love of God.
>
> We ask all this in Jesus' name. Amen.

November 17: St. Elizabeth of Hungary, 1207-1231

Diverse Patronage, Association with Roses

St. Elizabeth of Hungary was a princess whose great-aunt was St. Elizabeth of Portugal. Elizabeth was married at thirteen to Prince Louis (Ludwig) of Thuringia. She soon proved herself a force to be reckoned with. She had a hospital built near the castle shortly after their marriage, contrary to her new family's views, and attended to the sick herself. Elizabeth also gave bread and grain to the poor, and for this she is considered the patron of bakers.

St. Elizabeth followed the Rule of St. Francis of Assisi as best she could while her husband was still alive. She helped care for the sick, fed the poor, and gave away much of her wealth to those in need. Her husband encouraged her charitable acts, but he was also concerned for her safety.

Elizabeth's husband died during the Crusades in 1227, leaving her a widow with three children at just twenty. Her station at court was undermined by her brother-in-law, a cruel man who forbade her to continue her charitable acts.

The story is told that she would still take food to the poor and hide it under her mantle. One day she was stopped by soldiers, suspected of going against her brother-in-law's wishes. When they lifted her mantle, reminiscent of St. Brigid of Ireland, the bread she was carrying had been miraculously changed into a bouquet of roses.

November 17: St. Hugh, 1135-1200

Patron of Swans

This dear saint became an Augustinian monk when he was only fifteen and a Carthusian priest by the time he was thirty. As a priest he wrangled with three different kings in succession and staunchly defended the Jews from persecution.

St. Hugh would often visit the Carthusian monastery in La Grande Chartreuse. Carthusians are a solitary and austere order; each monk is given a hermitage cell, a workplace, and a private garden often referred to as the potager. These groupings of hermitages, or very small housings, were joined to a cloister that led to a centralized communal ground and formed their monastery. For this order, as with the Benedictines and Cistercians, working a garden and the labor of prayer led their attendants into a harmonious and whole life—a life of living and eating within the rhythm of nature. For St. Hugh, this was the way he felt called to serve our Lord.

On one of his visits he found the monks assembled in the dining room looking quite grim because they had nothing to eat. When St. Hugh questioned them further, he learned that someone had generously given them freshly butchered fowl to eat, but the Rule of their order strictly forbid them to consume meat. The only flesh the monks could eat was what came from the lakes and streams. St. Hugh understood their predicament, as he knew God would too. So he knelt in prayer right there in the kitchen and made the Sign of the Cross over the birds. Miraculously the meat of the fowls turned into the flesh of turtles. The men rejoiced and set about making soup.

As for the patronage to swans, the legend begins in 1181 at Westminster Abbey when St. Hugh became bishop. St. Hugh always had a love of animals, and many stories were told about how these woodland creatures would gather near his cell window at the monastery. On the day he was made a bishop, a large and fierce whooper swan came near. As it approached St. Hugh, its very nature changed to that of gentle adoration. But this gentleness was reserved only for the new bishop. The swan, a fierce and constant companion of St. Hugh, is said to have defended him against anyone who drew too near and remained awake to guard the saint even as he slept.

November in the Garden

> God has not promised a state of constant bliss or a prob-
> lem-free existence but has promised to be present in the
> silence and in the dark, to exist alongside us.
>
> —Philip Yancey

Practical Gardening: Dormancy and Readying for Winter

In early November I find myself preparing to nestle in for the winter.
My gardening frenzy shifts to calmer activities, such as writing and
cooking, and I gratefully look forward to time for reading garden
magazines set aside throughout the summer months. There are just
a few more tasks that need attending to before winter enfolds the
gardens.

For shrubs exposed to winter winds and prone to the desiccating
effects on their leaves, such as rhododendrons and dwarf Alberta
spruce, protect them with a burlap barrier. Place the barrier four to
six inches away from the plant's limbs on the south, southwest, and
windward sides. If a plant in a previous winter has shown injury on
all sides, surround it with a barrier. Always leave the top open for
air and light penetration. Never fill the space between the plant and
the burlap with leaves. The burlap also protects plants from deer
browsing.

Another way to protect small evergreens is to prop pine boughs
or Christmas tree greens lightly against or over them. This helps
catch more snow for natural protection and offers additional protection from wind and sun.

Young trees and those with a thin bark are often damaged by
sunscald. Sunscald is characterized by a long sunken or cracked
area of bark found on the south or southwest side of the trunk. On

a cold winter's day, the sun can warm the bark to the point where it becomes active. When the sun is blocked, bark temperatures drop rapidly, killing the active tissue. Sunscald can be prevented by wrapping the trunk in late autumn with white plastic tree guards or commercial tree wrap. This also protects the trunk from deer rubs when the bucks grow antlers. Be sure to remove wrappings in late spring.

Protect the lower trunk portion of young trees from mice and rabbits. Use mesh hardware cloth rolled and fastened into a tube around the base of the trunk, leaving about a half-inch space, and buried about two inches into the soil. Be careful not to damage the tree's roots. I often cut a notch into the wire as wide as the root so the mesh tube will set deep enough into the ground.

Mulch is great as a weed barrier, and it helps retain moisture. It also protects plant roots from freeze/thaw damage. This damage is caused by the sun warming the soil surface and "waking up" a shallow root system. As with sunscald, when temperatures drop suddenly the activated tissue is killed. Pile on extra leaves at the base of shrubs and trees to keep soil at an even temperature. For late-autumn-planted plants, the mulch will also help protect against heaving from freezing soil.

Faith-Filled Gardening: Devotional Gardens and Shrines for a Saint

Many of us already have an object in our homes that speaks of a particular devotion of which we are fond. My own favorites are the image of Divine Mercy that is mounted in my prayer space and the Madonna that stands in my outdoor garden. Many other gardeners have a shrine to St. Francis, who is the patron of animals and ecology, or St. Fiacre, the patron saint of gardens.

One of the most recognizable garden devotionals of a Catholic home is a statue of Mary, often inset inside a small grotto. In the mid-1900s, this was often an old cast-iron tub, partially buried, with Mary standing inside and flowers planted around it. This is a very American configuration to a devotion that is centuries old.

Roadside shrines, or grottos, are very common throughout Europe, Mexico, and the Southwest. They may be very ornate with mosaics and glass doors, simple little fieldstone grottos, or more reminiscent of folk art or the ethnicity of the region.

These little shrines are considered religious sites and are visited with appropriate respect and reverence. They are usually built on private property for the glory of God and are not associated with a particular church. Quite often their construction will include a small altar where the faithful leave flowers, personal objects, and notes or photos. Some shrines also include a small bowl of sand in a protected corner where visitors can place a lighted candle.

A shrine is different from the more recent development of roadside crosses. These crosses are memorial markers that indicate the site of a fatal auto accident or other similar tragedy where a life ended. Though these sites may be visited by mourners with prayers for the deceased, they are not considered a devotional site.

You can build your own shrine and grotto out of almost any material. Some basic rules apply: the statue or image you select should be recessed within a small structure, and a small ledge should be included on which the statue will stand. In some countries where weather is inclement, these shrines are often little metal boxes with glass doors. In other regions they are made of stones or simple wood frames.

If you prefer your shrine to be used for your own private purposes, place it so it faces your home and is out of public view.

Shrines and grottos that are near to and face a road are assumed to be available to anyone who wants to visit.

Besides statues, you could use a picture suitable for an outdoor environment or a representative symbol created in cement. For example, an open book is used to represent St. Ann, the mother and teacher of the Virgin Mary. St. Michael the Archangel, who triumphed over Lucifer, is symbolized by a sword.

Shrines that are dedicated to a particular saint or angel may also include referential plantings. A well-known example is from Our Lady of Guadalupe, who left the dark pink rose growing on a hillside for St. Juan Diego after his vision. This rose is the Castilian rose or damask rose, *Rosa damascene*.

St. Brigid's Cow

A lovely example of how a symbol can represent a saint is St. Brigid of Kildare's cow. St. Brigid, who was baptized by St. Patrick, was known for her generosity. Brigid's mother looked after her master's herd of dairy cows. At one point in her life Brigid took over for her mother and gave away a lot of the milk to those in need. Nevertheless, the cows produced enough milk for the druid master's own need. When he realized this, he saw it as a miracle and, as a result, released her mother from servitude.

The following table will help you find some plants that are associated with specific saints. Many flowers are associated with a saint simply because they were in bloom during the saint's feast day.

Saints and Associated Plants

Saint	Plant	Significance
St. Agnes of Rome	*Hellebore niger*, white Christmas rose	Thirteen-year-old virgin, martyred in late January when this flower bloomed; purity
St. Ann, mother of Mary	*Matricaria sp.*, chamomile	Beloved mother
Archangels	*Angelica archangelica*, garden angelica	Healing many illnesses
St. Athanasius	*Athanasia crithmifolia* or *Tanecetum crithmifolia*, Tansy	Immortality, to be saved from corruption
St. Benedict	*Geum urbanum*, wood avens or herb bennet	Causes evil to flee; five petals for the five wounds of Christ
St. Brigid of Ireland	*Taraxacum*, dandelions and also *Anemone coronaria*, windflower	First flowers of spring, honoring her feast day
St. Catherine of Alexandria	*Nigella damascena*, Love-in-a-mist	Reminiscent of the wheel that broke at her martyrdom and her deep love of Jesus
St. Christopher	*Osumnda regalis*, royal fern	Found near water; this saint carried the Christ child over a river

St. David	*Narcissus sp.,* daffodil (previously the leek)	Blooms on feast day
St. Dominic	Roses	Attributed for having invented the five-decade Rosary, possibly made from compacted rose petals
St. Dorothy	Apples and roses growing together	Gift of heaven
St. Edward, king	*Fritillaria imperialis,* crown imperial	Flower of the king
St. Elizabeth of Hungary	Roses	Grain or bread in her apron to feed the poor was turned into roses
St. Faine	*Viburnum sp.*	Flowers persisted as did she
St. Fiacre	Garden produce; altar flowers	Miraculous garden to feed the poor
St. Francis de Sales	A nosegay	Francis wrote, "At the conclusion of your prayer, walk about a little and gather a little nosegay of devotion from the considerations that you have made, in order to inhale its perfume throughout the day."[4]
St. Gabriel the Archangel	*Lilium candidum,* Madonna lily	Confirmation of message from God

St. George	*Campanula rotundifolia,* harebell	Blooming on his feast day; humility
St. Gerard	*Aegopodium podgraria,* bishop's weed, gout weed	Curative of gout of which this saint suffered and cured
St. James	*Senecio jacobaea,* staggerwort, ragweed	Blooms on feast day
St. John the Baptist	*Hypericum sp.,* St. John's wort, chase-devil	Dispels darkness; heals all
	Lychnis calcedonica, scarlet lychnis	Great candlestick or forerunner of light
St. Joseph	*Lilium candidum,* Madonna lily	Confirmation of message from God (same as St. Gabriel)
St. Juan Diego	*Rosa damascene,* Castilian or damask rose	Our Lady of Guadalupe gave these to Juan Diego
St. Margaret of Cortona	*Bellis perennis,* Herb Margaret, English daisy	A medicinal herb; she cared for the sick and poor
St. Mary Magdalene	*Tanacetum balsmaita,* costmary, maudlin-wort, bible leaf	Fragrant reminder, ardent love
St. Michael the Archangel	*Aster amellus,* Michael-mas daisy	Blooms on feast day; protection
St. Patrick	Three-leaf clover	Teaching of the Holy Trinity

St. Peter	*Rhinanthus minor,* cockscomb	Blooms on feast day
	Primula veris, cowslip or Herb St. Peter	Keys to heaven
St. Phocas	Carnation or garden produce	God's flower; fed the poor
St. Robert, Cistercian	*Geranium robertianum,* cranesbill, Herb Robert	Healing
St. Thérèse of Lisieux	Roses	Her gift for answered prayers
St. Thomas of Canterbury	*Campanula media,* Canterbury bells	Pilgrims journeyed to his shrine with bells on poles and horses' harnesses; these flowers looked like bells and grew along the way.
St. Valentine of Rome	*Crocus sp.*	Blooms on feast day

Biblical Reflections

And let us consider how to stir up one another to love and good works, not neglecting to meet together, as is the habit of some, but encouraging one another.

—Hebrews 10:24–25

None of us lives to himself, and none of us dies to himself. If we live, we live to the Lord, and if we die, we die to the Lord; so then, whether we live or whether we die, we are the Lord's. For to this end Christ died and lived again, that he might be Lord both of the dead and of the living.

—Romans 14:7–9

I consider that the sufferings of this present time are not worth comparing with the glory that is to be revealed to us. . . . We know that the whole creation has been groaning in travail together until now; and not only the creation, but we ourselves, who have the first fruits of the Spirit, groan inwardly as we wait for adoption as sons, the redemption of our bodies. For in this hope we were saved. Now hope that is seen is not hope. For who hopes for what he sees? But if we hope for what we do not see, we wait for it with patience.

—Romans 8:18, 22–25

The eyes of the Lord are upon those who love him, a mighty protection and strong support, a shelter from the hot wind and a shade from noonday sun, a guard against stumbling and a defense against falling. He lifts up the soul and gives light to the eyes; he grants healing, life, and blessing.

—Sirach 34:16–17

Put off your old nature which belongs to your former manner of life and is corrupt through deceitful lusts, and be renewed in the spirit of your minds, and put on the new nature, created after the likeness of God in true righteousness and holiness.

—Ephesians 4:22–24

Behold, thou desirest truth in the inward being; therefore teach me wisdom in my secret heart. Purge me with hyssop, and I shall be clean; wash me, and I shall be whiter than snow.

—Psalm 51:6–7

I will rejoice and be glad for thy steadfast love, because thou hast seen my affliction, thou hast taken heed of my adversities, and hast not delivered me into the hand of the enemy.

—Psalm 31:7–8

Prayer Focus for November

> Sacred images are intended to awaken and nourish our faith in the mystery of Christ. An image of a saint reflects that mystery at work in our world and guides us visually in the lessons of the world. The saints are our family, guiding us from eternity.

We are part of communities and families, whether we have extended family, are single, are childless, or are alone. But a family is more than DNA; it can be defined as those who make us feel wanted, accepted, and unconditionally loved. Who we are, how we live, and our faith have been handed down to us through our families. Nothing about our lives is done in isolation. Is there a particular person who modeled for you what it means to be a Catholic? If he or she is still living, have you expressed your gratitude for the gift of faith in your life? If deceased, have you spoken to him or her in prayer?

The seasons of our lives bring happy times and challenging moments. Which saint or saints have accompanied you in your struggles? What elements of their personal struggle led to your devotion to them? In what way have you honored your patron saint or a deceased loved one?

December: Discerning What Is of Value

> Not to accept everything, but to understand everything; not to approve of everything, but to forgive everything; not to adopt everything, but to search for the grain of truth that is contained in everything.
>
> –Elisabeth Leseur

Whether in a garden or in our lives, we evaluate things for their worth. When I chose to downsize and live more simply, I looked hard at my possessions and had to discern what was of value and why. A lot of dross came to the surface in the process—and dozens of carloads went to charity.

During December we are drawn into evaluating what we find useful and fulfilling and where we place worth. A lot of that discernment has to do with family, relationships, and what we cherish; after all, it is the Christmas season. We often let go of personal wants to do what is best for another.

The person who gave the gift of herself most fully was Mary. From the first moment of life in her mother's womb, Mary had a unique union with God. For this reason the month of December is dedicated to her immaculate conception. This closeness with God and her trust in him allowed Mary to fully submit to his request at the annunciation and allowed God's saving grace to work through her. And so, this month we enter the season of Advent and look ahead to the Nativity.

Traditions and Feasts of December

I note the echo each thing produces as it strikes my soul.

–Stendhal

The first Sunday of Advent marks our Church's new year—four weeks prior to the secular New Year in January. Throughout Advent we prepare to celebrate Christ's first coming two thousand years ago and look forward to his return for the final judgment.

It is customary for Catholics to have an Advent wreath, which points to the coming light of Christ in our world of darkness. A wreath, being a circle, has no beginning or end and symbolizes the eternity of God, the immortality of the soul, and the everlasting life found in Christ. The wreath, when decorated with evergreens, which are symbolic of life itself, points to God's gift of life even when the world grows dark with the lessening of sunlight hours.

Many kinds of evergreens are used when we make or buy wreaths, swags, and garlands for our churches or homes. Each type of evergreen has its own symbolic meaning.

- **Balsam:** The most commonly used evergreen for wreaths is balsam, and it has the symbolic meaning of eager anticipation.
- **Cedar:** One of the more fragrant and longer lasting evergreens, cedar indicates incorruptibility and healing, and so it is associated with eternal life through Christ.
- **Fir:** Frequently used in garlands as well as wreaths and swags are fir boughs, symbolizing a lifting up.
- **Holly:** This evergreen carries a few different symbolisms. In the language of flowers, it means to foresee, as in to understand in

such a way as to predict, to prophesy. Holly is also used as a reminder of where Jesus' birth and life will lead; its prickly leaves are reminiscent of the crown of thorns and the red berries of the blood he shed upon the Cross.

- **Juniper:** Symbolizing protection, it does that well! If you've ever had to trim juniper branches, you know how prickly and harsh they can be (a great shrub to plant under windows to ward off intruders).
- **Pine:** Pine conveys the meaning of eternal life.
- **Spruce:** Representing hope in adversity, spruce has a lovely sentiment when we think of what Holy Mother Mary faced before the birth of Jesus.

There are other non-evergreen plants often used in Christmas decorations. Bay laurel symbolizes a just reward, a victory over death. The delicate white-berry mistletoe is said to represent overcoming difficulties. And the unpresumptuous ivy holds one of the dearest images—that of clinging to God. It also symbolizes protection, joy, and fidelity—all consistent with "the one to whom we cling."

Any cones, nuts, or seedpods used in Christmas decorations symbolize new life and resurrection, pointing Christians toward Easter.

Within Advent we celebrate many feast days and memorials. On December 8, we honor Mary with the Feast of the Immaculate Conception in the womb of her mother, St. Ann. The miracle of this story was shared in the July chapter, of how her elderly parents, saints Joachim and Ann, were childless until God provided for Mary's conception. Her soul would be unblemished by original sin. Here is where the grace of God's salvation for us begins. From the immaculate concept came the Incarnation.

Another Marian feast this month on December 12 is Our Lady of Guadalupe, the patroness of the Americas. In 1598 the newly appointed bishop elect of Mexico, Bishop Zumárraga, wrote to tell the king of Spain that, unless there was a miracle, the continent would no longer be Christian. Between December 9 and 12, that miracle happened.[1] Our Lady appeared to Juan Diego not as depicted in European art but as an Aztec princess, a familiar image in his culture. Because of her apparition more than six million Mexicans were converted. This helps to explain the deep devotion Hispanics have to her; they owe their conversion to her influence.

The miraculous image that appeared on St. Juan's tilma, a blanket-like garment, and the only image that our Holy Mother gave of herself, is still visible at the Basilica of Our Lady of Guadalupe in Mexico City.

We all owe the Blessed Mother Mary our deepest gratitude. Without her there would not have been the Incarnation, the birth of the Christ. We celebrate his coming on December 25, the Nativity of the Lord—Christmas. On the following Sunday we honor the small family with the Feast of the Holy Family of Jesus, Mary, and Joseph.

December Saints for the Gardener

> We must be content in winter to wait patiently through the long bleak season in which we experience nothing ... believing the truth that these seasons ... are the most pregnant with life.
>
> –Caryll Houselander

December 1: St. Eligius, ca. 588–660

Patron of Horses

Born near Limoges, France, Eligius was trained as a goldsmith and worker of other fine metals, and as a blacksmith. His kind spirit and skill at his trade gained him a great deal of wealth that he used to help the poor and to build several churches and monasteries.

Because of his gentleness he was often called upon when there was a horse or mule too difficult for other blacksmiths to manage. There is a fanciful tale told that one day, when a horse was required to be shod, it stormed and kicked so much that it was said the devil had possessed it. Eligius was summoned, but instead of exorcising the devil he made the Sign of the Cross, took hold of the animal's leg, and shod it properly. After this he again made the Sign of the Cross, and the animal returned to its belligerent self.

Another legend tells of Eligius's favorite horse. Upon his death he bequeathed it to a dear friend who was the local abbot. But the bishop coveted the gentle horse and, as was the entitlement of a bishop, took possession of it for himself. The abbot was so distressed over the loss of the horse that he prayed to the recently deceased Eligius to intercede.

The gentle beast was being led to the bishop's home when it started to become ill. Within days the horse began to wither with its illness; it would not eat and barely drank the water set before it. The bishop called in several doctors to heal the horse, but each time they approached the gentle horse it would rage as if possessed. The bishop thought of another tactic to save the animal and sent it to a woman who was kind and handled all her animals with tenderness.

Soon the woman sent the horse back to the bishop with an angry note that scolded him for sending her a supposed gift that was instead a curse. The horse by then was so much worse in its sickness that everyone who saw it was sure of its imminent death. Finally a priest who had been aware of the situation from the start approached the bishop and, with carefully chosen words, suggested he return the poor beast to the abbot to whom it had been bequeathed. The bishop finally relinquished the horse, and it was taken back to the abbot.

The abbot, in tears at the sight of his sick and starving horse, gave thanks to Eligius for returning it to him and led the poor creature to a freshly cleaned stall. Immediately the horse began to eat and drink, and it tossed its head about playfully at the abbot. The miracle was recorded thus: that due to the prayers to St. Eligius, within days the horse returned to its former health and gentleness and remained so for the duration of its unusually long life.

December 2: St. Bibiana, d. ca. 361

Patron against Mental Disorders, Epilepsy; Association with Herbs

St. Bibiana and her sister lost their parents when they were still adolescents. Both parents were martyred for their faith, and eventually the sisters were too. Her sister, St. Demetria, dropped dead on the way to her cell. Bibiana was imprisoned in a madhouse for refusing to become a prostitute and renounce her Christian faith. It was there that she eventually died. A priest recovered her discarded body and buried her in Rome on land that had belonged to her parents.

The site of her burial soon became a place of pilgrimage. It was a beautiful area, having been part of the Roman gardens *Horti Liciniana*. By 467 a church was built over St. Bibiana's grave as a shrine to her unwavering faith. This same church was renovated several times, the last in the seventeenth century.

The church's beautiful gardens were maintained, and the plant selection was typical of that time period. The gardens included not only ornamental plants but also orchards and vegetables for food, as well as herbs for cooking, housekeeping, and medicinal use.

Legend has it that one of these herbs miraculously cured mental illness, epilepsy, headaches, and "the morning qualm" from excessive wine consumption, that is, hangovers. For this reason she became the patron saint of people suffering from hangovers and the mentally ill.

Records as to which herb specifically grew there that cured mental ailments have been lost. Native plants to that region of Italy that were used as herbal remedies for headaches are rue, sage, thyme, lavender, white willow, and linden trees. Some sources believe that the miracle herb was the Blessed Mary thistle, *Silybum marianum*, which was a common medicinal herb in monastery gardens.

If you have an herb garden that has been a challenge and you are given to headaches caused by trying to figure out why your garden suffers, then send up a few intercessory prayers to St. Bibiana. With her help, you may gain insight on how to grow a better patch of herb.

December 9: St. Juan Diego, 1474–1548

Association with Damask Rose

St. Juan Diego was a convert to the Catholic faith and the visionary of Our Lady of Guadalupe. While not associated with patronages to gardeners or farmers, the miracle of this humble farmer and the roses left by the Blessed Mother warrant his inclusion. The roses she gave him were the Castilian rose or damask rose, *Rosa damascena*.

Juan was a poor farm worker and field laborer who also wove and sold mats. He was a deeply spiritual man and took the name of Juan Diego when confirmed a Catholic. He was in his early fifties at that time and would be widowed a few years later in 1529. He and his wife were childless.

Once confirmed, Juan Diego would regularly walk to Mass, a four-hour journey each way. The church was fifteen miles south in what is now called Mexico City. It was along this route that he passed beside Tepeyac Hill, where the apparition of Our Lady of Guadalupe occurred. She told him that she wanted a shrine to be built at that site.

Juan Diego was awestruck and sought out the bishop to share with him what had occurred. The bishop and many others doubted his story and ridiculed him.

Juan later returned to the site, and the Holy Virgin sent him back to those who doubted with unquestionable proof that she had indeed made the request: the roses that Juan carried, besides it being winter and the wrong time of year for them to be flowering, were not from that region at all but from the bishop's home town of Castile, Spain. She also embedded her image in the fibers of Juan Diego's tilma.

The image on his garment of Our Lady of Guadalupe still remains and is hung in the basilica built at the site of the apparition.

Monsignor Virgilio Elizondo explained, "In the Indian cultures of that time, the tilma was the exterior expression of the innermost identity of the person. By being visible on Juan Diego's tilma, Mary became imprinted in the deepest recesses of his heart—and in the hearts of all who come to her."[2]

Though he died on May 30, St. Juan Diego's feast day was set to the day after the Feast of the Immaculate Conception and is followed by the Feast of Our Lady of Guadalupe on December 12.

December 24: Adam the Patriarch

First Human, Husband of Eve, Patron of Gardeners

Although Adam's memorial is no longer on the Roman Catholic Church calendar, it remains on the calendar of some Eastern Churches on this day. Adam was the second gardener on this earth, God of course being the first.

The name of Adam is derived from the Hebrew word *ha-adamah* ("the ground") in a similar manner that in Latin *homo* is related to *humus*. Both refer to him as being of the earth.[3] Adam was created not only of the earth but initially to attend to it in joy and recreation. It became a labor only after Adam and Eve disobeyed God and ate from the tree of the knowledge of good and evil.

In Christian legend, this tree became known as the tree of paradise and on this date was decorated with red apples that represented the forbidden fruit. At about the sixteenth century, people brought the tree indoors and hung Communion wafers on it to represent the Eucharist, the fruit of life. Shortly thereafter, the Feast of Adam was discontinued in the West, but the practice of having a tree continued. In Germany, it was called the *Christbaum* or Christ tree (Christmas tree).

Angels, hearts, and stars made from white pastry dough and figures of people and animals made from brown dough replaced the Communion wafers. Eventually fruits and vegetables were made from marzipan and added to the tree. In the seventeenth century, the Christ tree was nicknamed the sugar tree, and it is no wonder that children waited in eager anticipation for disassembling it on January 6.

There is also a story from *The Golden Legend*, a medieval book of the lives of saints, that tells of seeds taken from the paradise tree, which in this story is called the tree of mercy. A very aged Adam knew that it wouldn't be long before he died. Wanting to be forgiven by God, he sent his son Seth to the Garden of Eden to find an oil of mercy. The garden had been closed by God immediately after they were expelled, and only the angles that guarded the entrance were permitted to enter. One of these angels, upon hearing Seth's plea, recognized Adam's desire for forgiveness and fetched a few grains of seeds from the fruit of the tree of mercy; apparently no oil had been pressed.

Upon his return home, Seth found his father still alive and shared with him the story of the angel and the seeds: "And Adam laughed then died. And then Seth laid the grains or kernels under his father's tongue and buried him in the vale of Hebron; and out of Adam's mouth grew three trees of the three grains, of which trees the cross that our Lord suffered his passion on was made."[4]

We all know as Christians that it is through our Lord's passion that mercy was granted to us all, and Adam too was granted the mercy he sought so many centuries ago.

December in the Garden

> The secret of my identity is hidden in the love and mercy of God.
>
> –Thomas Merton

Practical Gardening: Evaluating the Landscape

Sometimes things don't work out as we planned, and we need to take a long hard look at why. This is true not only about the landscape of your garden but also the landscape of your soul. December is an opportunity to look back at the garden year that is coming to an end and be attentive to what encourages proper development.

As time goes by, whether it's a season or several years, you'll notice something in your garden is not working out right. Is it diseased, in decline, or not growing well where it was planted? Has the plant become overgrown or entangled with other plants? Was it the completely wrong thing to add to your garden, or has it taken over? Is there too much maintenance required to keep the plant healthy or in check? Or perhaps you have come to the point where you can't manage all the work and have to decide where to cut back and what to remove.

Evaluating our gardens and our souls is something we must do on a regular basis. We want to be sure things are growing properly and reflect the beauty intended. Let's start with the first question about decline. You'll need to discern what caused the problem. Consider the location of the plant. Check references and talk with other gardeners on how to grow the plant in your zone. In your researching you will want to consider the following: light, air movement, water, and soil and roots, which relate to nutrition.

Look closely at the plants' leaves and stems for pests. With some plants, especially hardwoods (trees or shrubs), look for small holes in the trunk or limbs that indicate borer infestation. When leaves are mottled you are probably looking at blight—a common name for any plant disease that can be a fungal or bacterial infection. If you are unfamiliar with the bugs or blight, take a sample in a tightly closed clear plastic bag to your local greenhouse, nursery, or county extension office for identification.

Over the years a mature hardwood can become overgrown, entangled with other plants, damaged by storms, or have excessive deadwood. Depending on its age and whether it can be rejuvenated, removal is often the best option. Here is an opportunity to redesign an area and add new life to an old landscape. Consider the cost, and if warranted, move forward with renovation.

The same action can be taken when you've added something that was completely wrong for your garden or has unfortunately taken over. Mistakes happen and must be rectified. I have sometimes bought a lovely plant on impulse and enjoyed it until its weedy habit was discovered. I remember well the mint that took a pickax and three years of herbicide to eradicate.

A garden requires that we be attentive, not only to resolve problems but also to maintain a healthy and pleasing landscape. This takes dedication to do the work, and discerning what to keep and what to remove often has more to do with you than the plants. Our lives change. Perhaps we once had free time to work in multiple gardens, but now there are new demands: a job, an aging parent, or children. Or perhaps the strength and stamina we once had for weeding, pruning, and mowing is now limited. As I discovered, accepting that we can't keep up with our gardens can be heart wrenching.

I thought my identity as a gardener was being lost as my neglected gardens became overrun with weeds. When I finally accepted that physical limitations demanded I garden less, I called in reinforcements. Friends came and joyously dug up twenty-five years of perennials from ten different gardens. They were all delighted with having their trunks and back seats filled to capacity. What remained were smatterings of plants and weeds, and several shallow potholes in what used to be flowering beds. The time for evaluation had passed, and I had to be ruthless.

I unlatched the double doors of the shed and pulled out the self-propelled lawn mower. Determinedly I walked it to the front yard, took a deep breath, and moved it into the gardens. Working around the potholes, I reduced to mulch what plants remained. I wasn't sure if it was harder physically or emotionally. It didn't matter. I had to clean up the mess as best I could. I shut off the mower and turned around.

There before me stood the basic structure of my gardens: the shrubs and ornamental trees. With all the perennials and ornamental grasses stripped away, the simplicity and beauty supported itself. The landscape was only adorned by the smaller things that added texture and color to the space. All the pretty stuff had been nice, but they had depended on a good foundation.

Take note of the plants that form the foundation of your landscape and build on that. Whether you need to make a small adjustment or a major overhaul, take the time to evaluate what is valuable and why.

Faith-Filled Gardening: Nativity Traditions and Stories

Advent

Advent is a time of peaceful waiting, of preparing our hearts. We prepare not only to celebrate the gift of the Incarnation, the Nativity of Jesus, but also in expectation of his final return.

Having an Advent garden is a wonderful testament to our own waiting for the time that we will meet our Lord. It can help us recognize the incarnation of Christ within each of us when we pray.

There are so many wonderful symbols related to Advent that the challenge will be to create a garden space using only a few.

Let's start with the colors of this season: purple violet for penance and healing, and rose pink for comfort and joy. Imagine your outdoor prayer space filled with plants following this harmonious color theme and then add just a touch of white here and there to represent the Holy Spirit.

Speaking of white, consider an all-white garden. Many celebrations for Advent occur after sunset where light is brought into the darkness. It is during the evening that an all-white garden really shows off its beauty. It can almost glow in the moonlight. Adding candles is always a nice touch. A white garden is also nice for reflecting on the Transfiguration, which is celebrated in August.

With the idea of candles comes the notion of the Advent wreath. Your garden could be a circular pattern with green plants delineating the areas. Perhaps you could use boxwood, *Buxus sp.,* or rosemary, with one grouping of pink flowers and three sections of purple flowers. Develop each grouping with a different texture or form, such as broad petals or spiked or globus flowering stalks. This layout is very striking even in a small private garden.

Another shrub that can be used to divide a garden space is holly, *Ilex sp.* I mentioned earlier in this chapter why holly is so often used during Advent: it symbolizes the fulfillment of Jesus' human life.

We sing "O Come, O Come Emmanuel" throughout Advent. The word *Emmanuel* can also be added to the garden as a plaque or stepping-stone. Handmade stepping-stones representing Advent can include purple or pink images, angels who announced his coming, or stars using small glass cabochons or mosaics. If you're feeling ambitious, there are twenty-five symbols for ornaments on a Jesse tree (representative of the family tree of Jesus), and these can be imprinted onto pavers or other elements for a garden too.

Jesse Tree Symbols

Family	Symbols
Creation of the world	Globe
Adam and Eve	Snake and apple
Noah and flood	Rainbow
Abraham	Camel
Sarah	Baby
Isaac	Ram
Jacob	Ladder
Joseph	Multicolored coat
Moses	Burning bush
Miriam	Tambourine
Samuel	Lamp
Jesse	Branch

David	Harp
Solomon	Crown
Isaiah	Throne
Jeremiah	Tablets of law
Angels	Angel
Malachi	Trumpet
Zechariah and Elizabeth	Dove
Mary	Lily
John the Baptist	River
Joseph of Nazareth	Hammer and saw
Bethlehem	Star
Birth of Christ	Crib

An empty manger is often seen during Advent with the Christ child being laid in it on Christmas. Add a small trough in your garden and plant it as a seasonal container filled with purple and pink flowers, rosemary, and *Dianthus sp.* (carnations, pinks, and Sweet William). Come Christmas, converting it into a crib will be effortless. Add some ornamental grass clippings to the center as straw and then a figure of the baby Jesus.

There is always the possibility of making a small grotto of the Nativity a permanent part of your outdoor prayer space. I can recall my own delight when, coming around the bend in a garden path on a warm July day, I found a small stable built under a fallen tree in a slope of ground not readily visible from the path. The creator of this manger display had taken advantage of a natural cavity in the earth to make his Christmas scene.

Christmas

A Christmas garden can be more than red and white, adorned only with poinsettias and holly. Think more about the purpose of Christmas: the Incarnation of God, the exemplary faith and obedience of Mary and Joseph, and the heavens opening for the angels to sing and for humankind to give praise.

It is a peace-filled time, contrary to the more secular observances. The Light of the World was born, and so we light candles—and lots of them. To line your garden path with light, use nail-punched tin cans, white paper bags, or glass jars with sand in the bottom to hold tea-light candles.

Why not take a birdbath basin, fill it with sand, and add three larger candles to represent the Trinity fulfilled by the Incarnation? You could use a green candle for eternity, a red one for the blood of Christ, and a white one for the Holy Spirit or the angels—and now you know why these three colors are used during Christmas. Think about adding smaller white tapers to this arrangement, one for each gift of prayer offered by you or one of your family members. This could become a new Christmas tradition.

An outdoor Nativity is a fairly common sight during this time of year. As I mentioned before, you could create a grotto of his birth to be a part of the garden all year. Remember the planter you made to represent the crib? Now is the time to lay the baby Jesus in it, and don't forget to add the rosemary branches as Joseph did at the infant's birth.

We can acknowledge the animals that were present at the birth of Jesus. The patron saint of animals and nature, St. Francis of Assisi, petitioned the emperor of his time to order corn and grain be strewn along the roads on Christmas Day. This way the birds and animals would all have food to eat and would celebrate God's gift with the faithful. In this same vein, I have often decorated a tree in my yard with food for the birds (and as a result, also the raccoons, mice, rabbits, and deer).

To create this feeding source, I select a distant tree, usually an evergreen, that is visible from my window. Then I decorate the tree with any number of things: field corn cobs cut into two-inch lengths; pine cones covered with birdseed mixed with suet or peanut butter; purchased birdseed bells; homemade animal biscuits cut with cookie cutters; handfuls of wheat or oat stalks tied together; and small sunflower heads. All these elements are hung with biodegradable twine. I also make red bows from outdoor ribbon to tie on the tree to make it look festive and add a few white wooden angels to complete the decorations. Keep additional food ornaments in an airtight container for replenishing your tree during the twelve days of Christmas.

There is another Christmas tradition about birds: on Christmas morning, before the household eats breakfast, a handful of crumbled bread or birdseed is sprinkled on the doorstep. In our willingness to share with God's creatures, legend has it that we are blessed in the coming year by their consuming our gift by nightfall.

The Christmas Rose (Helleborus niger)

At the time of the birth of Jesus, a young shepherd girl followed the Magi and wept outside the stable because she was poor and had nothing to give the baby. She sobbed, saying that she would have brought flowers if it hadn't been winter and the ground hard and white with frost: the only thing she could give the Child was her love.

Suddenly the Archangel Gabriel appeared and asked the young shepherd girl to follow him as he led her into the cold, dark night. Stopping, he struck the frosty earth, and at once the Christmas rose, *Helleborus niger*, sprang up and bloomed. The shepherdess was filled with joy and, drying her tears, plucked the beautiful white flowers and ran back to the manger to give them to the Holy Child.

In the same genus is *Helleborus orientalis,* and in some regions it is called the Lenten rose because it flowers between Christmas and Easter.

Epiphany

The celebration of the Adoration of the Magi includes the blessing of the home with the year and the initials of the Magi: (first two numbers of the year) + C + M + B + (last two numbers of the year), using chalk that is blessed. The three letters represent the names of the Magi: Caspar, Melchior, and Balthasar.[5] Part of the prayer for this blessing is *Christus Mansionem Benedicat,* may Christ bless this house, and again we see the lettering C + M + B.

In addition to gold, the Magi also brought gifts of frankincense and myrrh. These resins are very pungent and can enhance your prayer experience in the home or out in the garden. I am moved whenever I smell myrrh because it reminds me of the connectedness to Christ's life: it was present at the Nativity as well as at the tomb.

We are blessed as Catholics to have so many rich traditions through which to praise our God. Adding elements reflective of our faith to our gardens allows us to celebrate further the gifts that he has given. We also have stories that help to enliven our faith.

The Red-Breasted Robin (African Stonechat)

There are three legends about why the robin has a red breast, one of them taking place at the Nativity. After Jesus was born, the animals in and near the stable were the first to view the miraculous child. Joseph was desperately trying to attend to the needs of Mary and the infant in this cold and inhospitable lodging. He gathered clean straw and rosemary branches into a feeding trough for the baby's crib. He wrapped a cloak around Mary and their son to keep them warm as he tried to build a fire. But kindling was in short supply, and he dared not leave his family to search for more.

As the little fire was about to burn down once again, a little brown bird flew in beside the dying flames and frantically began flapping its wings. The air beneath its wings stirred the flames. As the fire grew hotter the little bird's breast turned red from the heat. Not until the fire was thoroughly stoked did the little bird put an end to its mission to help warm the Holy Family.

Biblical Reflections

And it is my prayer that your love may abound more and more, with knowledge and all discernment, so that you may approve what is excellent, and may be pure and blameless for the day of Christ, filled with the fruits of righteousness which come through Jesus Christ, to the glory and praise of God.

—Philippians 1:9–11

He has showed you, O man, what is good; and what does the Lord require of you but to do justice, and to love kindness, and to walk humbly with your God?

—Micah 6:8

For all men who were ignorant of God were foolish by nature; and they were unable from the good things that are seen to know him who exists. . . . Let them perceive from them [now] how much more powerful is he who formed them. For from the greatness and beauty of created things comes a corresponding perception of their Creator.

—Wisdom 13:1, 4–5

Thou dost show me the path of life; in thy presence there is fullness of joy, in thy right hand are pleasures for evermore.

—Psalm 16:11

With him are strength and wisdom; the deceived and the deceiver are his.

—Job 12:16

But he who looks into the perfect law, the law of liberty, and perseveres, being no hearer that forgets but a doer that acts, he shall be blessed in his doing.

—James 1:25

(For the fruit of light is found in all that is good and right and true), and try to learn what is pleasing to the Lord. Take no part in the unfruitful works of darkness, but instead expose them.

—Ephesians 5:9–11

Prayer Focus for December

> Yet we must experience our relationship with God between the poles of distance and closeness. By closeness we are strengthened, by distance we are put to the test.
> –Pope Benedict XVI

Over the years I've had to evaluate my landscape and as I've aged strip it down to the bare essentials. Look to the landscape of your soul. Is there something growing in your heart that is unhealthy, spreading like weeds or an infectious blight? Do you need to prune out deadwood and rejuvenate your spirit?

The removal of annuals and perennials from my garden allowed me to realize the importance of a good foundational planting of trees and shrubs. Name the elements in your life that may be crowding out your goodness. Ask yourself what are the elements for a spiritually sound foundation.

Acknowledgments

Imagine the seedpod of a milkweed. The pod contains hundreds of ripened seeds of faith that float on the wind, the breath of God, into our lives. The delicate seeds don't land all at once, they don't germinate at the same time, and some travel great distances before they reach the soil of our souls. Once rooted, that seed of faith grows—and spreads exponentially, if you've ever seen a field of milkweeds!

So how *do* I thank the hundreds of people who helped build my faith, encouraged my growth, and expanded my life as a writer? It's like trying to choose a favorite flower, determine which seed set the greater root, or determine if the first seeding was more fruitful than the fiftieth.

To name everyone who over the years contributed to the creation of this manuscript is daunting. They each in some way gave a gratuitous gift, and I am grateful to all who have brought me closer to God and the publishing of this book.

For seeing the natural progression from my first book to this, of gardens and Catholic traditions, I thank my first editor, Claudia Volkman.

The Holy Spirit then gently and persistently nudged me to seek God's will and do what I as a gardener never imagined was within me: to write. Attempting to find my way led to frequenting the Adoration Chapel, and for many months almost daily. I am most grateful for the Presence leading me on as I sat behind the pews at the small table with pen and pad. And I am grateful to the many adorers who came and went and would also pray for me during their holy hour.

Likewise, I am grateful . . .

- for friends who supported me financially, spiritually, and emotionally through the difficulties of unemployment and disability as I learned a new craft and identity;
- for the multitude of writers who came before me and whose work—in print, online, or spoken—collectively grew this book;
- for all the English majors who, as gently as they could, thoroughly impressed upon me the necessity of correct grammar and a good editor who helped me to develop a writing style; and
- to the dear Jean Lantis, former English teacher extraordinaire, who tirelessly helped edit the original manuscript.

I am grateful to those professionals who encouraged me, specifically Lisa Hendey, Pat Gohn, Monetta Harr, and Elizabeth Scalia, all who believed in me as a writer long before I believed in myself.

I also give thanks to all those at Ave Maria Press who brought their expertise in the crafting of this book, especially my editor, Bob Hamma.

The Catholic Writers Guild was instrumental in opening up avenues into an industry I knew nothing about. And from that association began a deep and lasting friendship with the unflappable Ann Margaret Lewis, who had mentored and continues to mentor and guide.

Most of all I am grateful to David Krajewski, to whom this book is dedicated, who encouraged, cajoled, cheered, lamented, and most of all prayed me through every failure and success along the way. I am grateful to his wife and daughters, who with him in intercessory prayers brought the water to the garden where the seeds for this book had been planted.

I am humbled and grateful to have been urged on by so many and realize that left to my own resources I could never have dreamed of or accomplished what God inspired.

Appendix A: **Liturgical Colors**

Vestments and liturgical colors are ascribed to specific days in the Church's year. My home altar reflects this, and I often carry these colors into the seating area of the garden, either by colored cloths or candles.

Color	Use	Symbolizing
Green	Ordinary Time: from Epiphany until Lent and the time after Pentecost	Symbolizes hope, fertility, nature, bountifulness, and freedom from bondage
White (Silver may also be used)	Season of Christmas	Purity, innocence, virginity, joy, virtue, and victory
	Season of Easter	
	Feasts of the Lord, Mary, the angels, and nonmartyred saints	The color of the pope's nonliturgical dress
	All Saints Day	Gold often accompanies white
	Nuptial Masses	
	Requiem Masses	
Red	Feast of the Lord's Passion (Passion Sunday, Good Friday)	Sacrifice (literally the blood of life), charity, fire, and zeal
	Feasts of the martyrs	Holy Spirit
	Pentecost	A cardinal's nonliturgical garb
Violet (Purple)	Season of Advent (blue-violet)	Preparation, penitence, sorrow, and mourning
	Season of Lent (purple)	

Rose	Gaudete Sunday	Rejoice
	Laetare Sunday	

Appendix B: Disposing of Sacramentals and Consecrated Materials

We as Catholics often have prayer items blessed. Things such as Rosaries, religious books, statues, and water are called sacramentals once a priest bestows a blessing upon them.

To prevent desecration of the material, that is, to avoid dishonoring it, a sacramental that is no longer usable or functional should be returned to the earth. The manner of disposal depends on the nature of the item. But in all cases, the item must be respectfully returned to the elements.

Contaminated holy water should be poured into a hole dug in the earth in a spot where no one would walk over it.

Combustible sacramentals such as wooden or paper icons, holy books, and palm fronds should be burned and then the ashes collected and buried, again in a spot where no one will walk over it.

Sometimes our garden statues become weatherworn and begin to crumble. These should be replaced with new ones that honor the holy persons they portray. The worn-out statue should be broken down into smaller, unrecognizable pieces. As with other earthen sacraments, it too should be buried in a spot without foot traffic.

Objects made of metals should be melted down and used for another purpose. A Catholic jeweler can help you with this.

On June 23, the Eve of St. John the Baptist, it is customary to build a bonfire and burn sacramental materials that are no longer usable. These ashes are then removed from the fire pit and buried.

Appendix C: Daily and Monthly Dedications

Daily Devotions

Sunday: Blessed Trinity, the Resurrection, Glorious Mysteries
Monday: the Holy Spirit, souls in purgatory, Joyful Mysteries
Tuesday: the angels, Sorrowful Mysteries
Wednesday: St. Joseph, Glorious Mysteries
Thursday: the institution of the Eucharist, Luminous Mysteries
Friday: the Passion of Christ, the Sacred Heart, Sorrowful Mysteries
Saturday: Mary, Queen of Angels, the Immaculate Heart of Mary, Joyful Mysteries

Monthly Devotions

January: The Holy Name and Infancy of Jesus
February: The Holy Family (Historically, this month had been devoted to the Passion of Christ.)
March: St. Joseph
April: The Blessed Sacrament (Historically, this month had been devoted to the Resurrection.)
May: The Virgin Mary
June: The Sacred Heart of Jesus
July: The Precious Blood of Jesus
August: The Immaculate Heart of Mary
September: The Seven Sorrows of Mary (Historically, this month had been devoted to praying for religious orders.)
October: The Rosary and the holy angels

November: The deceased souls who are in purgatory
December: The immaculate conception and the Nativity

Appendix D: **Labyrinths**

Although some see labyrinths as a New Age thing, they have been around for centuries. They have also been recorded as part of several unrelated cultures. The word *labrys* is a term for a symmetrical double-headed ax, a tool still used in forestry. If you look at a single circuit labyrinth of the neomedieval period, you can see the resemblance to the ax. The cathedral-style labyrinths are multicircuits, usually having four divisions.

Early and medieval Christians took Greek and Roman customs and made them their own, and the labyrinth was no exception. During the Middle Ages, people viewed the labyrinth as a symbol of redemption. It was not used as a form of pilgrimage as it is today.

The metaphor for redemption was that the path of sin leading to the center symbolized the route to hell and the only way back out was through the help of a woman—Mary.[1]

In time the labyrinth came to be seen very differently. "During the Crusades when Christians couldn't make visits to the Holy Land, and in the same manner that the Way of the Cross devotion developed as a sort of substitute 'pilgrimage' to the Holy City, labyrinths came to be used as substitute 'Chemins de Jerusalem' [road to Jerusalem]. Christians, barred from earthly Zion, would walk the labyrinths, often on their knees in penance, meditating on the Passion of Our Lord Jesus Christ."[2]

Labyrinths are designed in such a way that if you walk the path without veering off, you will reach the other end, the center, an achievement that is seen as the symbol for heaven. What a beautiful way to meditate on the way of Christ: there is only one way in or out, it is narrow, and there is only one path toward our God or away from him. "Though direct, that path, as in following Him as 'The Way,' is a winding road, full of turns and suffering and hardship . . . . But always, the Heavenly Jerusalem . . . is in sight from any place in the labyrinth, and one knows that if one remains on that path, he will find himself where he wants to be."[3]

Not everyone is comfortable with this type of meditative prayer. Many Catholics are concerned about the paganistic or New Age associations of the labyrinth. If you desire to walk a labyrinth that is not your own creation, never walk a labyrinth that is not in a Christian holy place or building.

With that said, there are many ways to incorporate a labyrinth into your garden. There are several Internet catalog sources for purchasing anything from small handheld labyrinths to full pattern sheets placed on the ground to guide construction.

If you are inclined to construct a small labyrinth in your yard, choose a simple shape of the neomedieval period that has seven or fourteen circuits or folds. Seven is always known to be a meaningful number throughout the Bible, and fourteen is the number of Stations of the Cross.

I have always liked the look and feel of a lawn labyrinth. The pattern is trenched out so that the path is the grass, set off with low-set fieldstones or narrow pavers. Setting the stones and pavers low enough allows you to easily pass a mower over the top for easier maintenance.

This arrangement is particularly easy to do at home because the outer edge of the circle can be surrounded by gardens. You can place benches at the starting point and in the center. Your labyrinth could also have a large tree in the middle with a circular bench around the trunk—this is my personal favorite.

For small spaces, consider a handheld labyrinth that can be traced with your fingers or stylus. You can make your own using a square piece of wood. Draw your pattern and then use a router or wood burner to outline it. You could also embed the pattern into one end of a wooden bench.

Creating a cement paver with the pattern in it would be a nice visual labyrinth. If you wanted to go a step further, consider creating four pavers resembling a simple quadrant-style labyrinth.

Notes

Introduction

1. Meredith Gould, *The Catholic Home: Celebrations and Traditions for Holidays, Feast Days, and Every Day* (New York: Doubleday, 2004), 2.

2. For additional online information about saints, visit SQPN's website http://saints.sqpn.com.

3. Hilderic Friend, *Flowers and Flower Lore*, vol. 1 (Bloomsbury, London: Swan Sonnenschein and Co., 1883), 139.

January: Seeding

1. Carl Lindahl, John McNamara, and John Lindow, eds., *Medieval Folklore: An Encyclopedia of Myths, Legends, Tales, Beliefs, and Customs*, 2 vols. (Santa Barbara, CA: ABC-CLIO, 2000), 788.

2. David Farmer, *The Oxford Dictionary of Saints*, 5th ed. (New York: Oxford University Press, 2004), 29.

3. Matthew Russell, S.J., ed., *Irish Monthly* (1907) 25, 60.

4. "St. Vincent Tournante," *Saint-Vincent tournante des climats de Bourgogne*, accessed September 12, 2014, http://www.st-vincent-tournante.fr

5. "Les origines," *Saint-Vincent tournante des climats de Bourgogne*, accessed December 2013, http://www.st-vincent-tournante.fr.

6. National Liturgical Office, ed., *A Book of Blessings* (Ottawa, ON: Canadian Conference of Catholic Bishops Publication Services, 1981), 141.

7. There is dispute as to biblical translations of plant names and species. Unwilling to enter the fray, I leave Greek, Hebrew, and all other

266

horticultural translations to the experts and merely list what plants are acknowledged as relevant.

February: Light

1. "Feast of the Purification (Candlemas)," *fish eaters*, accessed December 2013, http://www.fisheaters.com.

2. "Parable of Light of the World," *SQPN*, accessed December 2013, http://saints.sqpn.com.

3. Lindahl, McNamara, and Lindow, *Medieval Folklore*, 444–45.

4. Ibid., 117.

5. "Irish Blessings," *Irish Culture and Customs*, accessed December 2013, http://www.irishcultureandcustoms.com.

6. "Saint Valentine of Rome," *SQPN*, accessed December 2013, http://saints.sqpn.com.

7. Mike Aquilina, *Signs and Mysteries: Revealing Ancient Christian Symbols* (Huntington, IN: Our Sunday Visitor, 2008), 9.

8. Poetry Stone Deluxe Kit, Magnetic Poetry, Inc., PO Box 14862, Minneapolis, MN, 55414.

March: Pruning

1. "Feast of St. Joseph," *fish eaters*, accessed December 2013, http://www.fisheaters.com.

2. Marie des Douleurs, "The Annunciation," *Magnificat* 10, no. 14 (March 2009): 346–47.

3. J. H. Schlarman, "With the Blessing of the Church" (presentation, National Catholic Rural Life Conference, Des Moines, IA, 1994).

4. The story has many references; one source is Douglas D. Anderson, "The Glastonbury Thorn," *The Hymns and Carols of Christmas*, accessed December 2013, http://www.hymnsandcarolsofchristmas.com.

5. Gould, *The Catholic Home*, 60.

April: Preparing the Soil

1. Ambrose Mooney, "St. Valéry of Leucone, Abbot," *Celtic and Old English Saints*, March 27, 2009, accessed December 2013, http://www.celticsaints.org.

2. Peter John Cameron, O.P., "Psalm 139 (Commentary)," *Magnificat* 15, no. 2 (April 2013): 400.

3. Amy Steedman, "In God's Garden—St. Catherine of Siena," *SQPN*, accessed August 18, 2014, http://saints.sqpn.com.

4. This is the norm in the official Roman calendar, although many people still follow the end of Lent as on Holy Saturday when the triduum culminates.

May: Beginning to Flower

1. "May Crowning," *fish eaters*, accessed December 2013, http://www.fisheaters.com.

2. John Procter, S.T.L., *The Rosary Guide for Priests and People* (London: Kegan, Paul, Trench, Trubner & Co., LTD, 1901), 235.

3. E. Cobham Brewer, *A Dictionary of Miracles* (Whitefish, MT: Kessinger, 2010), 373.

4. Cornell University Department of Horticulture, "Bulb and Perennial Combinations," accessed December 2013, http://www.hort.cornell.edu.

5. A research site by the University of Dayton on Marian flowers throughout the world is Cindy Osborne, *Mary's Gardens*, last updated September 24, 2009, http://campus.udayton.edu.

June: Transformation and New Life

1. Scott P. Richert, "The Feast of the Sacred Heart of Jesus," *Catholicism*, About.com, accessed December 2013, http://catholicism.about.com.

2. "The Promises of the Sacred Heart of Jesus to St. Margaret Mary," accessed September 12, 2014, www.ewtn.com/library/christ/promises.txt.

3. St. Boniface was born in Crediton, in what is today England. This quote is taken from their records, accessed August 2014, http://www.creditonparishchurch.org.uk.

4. Martin Carver, ed., *The Cross Goes North: Processes of Conversion in Northern Europe, AD 300–1300* (Woodbridge, UK: Boydell Press, 2006), 570.

5. Farmer, *The Oxford Dictionary of Saints*, 422.

6. "Good Friday," *fish eaters*, accessed September 12, 2014, http://www.fisheaters.com/customslent14.html

7. The stigma is the part of the flower that receives the pollen and rises out of the top center of the passion flower.

8. The anthers are the pads of pollen.

July: Stormy

1. "Saint Gertrude Prayer," *Catholic Q & A, EWTN Faith*, accessed September 12, 2014, www.ewtn.com.

2. "St. Swithin," *New Advent*, accessed September 12, 2014, www.newadvent.org

3. *Irish Culture and Customs*, accessed September 12, 2014, http://www.irishcultureandcustoms.com.

4. Jacobus de Voragine, *The Golden Legend: Reading on the Saints*, trans. William Granger Ryan (Princeton, NJ: Princeton University Press, 2012).

5. Farmer, *The Oxford Dictionary of Saints*, 432.

6. International Commission on English in the Liturgy, Order of St. Benedict, *Book of Blessings: Ritual Edition* (Collegeville, MN: The Liturgical Press, 1989), 609.

7. Avinoam Danin, Alan D. Whanger, Uri Baruch, and Mary Whanger, *Flora of the Shroud of Turin* (St. Louis: Missouri Botanical Garden Press, 1999), 18.

8. More than thirty-six plants have been found on the shroud but await unequivocal species identification.

9. Danin, Whanger, Baruch, and Whanger, *Flora of the Shroud of Turin*, 12.

August: Fruitfulness

1. Jean Bainvel, "Devotion to the Immaculate Heart of Mary," *New Advent*, accessed December 2013, http://www.newadvent.org.

2. Pope Francis, *Lumen Fidei*, 26.

3. Francis de Sales and Jane de Chantal, *Letters of Spiritual Direction*, eds. Wendy M. Wright and Joseph F. Power, (Mahwah, NJ: Paulist Press, 1988), 158.

4. Ibid., 18.

5. Libreria Editrice Vaticana, *Catechism of the Catholic Church*, 2nd ed. (Washington, DC: United States Conference of Catholic Bishops Publishing, 1997), 870.

6. "Mary," *fish eaters*, accessed December 2013, http://www.fisheaters.com.

7. National Conference of Catholic Bishops, "August 15, Assumption Day Blessing of Produce," *Catholic Household Blessings and Prayers* (Washington, DC: United States Catholic Conference, 1988), 170.

8. Richard Stanton, *A Menology of England and Wales* (London: Burns and Oates, 1892), 393.

9. "Patron Saints for Girls: The Life of Saint Rose of Lima," *SQPN*, accessed December 2013, http://saints.sqpn.com/patron-saints-for-girls-the-life-of-saint-rose-of-lima/.

10. United States Conference of Catholic Bishops, *Compendium: Catechism of the Catholic Church* (Washington, DC: United States Conference of Catholic Bishops Publishing, 2012), 114.

11. BrailleTranslator.org, accessed December 2013, http://www.brailletranslator.org.

12. Saint Basil, "On Detachment from Worldly Goods," *Fathers of the Church: Ascetical Works*, vol. 9 (Washington, DC: Catholic University Press, 1950), 69.

September: Harvesting

1. Juniper B. Carol, "Ordinary Time: September 12," CatholicCulture.org, accessed December 2013, http://www.catholicculture.org.

2. Mick Hales, *Monastic Gardens* (New York: Tabori & Chang, 2000), 11.

3. Ben Johnson, "Michaelmas," *Historic UK: The History and Heritage Accommodation Guide*, accessed December 2013, http://www.historic-uk.com.

October: Preparing for Winter

1. Thérèse of Lisieux, *The Autobiography of Saint Thérèse of Lisieux: The Story of a Soul*, trans. John Beever, (New York: Image, 2011).

2. *Society of the Little Flower*, accessed September 15, 2014, www. littleflower.org.

3. Lisa M. Hendey, *A Book of Saints for Catholic Moms: 52 Companions for Your Heart, Mind, Body, and Soul* (Notre Dame, IN: Ave Maria Press, 2011), 48.

4. Bert Ghezzi, *Voices of the Saints: A Year of Readings* (New York: Doubleday, 2000), 676.

5. "Eurasian Magpie," *Wikipedia*, accessed December 2013, http:// en.wikipedia.org.

November: Dormancy and Rest

1. Zalman Goldstein, "The Yartzeit Anniversary," accessed December 2013, http://www.chabad.org.

2. Paul Claudel, *I Believe in God* (New York: Holt, Rinehart and Winston, 1963), accessed December 2013, https://archive.org/stream/ ibelieveingodame013460mbp/ibelieveingodame013460mbp_djvu.txt.

3. Richard Stanton, *A Menology of England and Wales* (London: Burns and Oates, 1892).

4. Francis de Sales, *Introduction to the Devout Life*, trans. John K. Ryan (New York: Image Books, 2003).

December

1. An excellent book about this miracle is by Carl Anderson and Eduardo Chavez, *Our Lady of Guadalupe: Mother of the Civilization of Love* (New York: Doubleday Religion, 2009).

2. John M. Samaha, S.M., "A Scientific Note About St. Juan Diego's Tilma," updated March 24, 2009, accessed December 2013, http://campus. udayton.edu/mary/meditations/samaha7.html.

3. Peter M.J. Stravinskas, ed., *Our Sunday Visitor's Catholic Encyclopedia* (Huntington, IN: Our Sunday Visitor, 1991), 39.

4. Rudolf Steiner, *The Temple Legend and the Golden Legend*, trans. John Wood (London: Steiner, 1985), 366.

5. Meredith Gould's book *The Catholic Home* and the website www.fisheaters.com both have excellent explanations of the ritual and prayers for this blessing.

Appendix D: Labyrinths

1. Some find here a similarity to the mythic hero Theseus. He enters a maze with his double-edge ax. There he traps the Minotaur and kills it. The hero's lover, Ariadne, gives him a thread so he can find his way back out.

2. See the excellent Catholic website fisheaters.com for this and more on traditional Catholicism: "Labyrinths: Symbols of Hell and the Pilgrim's Way," accessed August 26, 2014, http://www.fisheaters.com.

3. Ibid.

Bibliography

Anderson, Carl, and Eduardo Chavez. *Our Lady of Guadalupe: Mother of the Civilization of Love.* New York: Doubleday Religion, 2009.

Aquilina, Mike. *Signs and Mysteries: Revealing Ancient Christian Symbols.* Huntington, IN: Our Sunday Visitor, 2008.

Ball, Ann. *Catholic Traditions in the Garden.* Huntington, IN: Our Sunday Visitor, 1998.

Bartley, Jennifer R. *Designing the New Kitchen Garden: An American Potager Handbook.* Portland, OR: Timber Press, 2006.

Bartunek, John. *The Better Part: A Christ-Centered Resource for Personal Prayer.* Hamden, CT: Circle Press, 2007.

Benedict XVI. *The Environment.* Edited by Jacquelyn Lindsey. Huntington, IN: Our Sunday Visitor, 2012.

Bowden-Pickstock, Susan. *Quiet Gardens: The Roots of Faith?* New York: Continuum, 2009.

Brewer, E. Cobham. *A Dictionary of Miracles.* Whitefish, MT: Kessinger, 2010.

Carver, Martin. *The Cross Goes North: Processes of Conversion in Northern Europe.* Woodbridge, UK: Boydell Press, 2006.

Catechism of the Catholic Church. Liguori, MO: Liguori Publications, 1994.

Clark, Sally. "Flowers after a Wildfire." *Weavings* 27, no. 2 (2013): 10–11.

Claudel, Paul. *I Believe in God.* New York: Holt, Rinehart and Winston, 1963. Accessed December 2013. https://archive.org/stream/ibelieveingodame013460mbp/ibelieveingodame013460mbp_djvu.txt.

Curtayne, Alice. *Twenty Tales of Irish Saints.* New York: Sheed and Ward, 1955.

Danin, Avinoam, Alan D. Whanger, Uri Baruch, and Mary Whanger. *Flora of the Shroud of Turin.* St. Louis: Missouri Botanical Garden Press, 1999.

Davidson, Alan. *The Oxford Companion to Food.* 2nd ed. New York: Oxford University Press, 2006.

DeWolf, Gordon P., Jr., ed. *Taylor's Guide to Garden Design*. Boston: Houghton Mifflin, 1988.

Douleurs, Marie des. "The Annunciation." *Magnificat* 10, no. 14 (March 2009): 346–347.

Esolen, Anthony. "Food for the Journey." *Magnificat* 14, no. 4 (June 2012): 5–8.

———. "Time and Eternity." *Magnificat* 12, no. 10 (December 2010): 5–6.

Farmer, David. *The Oxford Dictionary of Saints*. 5th ed. New York: Oxford University Press, 2004.

Flowers of Mary: or Devotions for Each Month in the Year. London: Burns and Lambert, 1862. Accessed November 2011–December 2013. http://books.google.com.

Gemminger, Louis. *Flowers of Mary*. 1858 4th ed. Translat by a Benedictine sister. Baltimore: John Murphy, 1894.

Ghezzi, Bert. *Voices of the Saints: A Year of Readings*. New York: Doubleday, 2000.

Gould, Meredith. *The Catholic Home: Celebrations and Traditions for Holidays, Feast Days, and Every Day*. New York: Doubleday, 2004.

Hahn, Samuel J. *Stories Told under the Sycamore Tree*. Lima, OH: CSS Publishing, 2003.

Hahn, Scott. *Signs of Life: 40 Catholic Customs and Their Biblical Roots*. New York: Doubleday, 2009.

Hales, Mick. *Monastic Gardens*. New York: Tabori & Chang, 2000.

Hendey, Lisa M. *A Book of Saints for Catholic Moms: 52 Companions for Your Heart, Mind, Body, and Soul*. Notre Dame, IN: Ave Maria Press, 2011.

Hepper, F. Nigel. *Planting a Bible Garden*. Grand Rapids, MI: Fleming H. Revell, Baker Book House, 1997.

Hilton, Agnes Aubrey. *Legends of Saints and Birds*. 1908. Reprint, Charleston, SC: Nabu Press, POD Books, 2010.

Houselander, Caryll. *A Child in Winter: Advent, Christmas, and Epiphany with Caryll Houselander*. Edited by Thomas Hoffman. Franklin, WI: Sheed & Ward, 2000.

Iannone, John C. *The Mystery of the Shroud of Turin: New Scientific Evidence*. Staten Island, NY: Alba House, 1998.

International Commission on English in the Liturgy, Order of St. Benedict. *Book of Blessings: Ritual Edition.* Collegeville, MN: Liturgical Press, 1989.

King, Eleanor Anthony. *Bible Plants for American Gardens.* New York: Macmillan, 1941.

Klein, Peter. *The Catholic Source Book.* 4th ed. Orlando: Harcourt Religious, 2007.

Koenig-Bricker, Woodeene. *Ten Commandments for the Environment.* Notre Dame, IN: Ave Maria Press, 2009.

Krymow, Vincenzina. *Mary's Flowers: Gardens, Legends, and Meditations.* Cincinnati: St. Anthony Messenger Press, 2002.

Landsberg, Sylvia. *The Medieval Garden.* Toronto: University of Toronto Press, 2003.

Langford, Jeremy. *Seeds of Faith: Practices to Grow a Healthy Spiritual Life.* Brewster, MA: Paraclete Press, 2009.

Lawrence. *The Practice of the Presence of God and The Spiritual Maxims.* Mineola, NY: Dover Publications, 2005.

Lindahl, Carl, John McNamara, and John Lindow, eds. *Medieval Folklore: An Encyclopedia of Myths, Legends, Tales, Beliefs, and Customs.* 2 vols. Santa Barbara, CA: ABC-CLIO, 2000.

McBrien, Richard P. *Catholicism: New Edition.* New York: HarperCollins, 1994.

National Conference of Catholic Bishops. *Catholic Household Blessings and Prayers.* Washington, DC: United States Catholic Conference, 1988.

National Liturgical Office, ed. *A Book of Blessings.* Ottawa, ON: Canadian Conference of Catholic Bishops Publication Services, 1981.

Nollman, Jim. *Why We Garden: Cultivating a Sense of Place.* Boulder, CO: Sentient Publications, 2005.

Olson, Marsha. *A Garden of Love and Healing: Living Tributes to Those We Have Loved and Lost.* Minneapolis, MN: Fairview Press, 2002.

Prewitt, Ellen Morris. *Making Crosses: A Creative Connection to God.* Brewster, MA: Paraclete Press, 2009.

Procter, John. *The Rosary Guide for Priests and People.* London: Kegan Paul, Trench, Trübner & Co., LTD, 1901.

Pseudo-Macarius. *Fifty Spiritual Homilies of St. Macarius the Egyptian.* Translated by Arthur James Mason. London: Macmillan, 1921.

Realy, Margaret Rose. *A Garden of Visible Prayer: Creating a Personal Sacred Space One Step at a Time*. Englewood, CO: Patheos Press, 2014.

Sanders, Jack. *Hedgemaids and Fairy Candles: The Lives and Lore of North American Wildflowers*. Camden, ME: Ragged Mountain Press, 1995.

Schlarman, J. H. "With the Blessing of the Church." Presentation at the National Catholic Rural Life Conference, Des Moines, IA, 1994.

Simsic, Wayne. *Garden Prayers: Planting the Seeds of Your Inner Life*. Winona, MN: St. Mary's Press, 1995.

Stanton, Richard. *A Menology of England and Wales; or, Brief Memorials of the Ancient British and English Saints, Arranged According to the Calendar—Together with the Martyrs of the 16th and 17th Centuries. Compiled by order of the Cardinal Archbishop and the Bishops*. Philadelphia: Wharton Press, 2011.

Steiner, Rudolf. *The Temple Legend and the Golden Legend*. Translated by John Wood. London: Steiner, 1985.

Stravinskas, Peter M. J., ed. *Our Sunday Visitor's Catholic Encyclopedia*. Huntington, IN: Our Sunday Visitor, 1991.

Swenson, Allan A. *Foods Jesus Ate and How to Grow Them*. New York: Skyhorse Publishing, 2008.

Taylor, Gladys. *Saints and Their Flowers*. London: A. R. Mowbray, 1956.

Turner, Tom. *Garden History: Philosophy and Design, 2000 BC–2000 AD*. New York: Spon Press, 2005.

United States Conference of Catholic Bishops. *Compendium: Catechism of the Catholic Church*. Washington, DC: USCCB Publishing, 2012.

Margaret Rose Realy is a Benedictine oblate who made her final oblate profession on March 15, 2014, at St. Benedict Monastery in Oxford, Michigan. She has a master's degree in communications from Michigan State University, is a regular contributor to CatholicMom.com, and writes about spirituality and gardening for The Catholic Channel at *Patheos*. She is also the author of *A Garden of Visible Prayer: Creating a Personal Sacred Space One Step at a Time* and *Cultivating God's Garden through Lent*. Realy has been featured in *Catholic Digest; The Catholic Times; Jackson Citizen Patriot; Lansing State Journal; The Daily Reporter; Your Home, Your Lifestyle;* and on the *Among Women* podcast.

Realy is the owner of Morning Rose Prayer Gardens, a liturgical garden consulting and educational business. She is a certified greenhouse grower, an advanced master gardener, and the coordinator emeritus of the St. Francis Retreat Center Garden Society in DeWitt, Michigan. She has worked as a greenhouse grower and garden consultant, taught workshops at Michigan State University, and is accredited to teach MSU Master Gardener continuing education.

AVE

AVE MARIA PRESS

Founded in 1865, Ave Maria Press,
a ministry of the Congregation of
Holy Cross, is a Catholic publishing
company that serves the spiritual and
formative needs of the Church and its
schools, institutions, and ministers;
Christian individuals and families; and
others seeking spiritual nourishment.

For a complete listing of titles from

Ave Maria Press

Sorin Books

Forest of Peace

Christian Classics

visit www.avemariapress.com

AVE MARIA PRESS
Notre Dame, IN
A Ministry of the United States Province of Holy Cross